KLONDIKE TREK

James Hinkle as a Young man.

Klondike Trek

Jim Hinkle's Life in the Gold Rush of 1898

James W. Hinkle's letters and drawings

Edited by

Martha J. Bates

KETCHIKAN PRESS
2008

Copyright © 2008 by Ketchikan Press
Paso Robles, California
www.ketchikanpress.com

All rights reserved. No part of this book may be reprinted or reproduced or utilized in any form or by any electronic, mechanical, or other means, now known or hereafter invented, including photocopying and recording, or in any information storage or retrieval system, without permissions in writing from the publisher.

Cover & interior by Chris Hall/Ampersand

CATALOGING-IN-PUBLICATION DATA
Hinkle, James W., 1852-1899.
Klondike trek : Jim Hinkle's life in the Gold Rush of 1898 : James W. Hinkle's letters and drawings / edited by Martha J. Bates.
    p. : ill. ; cm.
  ISBN 978-0-9817584-0-4
1. Hinkle, James W., 1852-1899—Correspondence. 2. Gold miners—Yukon. 3. Peace River Region (B.C. and Alta.)—Description and travel. I. Bates, Martha J., 1917-1998.
  F1079.P3H56 2008
  971.23/105092—dc22   2008933105

ISBN 978-0-9817584-0-4 0-9817584-0-1

Contents

Preface
    Marcia J. Bates, *Great-granddaughter of James Hinkle* / ix

Introduction
    Martha J. Bates, *Editor and Granddaughter of James Hinkle* / 1

1. A Klondyke Outfit / 3
2. Athabasca Landing / 11
3. Ten Miles Up the Slave Lake / 21
4. Hudson Bay Post, Head of Lesser Slave Lake / 24
5. Peace River Landing / 29
6. Fifty Miles Up Peace River / 38
7. Twenty-Five Miles Above Dunvagen / 48
8. Pine River Camp, British Columbia, N.W.T. / 76
9. British Columbia, N.W.T. / 93
10. Pine River Camp in the Fall / 108
11. Pine River Camp in the Winter / 127
12. Christmas in Pine River Camp / 163
13. Move to Fort St. John / 182
14. Fort St. John / 215
15. Thirty Miles from Cust's House / 235
16. Otter Tail River / 259
17. Hudson Hope / 275
18. Questionable Assertions / 282
19. Later in Mattoon, Illinois
    Martha J. Bates / 294

Epilogue
    Martha J. Bates / 299

SKETCHES BY JAMES HINKLE

1. Sketch of the rapids / 52
2. Indians pulling the boat / 61
3. Inside of cabin / 135
4. Hinkle's cabin / 144
5. Grimston's cabin / 145
6. Hinkle's cabin *(detail)* / 146–47
7. Grimston's cabin *(detail)* / 148–49
8. Myrty at the typewriter and Peters rabbit hunting / 152
9. Peters cooking / 155
10. Harry and his sweetheart taking a rest after long ride / 156
11. A whimsical sketch / 159
12. James William Thomas McMullen Hinkle—Editor / 176
13. Fort St. John / 198
14. Sketch with Hinkle's poem / 208
15. Cutting trails through the mountains / 246

PHOTOGRAPHS

1. James Hinkle as a young man / *Frontispiece*
2. Methodist church / 7
3. Harry, Presh and Myrty as children / 17
4. Hinkle in camp / 36
5. Myrty at age twenty / 79
6. Hinkle's mining license / 295
7. Diagram of graves / 303
8. Martha, Marcia, and Myrtle, Edmonton, Alta., 1952 / 305
9. Peace River Valley / 306
10. Myrty near burial site in 1952 / 306

*Compiled and edited with appreciation
and memories of my mother who was Myrty*

Preface

WHAT FOLLOWS are the letters, drawings and diary of James Hinkle, a Mattoon, Illinois railroad engineer who became a prospector in the 1898 Klondike Gold Rush to the Yukon Territory of Canada. These materials came initially to his family, in particular, to his daughter, Myrtle, and then were passed on to Myrtle's daughter Martha.

Martha was fascinated with Hinkle's absorbing tale, and spent her spare time over the years transcribing his minuscule handwriting into typewritten form. As Martha's daughter Marcia, I can attest to the scrupulous care with which she endeavored to transcribe every word correctly, sometimes poring over the texts with a magnifying glass. This book is entirely due to her devoted efforts.

My mother, Martha Bates, selected the text, drawings, and most of the photos for the book. She wrote the Introduction and Epilogue as well, and constructed Chapter 19, "Later in Mattoon…" with the help of relatives who were there.

The text (Chapters 1-18) consists primarily of letters written by Hinkle, interspersed with his sketches and entries from his journal. A few additional texts related to his efforts are also printed. In reproducing Hinkle's drawings, I have endeavored to present the images as closely as possible to their real appearance today—ink drawings on browning paper, written on both sides.

Reproductive techniques that strip the details of aging also strip much of the charm and verisimilitude of his work.

In the early 1950's, Myrtle (1879-1954), Martha (1917-1998), and Marcia (1942-), Hinkle's daughter, granddaughter, and great-granddaughter, respectively, followed up on his story, driving far north into upper Canada. Our story is picked up in the Epilogue.

Martha Bates edited and prepared the entire manuscript of this book, but was unable to publish Hinkle's story during her lifetime. She very much wanted her grandfather's story to be available for anyone to read. For that reason, I have now arranged the publication of her manuscript. It gives me great pleasure to see her dream finally realized.

I wish to thank Nicholas Carroll, Sonja Erikkson, and Ron Gallagher for their talented assistance on this project.

MARCIA J. BATES

February 2008

Introduction

by Martha J. Bates

THE LETTERS AND DIARY of James Hinkle tell a complete story of his travels during the Klondike gold rush of 1897–98. From the time of his arrival in Edmonton, Alberta, Canada, he wrote day-by-day accounts of his experiences in letters to his family. As he traveled northward, he would write until such time as he met someone coming out of the wilderness who could take his letter to Edmonton to be mailed. Many times these would be Hudson's Bay representatives, who would occasionally have a letter for him from his family, although these were far too few.

Hinkle had lived in the small Midwest town of Mattoon, Illinois, and, even there, the talk and excitement of the gold rush had stirred in the hearts of many men the latent desire for quick riches. Some of the more prominent men who had just a little more money than the average person yet not quite enough to satisfy them, decided to form a company called the Security Mining and Investment Company.

Their idea was to send three men to the Klondike, outfit them completely, pay their expenses and expect a gold mine in return. To get this project on its way, they sold stock in the company and all who bought it also expected to get their fair share of gold in due time.

There were alternate land and sea routes available with the accompanying advantages and problems. Some thought the Inland Passage up the west coast was the better route, but this was expensive, with passage difficult to obtain and the mighty Chilkoot Pass to negotiate after completing the boat trip. Furthermore, six hundred miles of wilderness separated the pass from Dawson. Therefore, it was agreed the men would be sent to Edmonton and from there they would travel the rivers and existing trails northward, prospecting along the way.

The three men the company chose out of the several who wished to make the journey were James Hinkle, Charles Hardesty and Jack Peters. James Hinkle was my grandfather and was an engineer on the railroad. Charles Hardesty also worked on the railroad and he and Hinkle were friends. Jack Peters was not a resident of Mattoon but came from somewhere in the northwest part of the country.

Not much was known about his background but he was taken on as the third man of the party because he claimed to have knowledge of navigation. This was felt to be essential for their course of travels on the rivers of the north. He encouraged them to go by way of Edmonton, saying he knew people in the far north who could give them much help.

Much thought and planning went into the preparation of the expedition. Schedules and routes had to be worked out and enough food, clothing and supplies had to be purchased to last the three men for at least eighteen months. Peters and two of the directors of the company went to Chicago for the purpose of purchasing the outfit.

All the town knew Hinkle and Hardesty and the preparations for their trip were followed with much interest. As the time to start their journey drew near, the Mattoon Daily Star printed a humorous news item concerning their outfit. At last everything was in readiness and in the early part of April, 1898, the expedition left Mattoon by train for Edmonton, Alberta, there to await their outfit and start their trek northward.

Grandfather Hinkle, whose letters and diary have been passed on to me, bade his family goodbye. They were:

Mollie or *Mamma*—James Hinkle's wife,

Myrtle or *Myrty*—his only daughter, 19 years of age,

Harry—his elder son, 18 years of age,

Vernon or *Presh* or *Pet*—his younger son, 16 years of age.

1

A Klondyke Outfit

Mattoon Daily Star
Mattoon, Illinois

March 25, 1898

A KLONDYKE OUTFIT
KATZ AND KAHN BUY LOTS OF STUFF
For Peters, Hinkle and Hardesty

OF THE THOUSANDS of people who have the Alaska gold fever, very few have any conception of the expense necessary to secure a proper outfit. And even those who have unlimited means to buy an outfit are at a loss to know what to buy or in what quantities. Last week Louis Katz, Mark Kahn and J. R. Peters were in Chicago and purchased an outfit for the three men who will brave the terrors of the Klondyke for the next year and a half as the agents of the Security Mining and Investment Co. of this city. The men are J. R. Peters, Jim Hinkle and Charles Hardesty. All three are courageous men and seasoned to hard work and exposure.

    The Star takes it that a brief enumeration of the principal articles necessary for such a project will be interesting reading to its readers. Here are some articles of hardware: Augers, axes and handles, bits and braces, chisels, compass, butcher knives and files, gold pans and hammers, oakum and picks, rope, saw-set, gold scales and shovels, screw-drivers, pack saddles and tents, whip-saws and hand saws, jack and block planes, spool wire and nails.

Another very necessary article is buck-skin shirts which are worn next to the hide to keep out the cold, also buck-skin drawers and mitts. The former garments are $6 each and the mitts $1.25.

That the men will not go hungry is evidenced from the grocery list now before us. This list could run Uncle Amos' caravansary at the county jail for thirty years. Yet these three men expect to eat it all and more too if they don't die with the gout in eighteen months.

Some of the items in the grocery list are amusing. For instance these two: sugar 100 pounds, soap 70¢. Now imagine three men getting along a year and a half on 70¢ worth of soap. At the end of that period they would not be allowed to work in a glue factory if that is all the soap they used.

Then there are evaporated apples, apricots, bacon, baking powder, barley, extract of beef, candles, coffee, corn meal, matches, condensed milk, mustard, rolled oats, split peas, pepper, red and black, prunes, rice, salt, soda, tea, tobacco, evaporated potatoes, carrots, onions, soup cakes and various other articles more useful than ornamental.

A glance at the clothing list also has its interest. Blankets, caps, sheepskin lined coats, socks, sweaters, carrying bags, gloves, snow glasses, handkerchiefs, mitts, pants, bed sheeting, shirts, mackintosh coats, towels, drawers, laced boots, rubber boots, moccasins, snow shoes, sleeping bags, etc.

That the trio will be prepared to defend their outfit from marauding hands, the following items show: Thirty-eight caliber Colts rifle and loaded shells, Winchester shot gun and thirty-eight caliber rifle and cartridge belts together with many boxes of loaded shells.

A medicine chest and "Happy Rover" cook stove complete the list.

• • •

Note: In the following, Jim Hinkle's letters always begin with his location and the date. He frequently started and stopped letters several times before mailing them, each time dating the new material. His journal entries are labeled: "From Hinkle's journal."

A Klondyke Outfit / 5

SOUTH EDMONTON, ALBERTA, CANADA

Sunday, April 17th, 1898

My dear Mollie and Myrty and Boys,

As I have nothing to do only set around, I will write you. This letter will not go out of here until Tuesday as there are only three trains that go out of here a week and they are on Tuesdays, Thursdays and Saturdays. I will write today and talk about this place, the country, the people and things in general.

The city is on both sides of the Saskatchewan River and the side we are on is the side the railroad is on and is called South Edmonton. This is the finest farming country you ever saw for wheat, oats, barley and rye; no corn or apples but lots of small fruit along the river. The river is a sight to behold. It looks to be about two miles from bank to bank and down to the bed of the river it looks like looking down a hill twenty miles long. The banks are very rough and very thick with trees, small saplings called birch and fir.

The natives are a queer set but the politest people there ever was. They talk some like a full-fledged Irishman. If they get up or make a move, they will say excuse me and will answer any question you ask them. The girls are all big, raw boned and ugly and are all stuck on plain pink dresses without any trimmings. Everyone you see has a pink dress on. They all have big feet and never black their shoes.

This is a busy place. It is about the size of Gays west of Mattoon, only the houses are all bigger and made of brick and nearly all of them hotels or boarding houses and all of them are getting rich on account of the gold rush. If Harry had one hundred dollars and was here with you, you could get rich for this place will never decrease in business but increase. Everything is in cash. He could buy a team and dray between South Edmonton and Edmonton and you could keep boarders and make dollars here where you won't make cents there.

There are three big elevators, one bank, three churches and one schoolhouse. There are some Indians and lots of half-breeds and then about five miles out in the country there are a thousand of them. They have to get a pass to come to town and they all look like giants and the devil. They have nothing on but a blanket.

We went up the river three miles yesterday where some miners are washing gold on a sand bar. They make about a dollar fifty per day. We watched one man for an hour and at the end of three hours that he had worked, he cleaned up and washed it all out (I mean the sand) and it turned out seventy-five cents worth of gold. A little lump about the size of a corn grain. These men are here on their way to the Peace River and have not got enough money and this is the way they are getting money to get there. So you see we are in the gold regions. I would not take any amount of money for my chances of getting rich.

And now Harry and Pet, pitch in and make a good living for mamma and Myrty and I am sure that you will not have to work more than two years anyhow. Save every cent you make and I will fix you some day for it. Have you moved yet and what do you pay for rent and has Harry got a regular engine and what is Pet doing and Myrty, did you have your lesson and do you practice on the piano? Don't neglect the piano. Study hard and learn the shorthand and you will be all right. By good management you can get along nice and mamma, you must not work one bit; the kids can make a good living for you and I know they will, won't you Harry, Pet and Myrty?

We are boarding with a widow woman and she owns a little cottage close by. No one lives in it but us three Klondykers. There are four beds in it, a stove and three chairs, a stand and we have a lamp and a sperm candle, pen and ink, coal bucket and coal, a coal shovel and poker and some wood and the front door has red glass in it. There are three rooms. The front room has lace curtains hung on nails, no carpet on either of the floors and that is all.

We have pretty good grub. They set the table and we must eat a bowl of soup first (this is dinner) and then they bring the eggs and meat and then they bring the sauce and cake and then when we get about done they bring in the coffee. For breakfast we have a bowl of cracked barley first and then just meat and potatoes and bread and butter. For supper we have cold meat and mashed potatoes and coffee. For this we pay six dollars a week and think it is cheap.

Monday, April 18th, '98
Just got back from Edmonton. Hardesty and I walked down to the river and were taken across in a canoe. It is three miles over there and the banks of the river take up two-thirds of the way and I'm not one bit tired. This is sure enough healthy country and the air is light and my, but I can eat. If they would fry me some boot tops I could eat them.

We go from here to Fort St. John on the Peace River—400 miles—just as soon as our goods arrive. Will keep you posted as to how to address the letters before I leave here. Mollie, the mail is so irregular here I wish you would write me every two days for I want to hear from you as often as I can before I leave here and what I don't get here will be forwarded on to me. I have not heard a word from you yet. This leaves us in the best of health and the very best of spirits. Take good care of your health and have the kids do the work. Goodbye and many kisses from your
  Hubby Jim

South Edmonton, Alberta, Canada
Sunday, April 24th, 1898
My dear Mamma and Harry, Myrt and Pet,

Received yours of the 28th and will answer it now. Charley and I have just come from church, the Methodist, and as you will want to know how they do out here in this country at church I will tell you all about it as near as I can recollect.

Church takes up at 7:30 P.M. and it is just sundown; it does not get dark here until 9:00 o'clock. They had an organ, a choir, two ushers and a preacher. First the choir sang "Praise God From Whom All Blessings Flow". No one told them to sing but they just sang it. Then the preacher prayed, then he gave out the number of a hymn that everybody in church sang. Then he read the 73rd psalm and gave out the number of another hymn and it was the tune to the hymn the Masons sing at a funeral. Then the preacher gave out his text and it was all of the 1st psalm and he used the whole psalm in his sermon and I never heard as good a talk and as good an explanation in any church as he gave.

He is a young man. After he was done preaching the choir alone sang a song, there were five of them, three girls and two men and then the stewards passed the hat, the preacher said the benediction and we all went home.

At the door, we all had to shake hands with the stewards before we left the church and I will say we were very much interested. Everybody goes to church here. There are the Methodists, Presbyterians, Catholics and Baptists.

It is nice weather here but windy, no snow except on the banks of the Saskatchewan. There are no birds here except once in a while I hear a robin and I heard one peewee.

Our goods haven't come yet and I want you to know we are awfully tired waiting for them. We don't look for them before Saturday, then we will get out of this place. I will stop for tonight and finish tomorrow. Good night with a kiss to all.

April 25
I am stiff as a poker. We were jumping yesterday for exercise and I can hardly move this morning. Well we have a wedding in our town already this morning. Now think of a wedding on Monday morning by 7:00 o'clock. The bride is seventeen and the groom old enough to have five little children.

His wife has only been dead four months. He is a farmer and owns a big farm. The bride just went by our shanty to a neighbors all by herself. She had on her bridal veil.

Well I have just come back from up the river. And now Myrty I will tell you what I saw and what I did. I went the most difficult way I could go and I am as tired as a dog for I am as fat as a hog. I went all the way up the river along the banks and Myrty it is a sight to see. Wish I had a Kodak to have taken some pictures. The banks are a half mile down to the water and some places are straight up and

Methodist Church

down and just as thick with little trees as can be and right where I got this moss is the prettiest sight of all. The ground is covered with it so I send you some.

I went up the river for two miles through these kinds of sights until I came to where they are washing out gold. It is just a big sand bar that is along the river and they scoop the gravel and sand up in a screen and they have flannel cloths to catch the gold.

It is what is called flour gold and they work all day washing and shoveling and make about a dollar fifty per day to the man. I have gotten acquainted with two of the men. They have been up to our shanty and I asked them if they would let me use their gold pan to wash out one pan of gravel, that I wanted to send it to my Myrty. They said, "certainly". So I took the shovel and just put one shovelful in the pan and took it to the water and did like they did and washed it down to just what I send you.

This is not all gold but there are lots of bits of gold in it. John Catlen will call them colors. There is about one cents worth of gold in what I send you. Get a glass that will magnify and you will see it or get a black pan and put this in it and pour some water in it and shake the pan and let the water run around the pan slow and the gold will be the last to run after the water and black sand. Be careful and don't waste a bit of it. You will have to pour the water off and then dry the sand before you can handle it. So now this is my first gold digging but you just wait until I get up on Peace River and I will send you some nuggets.

Well it is about 5:00 P.M. and the mail comes in tonight and if I don't get a big letter from all of you I will be so darned mad.

That bride has been wearing her bridal veil all day around the house and just been cutting up with kids all day. She wears a loud colored dress. There is going to be a dance there tonight and we are invited. I don't think I will go for I have the headache.

Say, I want you to send me the Globe paper once in a while or else tell me some more news. We don't hear anything about war. Send me the Commercial if there is anything in it and answer my letters just as soon as you get them. Answer them so you can get them off on the first train. I expect by the time you get this we will be out of here but you just address them the same and they will be forwarded to me and I will tell you where to direct your letters after we leave Edmonton.

Tell me how things are and how much the boys are making and how much the watch brought you and if you are all well and Myrty you rascal, if you don't tell me something I won't send you a darned nugget. Any little thing you say does me a whole lot of good.

You must study hard with your lessons and you see when your Dad comes home from Scoopingdyke you can be my bookkeeper. I want to see you awful bad but there is a long time between scenes. So I will just have to imagine I give you a great big smack in the smacker. Well now don't forget anything that I have told you and I will say goodbye for this time with lots of love and kisses to all. This leaves me in the best of health with the exception of a headache and a cold. I am your Klondyker

Jim Pop
P. S. Mamma take care of yourself.

2

Athabasca Landing

May 21, 1898

Dear Mollie and Kids,

    We are one hundred miles northwest of Edmonton camped on the banks of the Athabasca River. This river is about as large as the Ohio. I will now tell you all about the trip from Edmonton and the country around this place, if I can keep the darned mosquitoes away. There are forty million in my tent right now and nothing will keep them away but the wind. I put Peneroyle all over me and they eat that off and then go for the hide. Hardesty is cussing them all the time.

    Well we had quite a trip from Edmonton over here. We left there Tuesday at 3:00 P.M. by wagon and arrived at the Landing Saturday at 11:00 A.M. and the crookedest, and up and downest, roughest, stoniest, longest, miserablest, doggondest, windiest, blamedest, tiresomest, dustyest trip that ever tripest. Oh it beats the devil! Dash* had his toe mashed the first day by the wagon running over it.

    This is beautiful scenery. We are right under a high bluff and right close to the water. There are two stores, two sawmills, two boat yards, two restaurants and one church that is made out of logs and

---

* *Dash was a dog that Hinkle acquired while in Edmonton awaiting the supplies. The circumstances surrounding his acquisition were evidently described in a missing letter.*

is as large as our barn. Also there are five dwelling houses, all made out of logs and covered with sod. There are lots of bear here, there were three killed yesterday and brought into the Landing. There are plenty of fish and they are easy to catch.

This is a lonesome day because there is nothing to do except sit around and look at the hills and river. We will buy a boat tomorrow or get one made and as soon as we get a boat we go up the river seventy miles to Lesser Slave Lake and from there we have to be hauled by wagon seventy miles to Peace River Landing. It will take us a week to go to Slave Lake and three days from there to Peace River Landing.

I don't expect I will hear from you more than a couple of times in a year but you will hear from me often for there is someone coming out very often where there is no way for me to get your letters only as McDougall and Secord make their trip and that is about twice a year. But you write often and maybe I will get some of them.

Later

I have just come from church, it is called the Church of England. There were seven white women and three half breed Indians, the balance was all kinds of people, French, Indian, white people and myself. They sang our old songs such as "Gathering Up the Shells at the Sea Shore". The preacher read the 68th psalm and his text was the 17th and 18th verses of the 68th psalm. The preacher prayed twice before he commenced to preach. I guess that was all right but I believe that he forgot that he had prayed once.

We are going to build a boat ourselves so I will have to stop and go to bed and in the morning we go at making our boat and I won't have any time to write much until we get it done for the days here are eighteen hours long and we want to get it done as soon as we can. I will be too tired to write of evenings until after the boat is built. It will take us about four days to build it.

Wednesday, 25

We have our boat about done, will finish it tomorrow and we will leave here for Lesser Slave Lake and Peace River Landing about

Saturday. We have been working hard since Monday and I am awful tired, too tired to write so I am going to bed and finish this before we leave here.

Thursday evening the 26th
Have been working all day on the boat. I am so tired I can hardly walk. When a fellow works eighteen hours a day and works like you know I do, he is pretty tired. We have the boat all done but the finishing touch, have it painted. We will put it in the water in the morning to see if it leaks any and finish it all up tomorrow. I don't know if we will leave here before Monday or not. I expect not for we will want to rest a bit. Goodnight now, I am going to bed.

Friday May 27th
And it is Myrty's birthday and oh but I want to see her bad, and all of you. But somehow I have been lonesome today for the first time, I guess it is because I have been thinking about her all day. I suppose you have had a little birthday dinner for her. I wrote to her and told her in one of my letters that wherever I was, I was going to kill a bear or a duck or something and have a dinner and eat it to her health so now I will tell you what I had.

We were so busy building the boat that I could not go out and kill a bear but this is what I did do. While we were working, I set a fish line in the water and caught three big fish, all we could eat, and that is what I had for Myrty's birthday dinner and every bite I took I thought of Myrty. Besides, I cooked a pot of beans and we had bread and butter, roast bacon, coffee and molasses made out of sugar and that's all.

7:00 P.M.
I am tickled so I can't see straight. I just got your letter, it was written May 13, just fourteen days coming from Mattoon. Now if I could get letters that soon all the time I would be satisfied. But I suppose after we leave here it will be a long time for me to get a letter from you but I am after gold and I will get that if I don't get any letters, but I am feeling lots better since I got your letter.

We have our boat done and it is in the water. We will pull out of here for Lesser Slave Lake and Peace River Landing Monday morning. Don't forget to address your letters to me like this — James Hinkle, Fort St. John in care of McDougall and Secord via Edmonton, Alberta, Canada. Well I will quit for tonight and go to my fish lines and see what I have caught.

Later

Well now you are not any more tickled to get my letters than I am to get yours. Every time I get a letter from any of you I cry all the time and Hardesty cries too. I will cut a lock of hair right off the end of Dash's tail and send it to you. It is as white as a sheet. Oh, he is the smartest pup you ever saw. He will do anything he is told to do. I will hide a stick or anything and let him smell it first and he will find it if it takes all day.

We have a steep bank to climb to where our tents are and I tell Dash to take some wood up to the stove and I believe he would carry wood up all day if I didn't make him stop. He will shake hands and he will speak—by a bark—every time I tell him to. He will go in the water after anything I throw in. It doesn't make any difference if I kill a duck and it falls in the water, he will get it. I will make him pull me before long or as soon as the snow comes. He sleeps in my tent every night and nothing can make a noise that he doesn't growl.

Now look here, I know I'm getting fat but you aren't going to shut me off from eating. I would just as soon have the fatty of the heart as the leany of the gizzard, see. Goodnight.

Saturday evening

And it is 9:30 and the sun is just down. I have just quit work and I am so tired I can hardly move. Have been all day getting the timber to make our oars for the boat and making them. Everything is ready now to start Monday morning.

I just got Harry's letter, written the 16th and I have been tickled twice this week. You bet Presh is the boy, he will take good care of you I'll bet, won't you Pet? I suppose you like it all right in your new home. Have the boys got you four good roomers and boarders?

I'll bet you did have a hard time moving, you always did kill yourself at such business. Tell Nute Reed hello and my regards.

Bully for Presh, he has got his job again, now don't let a brakeman go to sleep on you again or Doyle will cut your head off. I think I can see something brewing there between Frank Hart and Henry O'Bannon and my Myrty. It is either a fight or a sock. It will be a hole kicked in both of their pants when I come home if they aren't doggone careful. Myrty, remember what I told you, you know.

Hardesty is all right, he does just as much work as any of us, the only fault I find with him is that he snores in his sleep. You did just right to quit George Kinser, I would eat bacon and buy it at the store before I would buy a cents worth of him. Tell the Son of a B that I hope he will break up, lose everything he has and have to go to the poor house before I come back. He is no man at all. Well I hope you come out all right with your money.

I am so tired I believe I will go to bed. It isn't dark yet but what's the diff. By the way, tomorrow is the 29th and my birthday. Ha ha ha Myrty, you can't beat me around this time like you always do on my birthday. Goodnight—a kiss.

Sunday morning, May 29
I am 46 years old today and am as good as ever. I am a better man than I was at 21. Well what are you all doing there today, did you think of me? This is a beautiful morning, warm and nice although water froze in the water bucket last night.

Harry, we are not as near the gold fields as you think we are, we have the worst part of the road to go over yet. We have 600 miles to go and no railroad to go on. I will give you a description of the balance of the trip and what we will have to do to get there.

We are at the Athabasca Landing on the Athabasca River, just one hundred miles a little northwest of Edmonton. We have built a boat and are ready to go up the river. Our boat will have 5300 pounds in it. Now we have to go up stream all the way.

When we leave here we go to the Slave River and then through Lesser Slave Lake to the Peace River Landing. It is seventy miles to Slave River and two hundred miles from there and across the lake to Peace River Landing. Now two of us will pull the boat and walk on the shore and one will have to steer the boat most of the way except on the lake and there we can row the boat and all ride from Peace River Landing.

We go to Fort St. John and there is where I will get your mail after I leave here. It will take us fifteen days to go to Peace River Landing. From Fort St. John we go up the Peace River to Findlay River. So you see we have the hardest part of the trip to make yet.

I suppose you have the war fever too Harry but you must get that out of your head for you have to take care of the family you know and as prices have gone up in everything you will have to be saving with your money to make both ends meet.

I would like to have dropped in Mattoon on the day the engineers had their time out of a balloon. I suppose they had a great time. I suppose old Willie Bud was old splinter on a stick. I don't believe I would join the B. of L.F. yet for it costs something to keep it up. I suppose you will get a regular engine when they put the gravel trains on.

You must make it a rule Harry, to give mamma enough every payday to pay the rent and grocery bill even if you have none left for yourself. Of course Presh must do the same but he is not making as much as you. You must help Presh to get a steady job. I would like to know how you come out on your examination in the air car.

Well of course someone had to tear up the 364. I ran her twenty years and did not do that. What was the stoker that did it to her? Joke on the muskets when Charly Cox and Buck Cunningham went to war. It is very little war news we get up here. There are some people here that don't know anything about it, did not know there was a war. Be sure and give me all the war news and all the balance of the news.

Later

I walked about two miles out in the hills and timber, met a full blooded Indian with long hair and as ugly as the devil. I says, "How do you do", and he says "ugh" and went on. Oh it beats the devil, I had a notion to shoot him.

Harry, Presh and Myrty as children

I had my birthday dinner. It was baked beans, biscuits and some bacon baked with the beans, tea, gravy and fried potatoes and that's all. Joke on the pie and cake. What did you have? I can guess, you had roast beef, light bread, tomatoes, chocolate cake, corn pie and some dressing. Joke on Jim.

Monday morning, May 30
Well my darling girls and boys, I will have to bring this letter to a close. We are loading up our boat this morning to go in the direction of Dawson City so I suppose it will be a long time before I hear from you, but such is life in these large countries. Write lots of letters and I will get some of them. Hoping you will all get along

all right, I will say goodbye now for a while. Many many and heaps and lots of kisses and a whole lot of squeezes and one extra one for mamma and Myrty.

Goodby from your Klondyker papa Jim

• • •

FROM HINKLE'S JOURNAL

Tuesday, May 31, 1898   Left Athabasca Landing at 4:00 P.M. Made two and a half miles and camped for the night.

Wednesday, June 1   Made five miles. Had a hard time getting around the Seven Miles Island. Undertook to cross the river to island, water too swift, could not make it. After rowing for a half hour we crossed the river a mile below, had a bad tow path for one mile.

Thursday, June 2   Started out fresh, went along all right until dinner, after dinner had a tough time, made eight miles and have just had supper of pancakes, bacon and coffee.

Saturday, June 4   Caught twenty pounds of fish, had biscuit, fish and coffee for supper, are going into camp for over Sunday, nice place, thirty-five miles from Landing.

Sunday, June 5   Did my washing, had fish for breakfast, set yeast for bread, went fishing after dinner, caught six jack fish, about twenty pounds.

Monday, June 6   Very foggy, had a hard days work, in camp for the night, below a bad rapid, going to bed in sleeping bag.

Tuesday, June 7   Crossed the river on account of rapid, had a fuss with Hardesty on account of bread, he threatened to shoot me, got around the rapid and crossed back on other side. Had a bad beach, hard pulling all day, gone into camp about fifty miles from Landing.

Saturday, June 11 After a hard night fighting the mosquitoes and keeping out of the rain, we managed to sleep some, ate breakfast, good tracking. At 3:00 P.M. came in sight of the mouth of Slave River, all hands gave it a cheer.

Monday, June 13 Worked all day on boat, made a sweep, baked bread and tinkered around. Went down the river a mile and bought some Sucks coffee and other things amounting to $6.25 from a man that got sick and was selling out.

Thursday, June 16 Rained last night and in the morning. Started at 9:00 A.M. Went through five bad rapids. Jack took sick, got through all right, camped for night fifteen miles from the mouth of Slave River.

Friday, June 17 Rained at night, started at 8:00 A.M., went through the mile rapid, all day getting through, had to unload half of the boat and carry the goods six hundred yards. Had a racket with Jack on account of he wanted to go over another rapid to camp and I was too tired, would not go. Skinned my arm up lifting the boat through the rapids, camped for night twenty miles from the mouth of the river.

Sunday, June 19 Made bread, washed and mended clothes, caught five big perch, killed a pheasant in the evening, had supper and it is raining, forty miles from the mouth of the river.

Monday, June 20 Rain started at 9:00 A.M., had a hard days work, many rapids in the water all day, rowed one mile, camped for the night on an island.

Tuesday, June 21 Rained in the morning, went through one rapid and that is the last rapid, nice weather but a hard tow path, awful tired and the wind against us all day, camped for the night on a high bluff.

Wednesday, June 22 Had good water all day but a darned hard tow path, made twelve miles, awful tired, nice day, we are in sight of the lake we think.

Friday, June 24 Rained hard in the night, got good and wet, arrived at the lake at 2:50 P.M., awful tired, unloaded the boat, put up tents, gone into camp for a few days.

Saturday, June 25 Rained a little all day, killed two ducks, set yeast for bread, baked two prune pies, blow flies are about to take us.

Tuesday, June 28 Worked all day around camp overhauling the goods, smoked the meat.

Wednesday, June 29 Fixed sail, worked all day on boat.

3

Ten Miles up the Slave Lake

July 2, 1898

Dear Folks,

As there is a man just come from Smokey River and is stopped at our camp for dinner, I will drop you a few lines. We are twelve miles up the lake. We can't get any wind in our favor, the wind is all from the west and we want it from the east, therefore we can't sail. Have to row our boat and it is slow work. If we get a wind to sail we can row across the lake in ten hours. Last night we had quite a storm but we are in our harbor but had to unload our boat. The waves were six feet high. We are all well and as brown as saffron and can eat three pounds of bacon to the man per meal.

There are two other parties with us. One of five men and one of two men, and the five of us, twelve altogether. The lake looks just like a picture, the country is high, hills on both sides of the lake. We will not reach Fort St. John now until the middle of August unless we have good luck in traveling and I won't hear from any of you until I get there. That is a long time to wait for word from home but it can't be helped.

I hope I will get lots of letters when I do get there and I hope I hear that you are all well and in good spirits. Keep up good spirits and Harry and Presh save all of your money and work whenever you can for we all think that we are going to be lucky and get quite a nice thing of this trip in the way of money but we will have to go to Findlay River to get it in paying quantities and there is where we are going to first. We will just about arrive there this winter, and next summer dig gold out by the chunks. This is hard work but healthy work.

Remember me to all the friends. I suppose Myrty, that you are in a good position by this time. You dear girl, how I would like to see you, but never mind, I will make up looking at you when I come home. You must have a whole lot of new pieces to play on the piano for me when I come home and don't forget what I told you when I left home. I want to see all of you awful bad but can't. Well I am in a hurry to get this done before the man gets his dinner so I will have to stop for this time. I will write to you just as soon as I get to the other end of the lake or at Peace River Landing. So goodbye, lots of kisses. This leaves us in the very best of health. Bye bye.

Your papa Jim

• • •

From Hinkle's Journal

Saturday, July 2   In camp all day, awful windy, pulled out in the evening, made eight miles. Could not get around a bar, had to go back a mile to land, unload the boat, carry the goods two hundred yards, worked until midnight.

Sunday, July 3   Wind in our favor and are getting ready to start at 3:00 P.M. Got out a mile and got into a thunder shower, made sixteen miles with sail. Dave and Harry stayed in camp.

Monday, July 4   Nice morning, started at 7:00 A.M. Have not seen Dave and Harry. Rowed ten miles until dinner, started after dinner and made three miles. Wind came up, got by Swan River and did not know it, got around a sand bar, wind too high. Saw Dave and Harry coming across the Bay. They landed in the mouth of Swan River. Came up and told us so we pulled up stakes and went back and we all camped in the mouth of Swan River, unloaded the boats. Awful windy all night. Caught ten fish. This is the way we spent the 4th of July.

Tuesday, July 5   Still windy and are still in camp at Swan River. Jack just shot eleven times and killed one goose. Harry and Dave are up the river hunting.

Thursday, July 7   Still in camp at Swan River. Cleared off, started at 6:00 P.M., made Indians help us across the lake.

Friday, July 8   Started at 6:00 A.M. and rowed until 2:30 P.M. Caught up with Dave and Harry and the Hudson Bay Co. at dinner. Wind got in our favor, sailed all afternoon until 8:00 P.M. Made fifteen miles, gone into camp.

Saturday, July 9   Started at 6:00 A.M. Wind in our favor, put up sail, twenty-six miles to lake at 2:50 P.M. Went up to post office, got a letter from George and Hat.

4

Hudson Bay Post, Head of Lesser Slave Lake

July 10, 1898, Sunday evening.

My very dear brother and sister,

Oh how glad I was to get your letter yesterday and as well surprised, for it was by accident that I got the letter at this point. There were four Hudson Bay boats that passed us on the lake and camped one day with us but they were not allowed to look through the mail. So I wrote the captain a note for the postmaster at the head of the lake, to hold our mail until we called for it and that is how I came to get your letter at the head of the lake. I was awful glad to get it, first word I had from home since the 30th of May; On that day I got a letter from Mollie and one from Harry and that is the last word from anyone until your very welcome letter.

We arrived at the head of Lesser Slave Lake Saturday, July 9th, awful tired and with a whole lot of experience, George. This is the place to get muscle. My muscles are so big they have pushed holes through my shirt sleeves for the want of room. I'll bet I can lick anything that walks and talks unless it would be an educated hog.

I wish you were along, you would get a little touch of high life such as pulling on a three ton boat until your eyes stuck out like fried eggs. Or steering the boat over one of the few rapids and getting fast on a rock with the water running twenty miles per hour and

Hudson Bay Post, Head of Lesser Slave Lake / 25

have to get in it up to your neck to lift the boat around the rock. Then with three men pulling on the shore with a line one hundred feet long and you come to a high bank with brush growing as close to the edge as could be and in getting around the brush and small trees, you slip and fall in the mud and water ten feet below. Or having to wade out in the water a quarter of a mile in order to get the boat around a bend in the river.

That is what I call high life and that is what we had to do up the two rivers, one seventy miles and the other sixty miles. There were six rapids on the Athabasca River and fortysix on the Little Slave River and we were ten days going up the Athabasca and eight on the Slave River and nine days on the lake. And George, it is nice to be a sailor, anyone can be a sailor if he has staying qualities in him.

This lake is eighty miles long, twenty miles wide in places, then ten miles, then five. It is in and out all the way across it and at every one of the narrow places there is a sand bar that runs out in the lake from one to three miles with only about six inches of water. Our boat draws seventeen inches so we had to go out that far to get around them and we had the wind against us all of the time except the last two days. Then the wind got astern and we put sail, lit our pipes, sat back and talked about the war and other gab while the wind did its business.

As I said before, anyone can be a sailor. When a squall comes up, the sea would be perfectly calm one minute and five minutes later there would be waves as high as your head. All a sailor can do then is to get as close to the shore as he can and turn his boat with the bow in the same way as the waves come, jump in the water and mud up to his neck and hold the boat. Sometimes the squalls don't last long but sometimes they last for an hour but it is easy and one can be a sailor. The last twenty-six miles we sailed into the end of the lake and did not know it.

You just ought to be along, it is a picnic. If any of the boys has the fever to come up here, tell them to bring a two bushel bag of patience along for they will need it.

Well, we are over the worst of the trip. It will take us four days to have our goods hauled by wagon to Peace River Landing. We will start for there tomorrow and then push through the Findlay River as soon as our goods and ourselves are in first class condition. I am in good spirits but would be better if I could get more letters from my Mollie and kids. Why don't all of you write more often? It's worth a hundred dollars a letter to me.

Hat, your advice did me good. I had not forgotten how to pray, neither had I forgotten how our dear mother used to go out evenings in Uncle Jake Reeds' woods and how well I remember of going with her and there she would kneel down and pray for me and for all of her children. No, indeed, I never can forget that. It is as fresh in my mind as if it was last night. I have sinned but I can pray and never forget my good mother and her teachings. There is not a night that I lay down to sleep but what I pray for my dear family, my dear brother and my dear sister and father and for Him to take care of all of you and for Him to give me a safe trip and get me back to my family safe.

And Hat, I believe I will be successful in this great undertaking. I don't ask millions but just enough to be comfortable and for the rest of the stockholders to make out. I am in the best of health, have not been sick a minute since I left home and I think the good Lord has been merciful to me, all of which I am thankful for.

I do hope my family won't suffer while I am gone. It worries me but I am determined to be successful on this trip if the Lord is willing and I keep my health. So now don't worry about me and I think I will come out all right.

Was glad to hear that Warren did so nice and glad that my dear Myrty and Bertha visited you. Remember me to all the folks, lots of love to you all and Hat and George, write often. It is all that I have to encourage me up here in this wild country. I will stop now and write you again on farther on the trip. Let my folks know of your getting this letter. Keep me posted on the war news and now goodbye, lots of kisses to you all.

I am as ever, your brother.
Jas. Hinkle

From Hinkle's Journal

Monday, July 11, 1898 Working around camp, getting things ready to go to Peace River Landing.

Tuesday, July 12 Have hired horses to freight goods to Peace River Landing. Left Hudson Bay Post at 2:00 P.M., went five miles and camped. Awful warm.

Wednesday, July 13 Started at 7:00 A.M., made twenty five miles, awful bad roads. Have not seen Dave and Harry. Passed the Pabome party on Tuesday, they passed us on Wednesday and are ahead of us. The English party found them broke down and part of their horses gone. One of them went back to Post and got police after them. They caught up with us and we are all camping at the crossing of Heart River.

Thursday, July 14 Started at 7:00 A.M. and made about twenty miles. Stopped for the night. It is raining and looks like it will rain all night. We have been traveling all day through the forest, very bad roads. The English party are with us.

Friday, July 15 Have just got up and am setting down in my tent. It is raining and it rained all night. Charley is asleep and so is Dash, both in my tent. The water is very bad too, risen all along the trail, just mud holes.

9:00 A.M. Quit raining, had dinner at 12:30. Road is very bad and muddy. Made to Hudson Bay Ranch and gone into camp.

Saturday, July 16 Fifteen miles from the Landing. Nice day, nice country and good roads. We are in sight of the river. For three miles we are traveling right on top of the bluff, pretty scene. Arrived at Landing at 9:00 P.M., got five letters. Met Dave and Harry.

Monday, July 18   Bought a boat, got English party, Grimston to join us making eight men in the party. They pay for half the boat. Tried to whipsaw lumber after dinner and made a failure of it. Went up to Police station to buy lumber, had none to sell. Peace River is raising. Nice day and warm, got a mess of raspberries.

Tuesday, July 19   Nice clear day, Peace River is raising fast, river full of drift. Have just had breakfast and am going back to Police station to try and buy some lumber. Bought eighty four foot of lumber, been working on boat, dressing lumber and tinkering around all day. Washed dirty clothes.

Wednesday, July 20   River still raising fast. Warm and clear. Sawing knees for boat in forenoon. Went up to Police station in afternoon and bought one hundred foot more of lumber, took boat out of water, going to take two boards out of bottom and put an extension on boat.

5

Peace River Landing

July 21, 1898

Dear girls and boys,

    As we will be here a few days building a boat and waiting for the river to go down, I will write you a letter and send it when we leave this place. Peace River is not very peaceable since we came last Saturday evening. We call it the rare and tear river. It commenced to raise as soon as we got here and has just been raging ever since. It raised four foot in one night but today it is at a standstill.

    The whole river is as big as the Mississippi and has been for two days and nights, one solid mass of driftwood, whole trees, roots and all, green and dead trees, a sight that you could never imagine. I guess we won't have any firewood to burn this winter if it keeps on coming, have to burn gold I reckon.

    Well, luck is still on our side. I bought a boat for twenty-five dollars of a party that built it at Dunvagen, one hundred twenty-five miles up the river who are returning back for more grub. There's enough lumber in it to build a house as large as H.S. Clarkes' new one by you. Lumber is worth $60.00 a thousand here and none to be had at that. There is no saw mill and if you get lumber you go to the woods and whipsaw it by hand. There is about $100.00 worth of lumber in the boat.

We had another party of three join us here. They came all the way from Athabasca Landing with us, besides the two other men that has been our party helping one another from Athabasca. Of course we are three separate parties but are traveling together, helping one another over the rapids. Now the other three men have joined us and we will all three parties go up the river in one boat.

Each party pays his portion of the expenses for the boat and remodeling it so if you stop now and think for a moment you will see what a bargain I made. Our portion of the expenses is $11.00 to have a conveyance to haul our goods three hundred miles. Besides, we have eight big strong men to pull the boat — we will be equal to a steam boat and it won't be hard on us either.

The names of the two men that have been with us helping us are Dave and Harry Shaw and they are two English boys and live on the C.P.R.R. seven hundred miles from Calgary. That is the place we met Peters on our way out here. Two of the other three men are brothers and their names are Grimston. The other ones' name is Spencier and is a cousin to them and they are all English and live in Toronto, Canada and all three of them have been sailors all their lives.

All of them are nice men, all have good sound sense and judgment. We go together in the one boat as far as what is called the Twelve Mile Portage or at Hudsons' Post above Fort St. John. If we agree when we get there we will stay together and help one another over the portage. They have a small iron wagon.

We have to build another boat there at that place. We think with the eight men we will make about fifteen miles per day easy up Peace River. So you see if we would have had to build a boat, we would have had to saw our lumber out and worked like the devil to have made a boat in ten days and only five of us to have pulled it up the river. I am not looking for work such as we have had coming from Athabasca Landing.

Anyhow, if one of those jaspers in Mattoon had to pull a boat five hundred and fifty miles with four tons in it or go to jail, they would go to jail. That is what we have to do. Oh it is easy when you get your muscles well developed. We don't think anything about it, we are after gold you know and of course don't mind this little easy job.

If it was hard work like running an engine or being a round house foreman or that awful hard work of butchering or call boy or tending switches up on the hill or striking in the blacksmiths shop or studying law or cashier of some bank or boss in a clothing store or freezing ice cream or being a constable and having to walk so hard to get to serve a summons on someone in order to make 45¢ to buy a beefsteak with because he could not buy it on credit for he owed one meat shop $8.00 or having to work so hard as general foreman in the shop and strain every nerve in his body to look through the window of his office to catch some poor tired machinist loafing behind the fire box or having to practice on the piano (mamma, I won't say anything about you) or having to spade enough garden to make an onion bed, we could not complain.

But as we have a snap of a job we feel sorry and pity people that has such a hard time of it. Of coarse now we were not coaxed to take this job but just worked like the devil to get it and we intend to shoulder the cross and carry it to Klondyke and if there is any gold there we will dig it out ourselves.

You can stop and think for a moment if any of you would accept my position. The first thing you must do is to get on the cars and ride two thousand miles. That is easy when a fellow has never ridden the cars. Then the next thing to do is to go into camp for five weeks and take care of your two years outfit, that is easy too, especially if you bake a batch of bread and it won't raise. The next thing you have to do is to load your outfit up in two wagons and ride a hundred miles over the darndest pike that is on the north side of the equator. That is easy, awful easy, for you know I never navigated much that way.

The next thing to do is to go into camp again for two weeks (Athabasca Landing) and build a boat and work all day and the days are eighteen hours long. The next thing you must do that is quite easy is to load your boat up with your goods and hitch yourself up in harness just like a horse, only we are in single file and pull fifty-four hundred pounds, one hundred thirty miles. Oh that's darned easy, regular picnic. You can have so much fun switching your tail to keep the mosquitoes and buffalo gnats off you.

The next thing you must do is to go into camp for eight days, smoke your meat, dry your outfit and fight blow flies. The next thing you must do is to load up your boat again and row it across a lake eighty miles long against a head wind of course. You have it quite easy on this part of the job for when you camp for the night the closest you can get to the shore is six hundred yards. But a fellow can drive a stake in the water and tie his boat to it and wade to shore and pack his kitchen and bed with him. If you don't want to do that, you can stand out and hold the boat all night. You have to do that anyway when one of the squalls comes up and they come very sudden sometimes. It is the easiest thing in the world to get up at 2:00 A.M. and go out to the boat in a squall with the waves eight feet high and help the stake out for it would be too much on the stake for it to have to hold that big boat by itself. I always like to help anyone if he is hard at work.

The next thing you must do is to go into camp again for a few days and repack your goods and go up four miles to the post office to get a letter from home and don't get a darned letter. In this case your heart will pretty near fail you but you must remember what you started out after and keep up courage and say, "Well, I guess the folks did not write." The next thing you must do is to load up your goods in two wagons and haul them eighty-six miles over a worse road than any south of the equator.

The next thing you must do is to go into camp again and build another boat and wait for Peace River to get off its tear, then load up your boat and pull it three hundred eighty miles to Hudsons' Post just like we did the hundred thirty miles up the Athabasca and Slave Rivers. WE ARE AFTER GOLD. The next thing you must do on a job like this when you get to Hudsons' Post is to unload and pack your whole outfit over a portage of twelve miles, fifty pounds at a time. Oh that will be a regular picnic, something new you know. Won't I just link into it when I get there. The next thing a man must do on a job like this is to whip-saw enough lumber out to build a boat, build it and load up again and go on rejoicing as before.

Now we are in the gold fields and it is winter. The next thing to do is to build a log cabin, go into camp for the winter, four thousand miles from home and nothing to keep you company but the bears, wolves and deer and ten feet of snow. The next thing I will do is to trap and wait for spring and look for that gold mine I have started to hunt.

Of course Dash will be along with me. If any of the boys around there think they can stand a trip like this I would be pleased to meet them up here next summer. Tell them to send their card first for above all things I believe in style and if they don't send their card first they might be taken for a hobo and Dash would eat them up. He believes in style too for he won't let a redskin come near my tent.

I don't say or I don't want any of you to believe that I think that no one could make this trip but me for I know that any of the boys could. I don't claim to be the only pebble on Peace River. Yes, and a fellow has such a good appetite on a job like this after he pulls the boat eight hours, pine bark tastes awful good. I can eat dried apple pies up here and I never could in Illinois. Now don't let anybody say he just went on that trip to keep from going to the war for they lie every time they say it. I am past the age.

Well, lay all jokes aside, this is a trip for your whiskers. I have found out already that this is a large world and full of mosquitoes. How they do relish a suckers' blood. There are a thousand right in the top of my tent now thinking, "Oh, I will get some good blood tonight", but I will fool them when I give them a dose of Smogg.

The weather here is very warm when the sun shines but just as soon as it goes down you have to put your coat on. The air is very light and healthy. Any object that looks to be about a half a mile off is a mile and a half. The country all around as far as you can see everywhere is nothing but high hills or young mountains and valleys.

There is no fruit here but raspberries, wild strawberries and gooseberries, plenty of them. We found an Indian graveyard today. The way they are buried, they build a little coop just like a chicken coop and put the redskin in there and wrap him in some kind of cloth, just like a mummy, don't put any dirt on them and he is left there to dry up, gone to his happy hunting ground.

Saturday evening, July 23
I am going to be cook when I come home Myrty. I can cook anything that you can eat from brown gravy to a baked moose and I don't have to have all those knick knacks you have either. Oh, sometimes I use sand when the wind blows right hard. I do the most of the cooking. I baked cookies today (they are edible) the first of that kind I have baked, and I baked four apricot pies and a big chunk of bacon. The other men are working on the boat and when they came to dinner you ought to have seen them, the way Peters did sink his face into that pie would make the champion pie eater of the world hurry up.

He has always tried to make us believe that he did not like sweet things. The doctor told him that he must leave all sweets alone or it would kill him, He took one of the cookies and spread some brown gravy on it.

Says he to me, "What is them, biscuits'?

I says, "No, they are cookies".

He says, "I thought they were some cold biscuits left over."

And then he said, "They are too sweet for me", and then reached over and put two big heaping spoonsful of sugar in his coffee. Oh, what a liar. It is not the sweet that the doctor meant, it is eating so much sweet at once that made him sick.

I feel sorry for Hardesty, he has bad teeth and can't eat fast enough and consequently he doesn't get as much sweets as Peters does. I am going to pound his grub up for him with the tater masher. Of course the cook gets his share while he is cooking.

The river has gone down again and we will have our boat ready by Tuesday and then will pull out for Fort St. John. The boys are going across the river tomorrow hunting for bear and moose. And if Peters doesn't do any better than he did when he killed the goose at Swan River (shot eleven times and killed one goose) the bear will eat him.

He has been telling us ever since he was in Mattoon what a crack shot he was, that he could put five holes through your hat when you threw it up in the air. He has wasted a whole lot of ammunition up here and has killed but one goose. I told him he ought to have a cannon.

He can't make a success of catching fish as many as there are and as easy as they are to catch. He is afraid he will fall in the water. He has only caught two fish on the whole trip. He comes as near being no account as the fifth wheel on a wagon but we make him get in the harness just the same.

Ho, ho, another Klondyke outfit has just arrived by pack horses from the head of the lake. We have quite a lot of new arrivals. Well, the more the merrier. It will take them a month here to get their horses backs [sic] so they can go farther.

Sunday morning

The outfit that arrived here last evening are selling out and are going back home. They have come three thousand miles and have just found out they have enough grub to only last them this summer and that it will take them all summer to take them to where they want to go. They are asking Hudsons' Bay prices for their goods which is, "give me all the money you have and I will give you a few little things."

Flour is worth $9.50 per hundred, nails 40¢ per pound, tobacco, a poor quality, $1.00 per pound, sugar $20.00 for fifty pound sack and other things in proportion. Butter is worth 40¢ eight months old, that, that is not haired out yet 60¢. It would pay to run in a stock of goods here and start a competition.

9:00 A.M. Sunday

There was an Indian dance here in this place last evening, a very quiet affair which lasted all night. The tom tom string band played for the darned fools. The better class of people took the sights in because they could do nothing else. One dog shot.

A great many Klondykers have gone up in the hills bear hunting this morning. Nice place to rusticate if you don't pick any berries. If

Hinkle in camp

the peaks were just a little higher you could see Mattoon. One weasel killed in the Shaw brothers camp this morning. It took nine men and Dash to fix him. The mice are something that are bothering the boys at this place. Every one is killing the pests. No great damage done yet they ate one apricot pie for me. We have no traps or poison. At the east end of the lake it was blow flies, I wonder what it will be at the next camp ground, lice I expect.

Sunday evening, 8:00 P.M.
It is nice to wait a week for the mail to come in and have it arrive on Sunday and then wait all day for the post office to open and then don't get any letters. If some of you would just take half of your leisure hours of an evening and write the old man a letter, I would be able to get a letter every mail (once a month). I have not received the papers that Harry sent me and I haven't got any paper of any kind, I have no paper to shave with, I use green leaves.

Monday morning
Hardesty received packages that contained three Chicago papers, the Mattoon Journal of June 11th and the Mattoon Star of June 8th. Thanks to Mrs. Hardesty for sending so much reading matter, they will last us a long time.

We have our boat about finished and will leave here about Wednesday morning. The river has gone down. I will not be able to write any more after I leave here until we get to Fort St. John or else if we happen to get into camp for a few days before we get there.

So now I have a chance to send this back to the lake by a policeman. I will close for this time by impressing it on your mind that I would like to get more letters from you and more papers. This leaves us all in the very best of health, hoping it will find you all the same and getting along all right. I imagine I see Myrty pecking away on the typewriter. A few million kisses to you. Do your best all you kids. Goodbye with lots of love and kisses to all.

I am your Jim Hinkle

6

Fifty Miles up Peace River

Sunday, August 7, 1898

Dear Mamma and girl and boys,

I will now give you a write-up of our trip, the hardships and pleasures we have etc. As it is Sunday and we don't work on Sunday, we are in camp, all of us. That includes the two parties that joined us at Peace River Landing, a French party and another party of two that we have overtaken, fifteen men altogether besides the dogs.

We left Peace River Landing on Monday, August 1 at 10:00 A.M. We crossed the river to the opposite side and are tracking up the river on the right hand side. Our boat has seven men on board and eight men to pull it and man it. Four men pull the boat one hour and one hour off. We change every hour, that way we get to rest an hour.

There is a Mission and three houses and a few Indian teepees. We got three pounds of butter and some milk there, the first we have had since we left Athabasca Landing and the way we did go for that butter and milk. We paid just what we wanted to give for the milk and 35¢ for the butter. The country is uninhabited. The tracking is not as bad as on the Athabasca or Slave Rivers and the water so far is good.

On Tuesday the 2nd we left camp at 10:00 A.M. and made about eight miles, very bad tracking and swift water. The days are hot and nights are cold. Each side of the river has very high banks and thick timber.

On Wednesday the 3rd we left camp at 6:00 A.M. We did very well on this day but had bad tracking. What I mean by bad tracking is that the banks are full of brush and high steep banks and we have a hard time pulling the boat. But we are getting there just the same.

At 3:00 P.M. we had a thunder shower and a good wind. We tried our sail. It worked all right but the wind did not last long enough as it takes a strong wind to sail against the current in Peace River. So we drifted back about a half a mile, pulled into shore with the oars and tried the old way — the line, harness and main strength. Peters had a fit while we were trying to sail. Everybody on board was laughing at him and yet he has been telling Hardesty and me that he was a sailor and a steamboat man; he is, but a dry land sailor.

Three of our party are sailors and good ones at that. They sailed across the lake in nine hours and we were nine days getting across the lake.

Well, we made what is called the Seven Sticks on Wednesday evening. It is a landmark that the Hudson Bay Company has for their boats about twenty-four miles from the Landing. It is seven small trees cut off at the top thirty feet high and the bark peeled off them, no inhabitants, nothing but bears and they are thick, we see them every mile. One of our men killed one and we had fresh meat for a while. I have not killed any yet but have had no chance, that is I have not been close enough to them (but it was not my fault).

On Thursday the 4th we left camp at 6:00 A.M. This day we had good tracking and good water and made twelve miles. One swift place we came to we helped one another over it. We had thirteen men pull our boat through it. The line broke twice. We didn't do a thing except two of us on the boat went flying down the river at the rate of twenty-five miles an hour for a mile but we landed the boat all right each time and tried it the third time but put on a bigger line and got her through all right. One more fit had Peters. It is a good thing he was not on the boat or we would have had a funeral.

On Friday the 5th we left camp at 6:30 A.M. Tracking fair and water good. On both sides of the river, the hills are a thousand feet high. The prettiest sight I ever saw. I would give fifty dollars for a Kodak. On the right side the hills are bare and on the left side heavy timber. There is a big timber fire ahead of us and it is awfully smokey. We go into camp at 6:00 P.M. every evening. The days are getting shorter, the sun sets at 7:40 now, that is 6:00 your country.

On Saturday the 6th we left camp at 6:20 A.M. Good tracking and good water. Passed Burnt River at 3:00 P.M. Hills and country just the same. We camped for over Sunday and are about fifteen miles from Dunvagen. We are all very tired but all in the best of health and will be rested up by Monday morning. We are a jolly party, the three sailors are all right in every respect.

Sunday noon, the 7th
Have just had dinner of soda biscuit, fried Armours bacon, fried hominy, cold beans and tea. The three sailors had stewed prunes, prune pudding, baking powder biscuits, fried bacon, beef extract and tea. The Shaw boys had baking powder bread (hard as iron) fried bacon, tea and molasses. I didn't see what the French party had.

I was up at 8:00 A.M. and some of the boys are just getting up. We camped along side a bank twenty feet high. Back of us the hills are a thousand feet high. The sun is very hot today and it is still very smokey. Just now a party of three has just come into our camp. We left them when we had the hard pull when the line broke. We will reach Dunvagen tomorrow evening. It is called 60 miles from the Landing as the crow flies but about seventy-five miles to go around the creeks in the river.

I hope you have gotten all my letters I have written since I left Athabasca Landing. I wrote you four or five with twenty-four pages giving you a full description of the country and the trip that we have gone over. Mr. White said in one of his letters that the directors had asked him for my letter to have it published in the papers. Did they do it and have they published any of my letters? If they have, send me the clippings.

Presh, you and Clarence ought to be here to take a ramble up the hills. You could climb all day and then not be at the top and Harry, if you want any big game to shoot at, come up and bring a gun that will shoot harder than the shot gun or you will get into a fight that won't last long on your side. Myrty, there is nothing in the way of relics so far unless I would send you one of these hills, it would be a good thing to slide down in the winter. Joke on the sled and the girl too when they got to the bottom of the hill.

We expect to reach Fort St. John by the 25th, Harry's birthday, and I expect to get a whole lot of letters from you all there or there will be a fuss. Well I am going to take the gun and Dash and go to the top of this hill, the highest one there is. I have a curiosity to know what is on the other side so here I go.

Later

Well, what a world this is. I went to the top of the hill to see what was there. I thought maybe I could get a bear or a moose or look for gold or find something to send you. On top I found it to be as level as a floor, a space as big as a twenty acre field and nice grass, no trees. Beyond that there is another hill just as big. I did not go any farther to satisfy my curiosity. I was afraid that I would drop into the moon and could not get back to Canada again. Joke on mamma if I had not.

Well, I did not see a bear or a moose or anything that I could send you but this flower, it was right on top of the hill. I don't know the name of it. I guess we will call it the Out of Sight Flower. Anyhow, there is where it came from, 446 miles northwest of Edmonton and 2461 miles northwest of Mattoon. Take good care of it. The air is so light up here that you have to think a bit if you have lost your breath.

Some of the boys have been prospecting today, found lots of colors. Colors mean just what I sent you when I was at Edmonton, flour gold, a man could make $2.00 per day at it. That is not rich enough for me. So you see we are on the right track to find the yaller stuff. What is found here has come from the headwaters of the river and that means Findlay River, the head of which is on the other side of the Rocky Mountains and there is where we are going. We will not reach there this summer but will be close this spring. We are trying to make Fort Graham before winter sets in, anyhow we can make the mountains. The mountains commence at Fort St. John.

I am going to trap this winter, I think I can make a couple thousand. No doubt you have all formed an opinion as to how soon we will be in the gold fields and how soon we will be digging gold. Now I will tell you just as it will be. We have one hundred eighty miles to go to Fort St. John from there to Hudson Hope or Cust's House or what is known as the Canyon or Twelve Mile Portage is fifty miles and from there to Fort Graham is a hundred fifty miles. We will not average more than ten miles per day unless it is better than what we have gone over already.

Monday, August 8
Left camp at 6:40 A.M. and have made about nine miles today. We are eight miles from Dunvagen and will reach there Tuesday evening August 9. It is sixty-two miles from the Landing so you see we have only averaged about eight miles per day. There are a great many islands all along in the river and we lose lots of time getting around them. So now all you can do is to pray for us to have good luck and health and we will do our best. Anyhow we will travel as long as the weather will permit us and then go into camp for the winter.

But we think we will be across the Twelve Mile Portage before we go into winter quarters and if we do we will be in the gold fields but not as far as we will go. We want to get into the mountains on Findlay River to find lots of gold. So now you can judge just what we have to go through yet and as to about when we will get there. If the tracking turns out to be better we will get there that much sooner. We work every day except Sunday, ten hours per day and it is hard work, awful hard work, as hard as any work I have ever done. But all we ask is health and we will get there the same.

It is smokey and has been for three days, so smokey we can only see about a hundred rods, just like a thick fog, it is caused by a forest fire. We have left the high hills and are in a wide valley with pine and poplar forests on both sides of the river. We are in camp for the night and I am sitting on the boat writing. The boys are sitting around the camp fire telling their big yarns. Some of them have gone up into the wood hunting. I am cooking a pot of beans and stewing a kettle of dried apples. I am going to make preserves of them and have the beans cold for tomorrow.

Tuesday, August 9
Left camp at 6:10 A.M. Nice day but awful smokey and foggy.

1:50 P.M.
Just arrived at Dunvagen. We have gone into camp to fix our boat. We are going to unload it and stop the leaks and examine our goods to see if they are all right.

Dunvagen is on a bank, prettiest place we have come to yet, prettiest sights you ever saw. All around there are seven log houses, a Hudson Bay store, a mission and some Indian teepees. The mountains on the right are two thousand feet high. There are gardens planted by the priest. Lots of vegetables but he won't sell them. If we steal them we get hung so we look at them through the fence and say, "Oh I wish I had some of those onions and lettuce." Sounds natural to hear the cow bells jingling or to see one. Five Indian squaws just went by, they have been fishing, they look like the devil.

Wednesday, August 10
We are in camp and have got the boat unloaded out on the bank and have been all day working on it. We have just loaded the goods up again and we are ready to start in the A.M.

Myrty, I was sewing all forenoon. I made me a cover for my gun and a pair of suspenders out of moose skin. You ought to see the suspenders. They are the old fashioned kind like Dan and Leander Weidner used to wear when I was a boy (of course

I did not wear them). They are two inches wide and just a straight strap with button holes worked in each end of them and they are yaller. That's all right we don't put on any style. The smoke has cleared away and we can see the country.

Thursday, August 11

I was up at 4:30 A.M. and got all hands up. Everybody got breakfast and left camp at 7:15 A.M. It is our hour on the boat and we have good water so I thought it would be a novelty to write some while traveling. The smoke is all gone and we can see everything now with some satisfaction. The hills on both sides of the river are getting higher. The Hudson Bay boats are six days ahead of us and we will meet them about Saturday going back so when I meet them I will send this letter back with them. I am acquainted with the foreman of the boats. His name is Ferguson and is a half breed. His teams hauled us from the head of the lake to Peace River Landing. Got acquainted with him while we were camped in the mouth of Swan River on the lake. Excuse me for an hour. It is my time to get out and pull on the line.

Well here it is 11:00 and our dinner time. The tracking is pretty good this morning, we made five miles. Can't see the top of the hills where we are eating dinner.

6:40 P.M.

Well, I have just had supper. Hardesty said he would wash the dishes so I will write some more. Well, we made fifteen miles today, the most miles we have made in one day yet. We are seventy-seven miles from Peace River Landing.

I suppose you are suffering with the heat there. It is nice here, not too cold or not too hot. We get hot while tracking but get cooled off when it's our time on the boat.

Just as soon as the sun goes down we have to put on our coats and we don't have any rain only just a few thunder showers. There was frost last night a little. It gets fifty-two degrees below zero here in the winter, so the Hudson Bay man tells us at Dunvagen.

We have not killed any wild game yet on this river although there are lots of bear and lots of moose. We see fresh bear tracks everywhere and see the bears but as yet have not got a shot at any of them. We make so much noise that they get in the timber and that settles it, for the timber is so thick that you can't see ten feet.

But I will have one some day if I have to put salt on his tail to catch it. Joke on the tail.

I suppose you are talking street fair. I am awful anxious to get to Fort St. John to get some word from you. I will tell you something now that you will have to do after we reach Hudson Hope, but not until then. Hudson Hope is as far as mail comes in this way and it is fifty miles the other side of Fort St. John. When we get beyond there the mail goes into that part of the country some other way and I think it will be via Ashcraft. So now remember this and if you should not get any word from me for a long time, you address your letters like this, James Hinkle, Fort Graham via Ashcraft in care of Hudson Bay Company.

Now don't address any mail that way unless you get another letter from me headed at Hudson Hope and telling you to do so unless you should not hear from me until spring. Keep on sending your mail as you have until further notice. We may be in winter quarters at Hudson Hope.

Well, I expect we will meet the Hudson Bay boats tomorrow. So if I do I will try and send this letter back by them. You must excuse this poor writing for I have nothing to write on standing up, sometimes writing on my knee and every other way. Well I will quit for tonight.

Goodnight

Friday, August 12
Now this has been simply awful. We have been all forenoon going one mile. We came to a rapid and we had a time, had to put a block and tackle on the boat and pull the old tub over that and we just got her over at 12:05. We just had dinner and I am on the boat writing letters and one of the Grimstons are over on an island in the middle of the river prospecting. The other men are sitting on the bank smoking. We have just heard by an Indian that the next fifty miles is good tracking. That's all right too, we aren't kicking.

Mamma, I do hope that you are not sick and I do hope that you are getting along all right and I hope that Myrty has finished her school and has a good position and Harry has got all right with his ankle and Pet has a good steady job. I am awful anxious to know how you all are.

We are now four hundred seventy-five miles from Edmonton, eighty miles from Peace River Landing and eighteen miles from Dunvagen. We will be about one hundred miles from Peace River Landing Saturday evening if it is so that the next fifty miles is good tracking. We will be at Fort St. John about on Harry's birthday. If we do, that will give us another month to travel in before we go into winter quarters and ought to put us on the other side of Twelve Mile Portage or Hudson Hope. That is in the mountains and in the gold fields and all we have to do next summer is to look for gold.

Now mamma, I am going to find this gold while we are up here even if we have to go farther and it takes me five years to do it. I am not going to leave anything undone or let any time go by without trying to find it. It may be that we'll have to go to the Liard River, it won't pay to come out after all we have gone through if I have to go clear to the Klondyke country and I want you to tell that to Mr. Katz, Mr. Montague, Mr. Clark and all of the directors, that should we have to go farther that we want them to buy us another years outfit to do it with. You can tell them, as for myself, I won't give this hunt up as long as they will feed me.

We are not out of money yet, have lots of it, but this is in case we run out and have to go farther. But I don't think we will have to go any farther than the mountains 'til we find a good mine. We have reports from there that they are washing out from $5.00 to $30.00 per day on the sand bars in the river. If that is so there is a gold mine there in the mountains someplace.

I will keep you posted as fast as I find out and will give it to you all just as it is. Write me often and tell some more of them to write me. You must know how lonesome I am without hearing from home for so long. There is nothing up here to keep me company but the hills, the river and the bears. It is nothing but a forsaken country. Even the trees look lonely, it is a sight to see.

Well, I am looking for the Hudson Bay boats every minute so I must have this letter ready to send back. This leaves us all in good health and full of hopes, hoping it will reach you all right and find you all in as good health as I am myself. So now I will quit for this time and will write you again at Fort St. John and more good luck to you all is my sincere wish. Many kisses to you all and a big squeeze for Myrty. Goodbye. We are ready to pullout right now.

Your Hubby James Hinkle

7

Twenty-Five Miles Above Dunvagen

Sunday, August 14, 1898

My dear Mamma and girl and boys,

    I just got through writing you a letter yesterday and sent it back by the Hudson Bay boats and I will commence now on another one and give you kind of a memorandum of the balance of the trip to Fort St. John and will mail this letter when I get there.

    This is Sunday and we are all in camp. We don't work on Sunday. There are six parties of us altogether. There are three parties of us on one boat, eight men, we change off every hour, four on the line and four on the boat. We get some rest that way but we don't get to rest the whole hour for one man has to guide the boat and when we come to a bad place one of us has to use poles or get out in the water and help to push the boat off. But some places we have nice water for miles and then we get to rest the hour.

    We all seem to be lively enough today. There are eighteen of us camping. Some are washing dirty clothes, some are mending, some cooking, some gone hunting. I have just got done playing the fiddle. We will all be rested up by morning and ready for another week. We are just half way to Fort St. John and will reach there in ten days or by the 25th, Harry's birthday.

    Talk about sights, this is a sight that everyone should see. It looks like the mountain had been cut in two for the river to run through. I went up on top of a hill and found it level for one eighth of a mile back and then there is another hill just like the one next to the river. I suppose ten miles back from the river one could step off on the moon.

The beach is sometimes rocky and big rocks at that, some of them as big as a house, sometimes sand as level as a floor, sometimes mud, sometimes brush, but it is not as bad a river as the Slave River was to get up.

Wednesday, August 17, 12:30 noon
Well old cuteness, as I am behind three days in writing I will write some this noon spell. The reason I am behind is simply because we have had the very devil for the last three days, rapids, bad tracking and crossing the river back and forth to get around bad places. Yesterday we were all day going two miles and worked just as hard as we could. We came to a place where the river from bank to bank was about a mile wide and right in a big bend there were eight islands all close together. Talk about work, we didn't do a thing but work. We got by the bad place last night just at quitting time and we did not have to wait for someone to say, "Boys, it's 6:00 o'clock". None of us was able to go ten feet farther. We camped on the last island.

This morning we left camp at 6:45 A.M. and have made five miles up to the present writing and so far as we can see it looks good for us. We are about thirty-five miles above Dunvagen. The weather is fine, not too hot or too cold but the mosquitoes are very bad. There are lots of bear and moose all along but we are too tired to go and shoot them and we make so much noise going along that we don't get in shooting distance of them. A man killed one grizzly bear a few days ago. They are man eaters and are scarce but there are lots of black bear and cinnamon bear. They won't attack you unless you cripple one of them or kill one of their cubs.

The hills are high and rough and of sand stone. They cave in from the top and roll down way out in the water and that is where we have the devil to get our boat around. Some of them are just under the water and we can't see them until we get our boat fast on them. Then it is a case of wade out and lift her off. I still think we will reach Fort St. John by the 25th. The Hudson Bay boats are due there the 26th and I know they will have lots of letters for me from home, they had better have.

There are only two boats in our gang now. The other two have left us and gone on. Their boats are light and can travel faster than we can. There are thirteen of us together, two boats, eight in our gang and five Frenchmen. Well it is time to go to work so if I have time this evening to write some more and am not too tired, I will. It is my time in the harness so here I go to hitch myself up to the steamboat, oh, I mean the pull boat. A kiss apiece.

7:30 P.M.
Well, we have gone into camp and have made about nine miles today and are at the foot of a darned sight harder rapid than we were in yesterday. We have crossed over the river to the south side. The river is over a mile wide and full of sand bars and islands and we have to go first in the morning and find out how we are going to get through this Peace River place. The man that named this river is a damned liar, if he had of said quarrelsome river he would have been a gentleman.

Tell John Cantlon that we crossed over to one of the sand bars and found a hundred colors but tell him it is flour gold. We prospect every sand bar, find some gold in all of them but have found the most in this one. The farther up we go the better it gets. It has just commenced to rain and I will quit for tonight and cover up the boat and tell you tomorrow how we got through the rapids. On the next page you will find a sketch of this rapid, the river and where we are camped. I am writing now on the boat and these blots are caused by the rain drops.

Thursday morning, August 18, just after breakfast.
I will write while some of them are eating. The sun is just peeping up from behind the mountain. If I was over there I could step off onto it. I find that the rapids are still here and we have to go through them yet. Well there is nothing yet that has stopped us so I guess that we will get through this place. Myrty, this would be a nice place

to take a walk on Sunday evenings with your beaux. Joke on the time it would take to come here to take the walk. Joke on the girl if she didn't have any beaux.

Thursday noon
Well look at the sketch I drew and read all the reading and you can form an idea of what kind of a place we are in. We left camp this morning at 8:30. Have been until 11:30 coming one mile where the boat is marked on page five and now we have to cross sand bar #3. Understand, we are pulling seven tons through this. We had beans, cornbread and molasses for dinner. Now we are going to hitch ourselves up. One more kiss apiece.

6:00 P.M.
We have been all afternoon getting across this channel and to sand bar number three. We came to a place we could not get around so we have just finished unloading half of our boat and we are all tired out so we have gone into camp for the night. We carried our goods about five hundred yards and will try it again in the morning.

Friday, August 19
Five hundred miles northwest of Edmonton, one hundred and ten miles up Peace River and stuck on a rapid tighter than Billy be damned. After working all day Thursday and coming through one mile of rapids we came to a bad place that we had to unload our boat and portage our goods five hundred yards, seven tons of it.

We got just half of the boat unloaded last night, everybody wet and tired. Made our beds on sandbar number three and laid ourselves down to rest with the stars and heavens above us and enough gravel and water below us to build a railroad around the world. We are all in the very best of health and spirits but the most tarnation stiff in our joints. We have all decided to get our boat around this place, load up and go about a half mile to sand bar number five and go into camp for over Sunday and prospect this place thoroughly.

We have found lots of colors here on these sand bars. Yesterday we found in a pan, forty colors and some of them as big as pin heads.

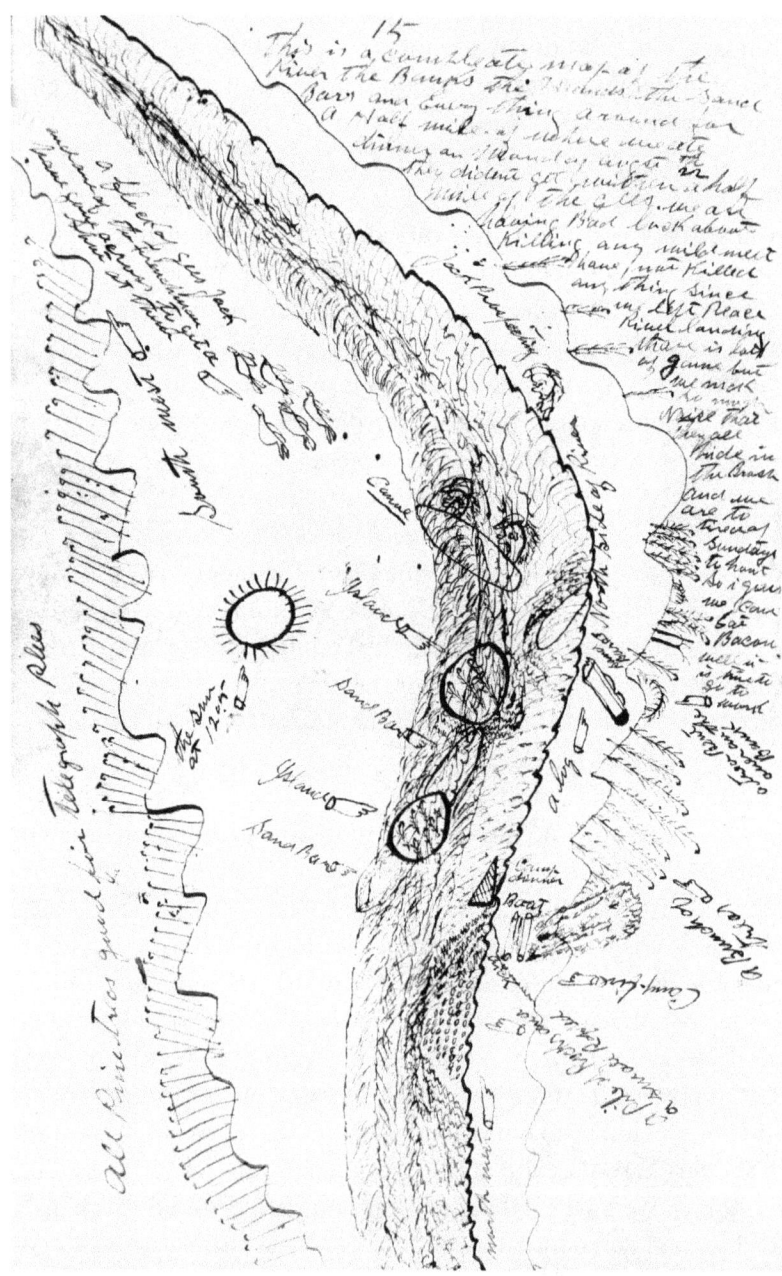

Hinkle's sketch of the rapids

The river here at this point is over a mile wide and full of sand bars and islands. We may find a good thing right here. We are going to work now to get the empty boat around to where the goods are.

Friday, at noon
We got our boat around the bad place, loaded up again and pulled around to island number five. We will be in camp until Monday. We are all very tired and we are going to prospect and hunt some fresh meat, bear and moose are good.

Mamma, I will look for your heart here at this place. The farther we go the better the prospect looks. But I don't think now that we will get much farther than Fort St. John before the cold weather sets in. It is a very difficult river to navigate and we are seventy miles from Fort St. John yet. I am awful anxious to get there to get word from home but we must not overdo the thing and make ourselves sick.

7:00 P.M.
I went bear hunting this evening, did not see any or kill any. Tomorrow I am going to prospect. We are camped at the middle of the island and up on a bank fifteen feet high in among the trees. They are as thick as they can stand.

Saturday evening, 6:00 P.M.
Just ate supper and I will write some more. I ate so much I am in misery. I stewed some dried apples and made apple dumplings (whope, how good) I made biscuits, I cooked split peas and sliced some Armours breakfast bacon right thin in them, opened a can of condensed milk for the apple dumplings, had cold beans and dried applesauce. There, can you beat that? I like to have busted myself.

Well we have all been prospecting today all around the islands and sand bars. We found lots of colors but nothing that would pay more than $1.50 per day unless we had machinery to work it with. Every indication is that the gold found here on the bars has come from up the river farther and that means the head of Peace River or its tributaries. But it is a sure thing that there is gold in this country and we are on the right track.

We will prospect everything that we come to as we go forward and try and make it to the Rocky Mountains or Hudson Hope before winter sets in. The Rocky Mountains are fifty miles from Fort St. John and are right at Hudson Hope. We are twenty-five miles from the British Columbia boundary line now. We will all be rested up by Monday and will start fresh and try and reach Fort St. John on next Saturday, the 27th.

Sunday, August 21, after breakfast.
Well, this is a beautiful day and the hawks are screaming across the river. Some of the men are in bed yet. We are pretty well rested by now. Here come the Hudson Bay boats sure enough, they are on the north side of the river. Oh I bet they have a dozen letters for me. Wait until I get in our canoe, I will go over and see if it is Ferguson.

I went over and as luck would have it, they stopped for dinner and I got Ferguson to look through one mail bag. I got a letter from Hat written on the 5th of July and the picture that Ollie took with a Kodak. I don't see why I didn't get a letter from you — have you quit me?

I was awful glad to get Hat's letter but I don't see why you don't write lots of letters and then I would get one every time some one came along. Now I can't hear from you until I reach Fort St. John. Hat said in her letter that we had a hard fight at Santiago and that there were between five thousand and ten thousand killed and wounded. That is the first war news we have heard since Dewey had his fight. Have not had any papers since I left Edmonton.

This is Ferguson's last trip this season. He will meet us on next Saturday on going back and we are going to get him to take our boat to Fort St. John for us, that is if he will. We were talking to him about it, he said if his men would, he would do it. He said his men were all about tired out but he thought he could get them to do it. Don't know how much it will cost us but not much. He says that the next thirty miles is good but the balance of the way to Fort

St. John is full of rapids. They know the river better than we do. It takes them four days to go from here but they are just like mules. It will probably cost us twenty dollars.

I don't see why Hat didn't write me a bigger letter. She only wrote on both sides of a half a sheet and didn't say anything except about the war. I haven't heard a thing about anybody around home since I got your letter at Peace River Landing. If you were all clear away from civilization for two months you would be awful glad to get big letters, I bet you would. Of course the few lines did me lots of good but lots of lines would do me gooder.

Ferguson wouldn't open all the mail bags, he is not allowed to open any of them. I know there were more letters for me, so near and yet so far. But people that are after gold can't expect all the accommodations so I will keep on hunting gold and sawing wood.

I baked ten loaves of bread since dinner and they are nice, puts me in mind of mamma's big loaves. Oh Myrty, I am going to be the cook. Now when I come home I can cook anything from roast moose to a pan full of sand. I can make apple dumplings out in the woods just as well as if I was in a bake shop and just as good too, so I can.

Myrty, these wild roses are all around where I am sleeping and just thick all through the woods. The blossom has fallen off and left the red bud just as big as a cherry and just as red. They are as pretty as a flower garden and look like they were good to eat. The bears do eat them. I will press one and send it to you in the letter.

After supper

I feel somewhat better after a beautiful supply of fresh light bread and milk gravy made out of condensed milk. It was a little bit sweet but we can eat anything sweet or sour up here.

We are all rested up and will start at 6:00 o'clock in the morning and try and reach Fort St. John by Saturday night if we can get Ferguson, the Hudson Bay man to take us after we meet him coming back. If we don't it will take us two weeks to reach Fort St. John.

Harry, there are a lot of beaver on this island. I watched for them for two hours but they were too cute for me, I could not get a shot at one.

There are lots of pine squirrels here but they are not fit to eat. They eat the buds of the pine and it makes them taste like balsam. They're between a ground squirrel and a grey squirrel.

There are no frogs here, but a few birds, some butterflies, a few snakes and a million mosquitoes. There are a good many ducks and geese and hundreds of hoot owls. I have not seen a buzzard since I left Edmonton. Nothing stinks here to bring them here. Have not seen a crow since I left the Slave River. There is a bird here that looks like the jay bird only it is larger and they will light on your head. They don't know what we are. There are birds that fly up the creeks, some call them king fishes. Goodnight. Three kisses apiece.

I lay myself down to sleep.

Monday morning, August 22
Left camp at 8:15. We have come four miles this morning. It is so smokey that we can't tell what is ahead of us. Some of the boys have gone up the river prospecting. We all feel good today and will be able to make several miles this week. We are getting ready to start so I will write some more this evening. Tra la la.

Hold on, we are not ready to start. Two of the boys have come back from up the creek and brought a dozen nice colors. Everybody grabbed a gold pan, a shovel and a pick and started on a dead run for the creek. But it was allover in an hour. We did not find any colors down where they found the first colors. So we came to the conclusion that what colors we did find in the creek were put there by high water from the river at some time. So we started at 5:00 P.M. and pulled a mile farther and are in camp for the night.

6:45 P.M.
A great excitement in camp, just as we sat down to supper Dash got after a pole cat. Well if you ever saw a scrambling, there was one. I threw rocks at Dash to keep him away from it and broke the cat's leg. Then, oh then what a stink there was raised in this camp. The cat got away very easy after that. Goodnight. Four kisses apiece.

Tuesday morning, August 23
Left camp at 8:00 and had good beach and good water up until dinner time. We are stopped now for dinner and it is a nasty looking place ahead of us. Don't know but it looks as if we have trouble ahead.

Tuesday evening, 6:00 P.M.
Have had supper and have gone into camp for the night. Well it was not so bad after dinner as it looked to be but it took six men to pull the boat for a half mile. After that we had good water for four miles and we are now at the foot of some more islands. All of our camp happens to be on a bend or at the beginning of a bend in the river. Part of the time we are going southwest and then to the northwest. We are now sixty miles from Fort St. John. Can't tell you when we will get there, but it won't be on Harry's birthday.

Wednesday, August 24, 12:00 o'clock noon
We left camp this morning at 8:30 and have made three miles up to dinner. We will meet the Hudson Bay boats about tomorrow evening and I must have this letter ready to send back unless they will stop and take us to Fort St. John. Anyhow I will have this letter ready in case he does not and then I will commence another one and mail it at Fort St. John on our arrival there.

This is a trip that many and many a human would dream about and it is a trip that many and many a man could not take for the reason that he could not stand it and do the work we do. It is a trip worth seeing but a hard one to make.

It has gotten very smokey again, looks like Indian summer only it is more smokey. It is our turn on the boat so I will light my pipe and proceed to navigate onward. For the night, tra la la.

After supper, Wednesday evening, August 24
Well I have had a supper of pancakes, cold beans and pork with sugar molasses. I feel all right only somewhat tired but will write some more. We are now about five miles from the British Columbia

border line. The mountains all on the north side of the river are very nearly bare and nearly straight up with all kinds of coarse rocks.

Now I will go out and hunt a place for my bed. We just hunt a level place and put our beds down on the ground and that is where we sleep. My bed consists of a tent first for a ground sheet, then the sleeping bag, then a double blanket on the bag and a double blanket for a cover, then the tent pulled up over that. If it rains we let it rain. I use my overcoat for a pillow, sometimes a flat stone. Six kisses apiece.

Goodnight.

Thursday morning just after breakfast.
If I were there this morning, Harry would get a thumping and don't you forget it either. I suppose you think you are a better man than you were one year ago today, but you wouldn't make a handful for me. Keep on growing and take a few trips like this and you can then begin to study about the matter. When I left the Landing I guessed that we would make Fort St. John on this day but I have missed it at least ten days.

The trip has been harder to make and there is no push in the crowd but myself and Charley. We are up every morning at 5:00 o'clock, get breakfast and then wait for the balance of them to take their time. If we didn't push the thing along we wouldn't get to Fort St. John in two years. Peters is actually not worth taking to a dog fight. He is what I call a first class know nothing, shirker and liar. He would be the last man I ever would want to take on a trip like this. The party would be better off if he was out of it. They are ready to start so I will stop. Tra la la.

We have just had the devil all morning and only made one and a half miles. We have two big bars to get around and they are as bad as a rapid. The points run out half way across the river and the water is so shallow that we have to wade out in the water and pull the boat.

Harry, I am thinking of you. I had pancakes and cold beans for dinner and I thought how you would bite a half moon in that pancake if you had it. I suppose that if you were at home, mamma made you a little dinner of some kind and I suppose you were all thinking about me.

When I started this letter, I thought we would be in Fort St. John today but we lack fifty-five miles of doing it and I can't tell how long it will take us yet. We are having a tough time of it and making slow progress. But we are doing our best considering what we are working with. If I had three more good men like Hardesty and myself we would have been there long ago. It is time to go to work. Tra la la.

Thursday evening just after supper. 6:30 P.M.
If I stop this letter short you will know that the Hudson Bay boats are coming. I will have to have it ready or I won't get to send this letter back. We are looking for them all the time now unless they have concluded to stop and take us to Fort St. John. I made a new rule in camp this noon spell and it was voted unanimous and it is that we work six hours instead of ten, commence at 8:00 A.M., quit for dinner at 11:00 A.M., go to work at 1:00 P.M., quit for the day at 4:00 P.M. and six men pull on the line instead of four and two men on the boat permanently and that the steersman should give all orders and everybody obey his command.

We elected Digby, one of the Englishmen and Hardesty for on the boat, this rule to go into effect immediately. So we started that way and you ought to see us go until we came to this bad place and we were there for one hour and a half but finally got the old tub over it. It is a sand bar running out into the river with a bay on the west side and the water very swift and very shallow.

Friday morning, 8:30
Here comes the Hudson Bay so I will say goodbye and wait and see if they will take us. We are in British Columbia. Lots of kisses.

Jas. Hinkle
Write me lots of letters and direct as usual.

August 26, 1898

A leaf of a wild rose just in front of my tent.
My dear Babies,

I promised to write you another letter after the one I sent back today by the Hudson Bay Company so I will commence right after we have left them and give you a sketch and letter too as we go along.

We could not get Ferguson to take us to Fort St. John but we hired six of his Indians and they take our boat and pull it and ourselves there. We give them $3.00 per day per man and board. It will take them three days to make it, making $54.00 and what it costs for the grub.

The grub consists of two pounds of flour, one pound of bacon and enough tea per man per day, altogether sixty pounds of flour, thirty pounds of bacon and about one pound of tea. We have to board them the two days it takes them to go back from St. John to the Landing. So now you know all about it and all we do is to sit on the boat and look on and take a free ride. So while we are going I am writing and will draw some sketches of the river as we go along.

We will be at Fort St. John on Sunday evening the 27th. I will make you a sketch of this place we are going by with the six Indians pulling us. There is a big bend in the river to the south side with a big island on the north side called by the Indians, Moose Island, with two sand bars and two bays and at the west end a bad rapid and still farther on, a house up on the bank with a man and his wife living there. It is the first house we have seen since we left Dunvagen. He is a trapper. We have a field glass and we all took a peep at the surroundings. The woman wasn't bad looking, the man looked like a Texan. He had seventeen dogs, a wagon and that's all. He looked lonesome and so did his house.

Well now we are going like something. These Indians are just like mules and can pull anything that is loose at one end. There is only one of them that can understand the English language and all he can say is yes, good, cheap, St. John and a few other words. They

Twenty-five Miles Above Dunvagen / 61

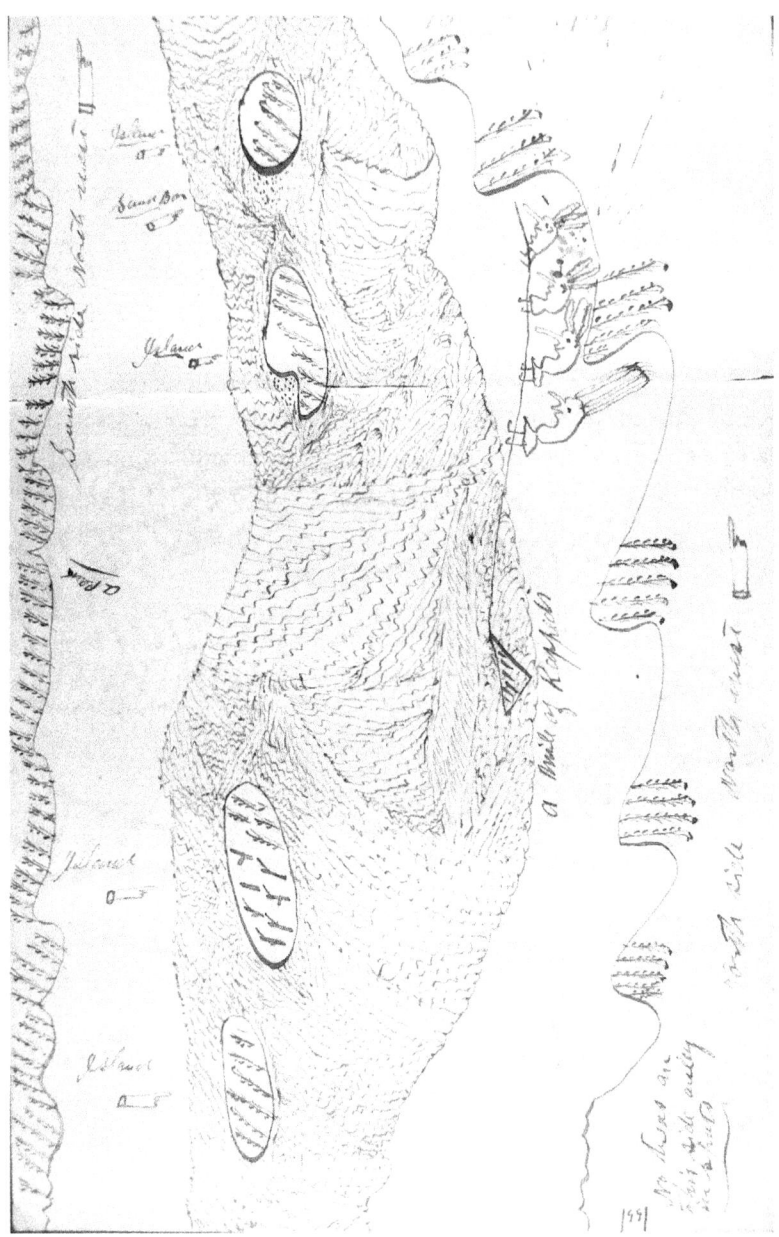

Hinkle's sketch of Indians pulling the boat

pulled the boat right through that rapid and were not more than ten minutes and it would have taken us a half a day and how.

This is the right way to travel up here and if ever I go again in any country like this I will be by hiring the natives to take me there. We would have been to the head of Peace River if we had hired six Indians to pull us. They go from Peace River Landing to Hudson Hope, two hundred thirty miles, in eleven days where it would take us two solid months hard work so you can see how it is.

Saturday, August 27
Everybody and the Indians are up at 5:00 A.M. They start at 7:00 A.M. They eat four times per day, breakfast at 6:00, then again at 10:00 A.M., then at 2:00 P.M., then again at 6:00 P.M. I cook for the Indians. Each meal is just the same, it consists of what they call bannock, fried bacon and a two gallon pot of tea.

Now as you tender feet down there don't know what bannock is I will tell you. I take six pints of flour, a tablespoon of salt and enough Peace River water to make it into dough. I hammer it with my fist until I make each bannock the size of the skillet and one inch thick, set it up end ways by a hot camp fire and bake it brown. Burn it or any old thing will do. They are not a bit particular. They eat ashes, dirt or anything that goes in the bannock. I have seen them make it and take their bare feet to flatten it out and when it is baked the print of their foot is stamped on the bannock. Presh, you try one and see how good it is. I cook four times a day for them just that way. Oh Myrty, you bet I can cook anything. I will make you ashamed of yourself when I come home.

We are traveling right along. We have just crossed the river to the south side and will keep on this side for eight miles. Today it is very foggy and damp. The hills are not so high along here and the trees are thick on the north side. The water is much swifter and gets more so as we get farther up. We must be all of twenty miles higher than Mattoon for we have been going up hill ever since we left Edmonton. We are two hundred miles west of Edmonton and five hundred fifty-six miles northwest of Edmonton. It is just lunch time, 10:00 A.M. and the Indians are pulling in to shore so I will stop and cook bannock for a while.

Lunch is over, the Indians are hullowing all about so here we go, I see some islands ahead. I can't see far enough ahead but from here it looks like the river stops and we are at the jumping off place.

We are thirty miles from St. John and are making good time. Oh my but there had better be eighty-five or thirty letters there for me or I will step off one of those peaks onto the moon and then you won't have any chance to get a letter to me. We will travel tomorrow, Sunday, and the Indians think they will make it to St. John tomorrow evening late. I hope so. Now we are coming to something else. Sure enough it is islands, rapids and the very devil itself.

Sunday morning, August 28
Have just cooked the Indians breakfast and our own and everybody has eaten their bannock and we are on our way. This is the first Sunday we have traveled since we left the lake. The Indians don't know any better, they want to hurry to St. John so as to get twenty seven skins. Twenty seven skins are equal to nine dollars. A skin is 33-1/3¢. Well they don't want to get there any worse than I do.

This morning is cold, everybody is shivering. I don't know what we would be doing if we were tracking our own boats and in the water to our necks. We will not reach St. John until Monday night. Our boat is too heavy and the water too cold. The Indians can't make as good time as with their own boats. The three days are not up until Monday noon.

I hope I will find everything all right at home when I get my letters at St. John. I can hardly wait to get there. There is a mail man that travels from Edmonton to St. John once a month and he is due at St. John the last of each month. We will just meet him there. His name is Livingston and he travels with two pack horses. Each man that agrees to pays him one dollar per month so he will have all my letters that were in Edmonton and all those along the road and posts that we came by. He gathers them all up and takes them to St. John and then collects his dollar from each man whose name he has.

10:00 A.M.

Just after lunch and be gory the Indians have struck on us. We are twenty-six miles from St. John and the water is very swift for the balance of the way and they say they can't make it in the three days so they have struck and we can't make them understand that we made a contract with their boss, Mr. Brick, that they would land us in St. John for $54.00 and five days grub. If they don't want to go any farther they can quit. If they do they won't get a cent for what they have done and besides we will shut their grub off and starve them into it.

It is an old game of theirs. They have played the same game on other Klondykers that we know of but we are too smart for them. There they sit holding a pow wow now. They will come to their milk I think, if they get hungry, we will wait and see. It looks kind of lonesome six hundred miles from no place with your engine broken down. Well such is life in large countries like this northwest. It is raining.

Well I'll just be darned if they haven't quit. I am a liar. They have packed up their traps and have gone back down the river toward Peace River Landing and it is a hundred fifty miles. They haven't got a bite to eat and no way to go that I know of except to walk. They are game just the same. Well we got two days work out of them for nothing, or rather for just their board.

But they have left us right in the worst place on the river to go through. We are twenty-six miles, so they say, from St. John and Peters and one of the Grimstons are down the river about ten miles prospecting. They stopped on our way up after the Indians took us and now we have to wait until they come and they were going to be gone a week. Darn if all things are not coming my way. I wouldn't care if we were at St. John or close there but it is too far to walk after the mail so I guess we will have to wait until Peters comes and then pull the boat ourselves. We have pitched our tent and gone into camp. Darn the redskins anyhow. It is a cold rainy day. I will quit for this evening and tell you later what happens.

Monday morning, August 29
Hardesty is going to walk to St. John and get the mail. It will only take him ten hours to walk it. He will go up today and back tomorrow as we have to wait for Peters until the last of the week. The French party has left us and gone on to St. John and one of the Grimston party has gone with them so that only leaves four of us here in camp, myself, the two Shaw boys and one of the Grimstons. Kind of lonesome, especially of evenings when these darn owls start to sing their mournful songs. (I don't care, I'm not afraid). It is 8:00 A.M. and I will take the gun and go a piece with Charley.

9:00 A.M.
Charley and I are four miles up the river from camp. I have concluded to stop here. Hardesty has gone on like a quarter horse. There he goes just around the bend and is out of sight.

Tuesday, August 30
I took the gun and went about five miles up this creek we are camped on to see if I could kill a bear or moose or something in the fresh meat line. I did not see a bear or moose but there are lots of bear tracks and some that looked like they had just been made. I killed a blue hawk and a small bird, bound to have fresh meat of some kind. Brought them into camp but Grimston says he can't eat the hawk because it was a bird of prey. I said I didn't care if it was a buzzard I was going to have fresh meat anyhow. So I cooked it.

I boiled it awhile to get the stink out of it and then I baked it. Got to thinking about dead horses and rats and the more I cooked it the more I thought. So when I got it cooked I gave it to Dash. Joke on the bacon. Myrty I am going to cook me a new dish today and it will be apricot dumplings, use the apricots in place of apples. So I will quit now and go into the bake shop.

Later
Well I put on a pan of apricots to cook and then went down on the boat tinkering around and I had the inside of one of our flour

sacks laying in the edge of the water to soak the old dry flour off it and I saw a dozen big fish around it eating the flour so the thought struck me I would like to have a mess of fish. So I rigged up a line out of twine and cut me a pole and put a hook on it and mixed up some flour into dough for bait and cast it into the water and behold I drew out fish for father. Notice I got so interested and the fish were such a good size that I forgot all about the apricot dumplings. I caught sixteen bushel of fish and had fish instead of dumplings. Joke on the apricots.

Wednesday morning, August 31
Well I am up and had breakfast thank you and now I will give you some news, news that is not at all encouraging. I will give it to you just as we get it and as it looks to me. When we arrived at Peace River Landing we were there sixteen days. We began to hear reports that there was no gold in this part of the country. We heard it from parties that were coming out, from parties that claimed to have been up as far as Fort Graham and a hundred miles farther, all of which we would pay no attention to, thinking that they were only telling us that to keep us out.

Other parties that were headed the same way we were and were right with us at the Landing and up the river paid no attention to the reports either and are still going on the same as we are. At the Landing we met a party that was known as the Good Hope Party and consisted of twenty-five men. We bought the boat that we now have from them. There were nine of them returning and they told us that the gold craze was all a fake, that a man could only make from $1.00 to $5.00 a day on the bars on Findlay River and that they had returned on account of not having enough provisions for all and had left the balance of the men up on Findlay River.

Ever since we left the Landing we have been meeting parties every few days that were going out and claimed that they had been up on the Findlay River and there wasn't much gold up there. Still we paid no attention to their reports and kept on going with a determination to go and see for ourselves. This morning we have met five more of the Good Hope Party returning home. They stopped at our camp for an hour and we pumped them about the country and everything about the gold craze.

They told us that nine of their party were still up above Fort Graham and that they were going to try and go across to the head of Black River in the Liard River to the Pelly Banks, that they came out because they did not have enough provisions for all and that they agreed to fit out the nine men with grub and then return home. They told us that they made $6:00 per day one hundred miles above Fort Graham on a sand bar on the Findlay River and that it was a small bar and they worked the whole bar until it was worked out and that was the best they had found.

Now we don't know what to think or to do. If I had two good men, men that are stayers, two men that would work and not get sick, I would keep on going as far as I could get this winter and then go into winter camp, build a log house and trap through the winter and make as much as I could, then next summer hunt for gold.

Hardesty is a good man, would not want a better man to work but he is troubled with reumatic and is pretty near give out. He is discouraged and is talking of going home. I think the biggest part is homesickness. Peters is not a man for this kind of a trip in any sense of the word. I would not take him to a dog fight.

Now dear girls and boys, I want to see you just as bad as ever a man wanted to see his family and just as bad as Hardesty wants to see his. But now look at it on the other side. I gave up a job that was paying me $5.00 a day to see if I could do better and I've worked for months as hard as ever a human could work and we are six hundred miles northwest of the nearest railroad (Edmonton) and over half of the way into a country where there is gold (the Klondyke) and we have eighteen months living in as good shape as if we were there in Mattoon.

I think we would be a big fool to turn back now at this stage of the trip without going on and making something in trapping and digging gold and running a chance of finding a good thing. There is gold in this country in paying quantities if we can find it and I don't propose to give up now until I give it a good test. Now I can't tell what Hardesty is going to do until he comes back from St. John but I think he is going home. And as to Peters, I don't know what he is going to do and I don't care.

If Hardesty goes home and Peters comes to the conclusion to go ahead with me and does his part of the work I am willing to keep on with him. But he will have to do different from what he has done since we left Edmonton. I propose to take care of the men that staked us, let come what will, and I propose to make something out of this trip if there is any way to do it. I keep a book of everything that is bought and every cent of the whole $2400 and will be able to show them an itemized account of the whole thing.

Mamma, I want you to tell Mr. Katz, Mr. Tivnen, White, and whoever else you want to that I am up here for business and their interests. Although it is a hard trip, I am just the same as that much iron and as long as I keep my health I will continue as such. I am not one bit discouraged but I think that I should have gone the other way over the Chilkoot Pass by the way of Juneau into the Klondyke country.

I would have been in there now and stood a thousand more chances to have gotten a gold mine. That is the way I wanted to go in the first place but you know Peters would go via Peace River and that he said he had friends on Peace River that had sent for him and that they had a good thing on Peace River all of which is a damn lie. There is gold in this country but so far in very small quantities and it is only flour gold but leads me to believe that if we go far enough we will find a gold mine. I will stop now and tell you what conclusion we have come to when Hardesty comes from St. John. I am looking for him this evening.

Wednesday evening, August 31
Peters and the Englishman have arrived at camp from prospecting. They found lots of colors but nothing that would pay more than from $1.00 to $2.00 per day. We are waiting now for Hardesty and one of the Englishmen that went with the French party to St. John. Then we will proceed to St. John anyhow.

7:00 P.M.
Hardesty has not come yet and I don't look for him tonight. I suppose he is waiting for the mailman, Livingston, to come before he leaves there. Then I think he is going home. One of the men that stopped here this morning in the Good Hope Party told me that he saw Hardesty in St. John and that Hardesty told him that he was going to get out of this damn country right away so I guess that settles it and goes to show that he is not the man to undertake this trip and should have stayed home in the first place.

It makes me so darned mad to think that there were lots of good men there that wanted to go and that I would pick out someone that could not stand the trip. I will know the next time what kind of men to pick and I will know what kind of stuff there should be in a man for this kind of trip. I wish I had George Stires and George Hinkle. Well I will have to do the best I can and that is all they can ask.

There is lots of game in this country such as bear, moose, silver fox, red fox, otter, beaver, skunk and fish. A good bear skin is worth $25.00, a moose hide is worth $10.00, a silver fox is worth $75.00, a black fox is worth $100.00, a red fox $150.00, an otter is worth from $5.00 to $10.00, a beaver is worth from $10.00 to $25.00 and a skunk is worth $1.00.

So you see if I have any kind of luck I can make a good thing out of it for I have the traps and I have prepared my bait for the season. The bait is fish put away in cans until it rots. The more it stinks the better it is. The best way to use it is to put some on your shoes and hands when you set the trap and a little on a rag hung over the trap. You don't dare to leave any of your own scent with the trap or going away from it. That is the reason for putting it on shoes and hands. A fox is cunning you know. I am all ready for business. The days are getting shorter and the sun sets at 6:30. Tra la la.

Thursday, September 1
11:00 A.M. and Hardesty has not come yet. I had a talk with Peters about Hardesty going home and asked him what he thought about it. He said he is not going home until the grub runs out and the way he talked I think he intends to keep on going with me. He does not

say anything about trapping and I do not care if he does or not. He understands that I am up here for business and I think he will try his best from this point on to do the right thing.

If Hardesty goes home we will have enough provisions to last three years and it is all in the best of shape and worth its weight in gold up here. Flour is worth $15.00 per hundred. We have 1600 pounds. Bacon is worth 28¢ per pound, we have 500 pounds. Sugar is worth 25¢ per pound, we have 300 pounds. Corn meal is worth 10¢ per pound, we have 100 pounds. Beans are 20¢ per pound, we have 150 pounds. Fruit is not used or sold up here, it is too dear but worth all you ask for it. We have 100 pounds of dried apples, 25 pounds of dried apricots.

Evaporated vegetables are not sold up here and are only used by parties that bring them in and are just the same as that much gold. We have 200 pounds of different kinds such as onions, potatoes, carrots, peas, turnips, etc.

So you need not worry about me starving. We have clothes that we can't wear out in three years so taking everything into consideration we are well fixed for the occasion and I intend to make something out of it if it can be done. Besides all that we have $600.00 in money.

Now mamma, I hope you and the kids will make it all right and I will stay here until next fall anyhow and every cent I make I will bring home with me. There is no way to spend money up here except for grub and that we have. I am certain that I can make a lot of money trapping and I am certain that we will hear of a rich strike in gold either by ourselves or someone else. If we do you see we are right in the country and can fly to the place in a short time. So I am not one bit discouraged unless Hardesty comes and brings me some word from home that will make me change my mind and I am praying that he will bring me good news.

3:00 P.M.
I have just come back from a little hunt up this creek that we are camped on. I have named this creek Struck Creek on account of the Indians struck on us here. We are sitting around the camp like

a lot of bumps on a log. Can't do anything until Hardesty and the Englishman come back.

Friday evening, 3:00 P.M., September 2
No sign of Hardesty yet. Jack has gone hunting and one of the Shaw boys has gone up the river as far as Pine River. The two Englishmen are sitting around their tents, the other Shaw boy is baking bread and I am sitting in my tent writing. It's pretty damned lonesome — a fellow gets lonesome sitting around waiting on someone. If I was on the go I would be all right.

I wish you could see where we are camped. Our tents are pitched right on a big high sand bar in the mouth of this creek and the wind blows a hurricane every hour and you ought to see our grub box, stove, bed and everything, it is just covered with sand. I made biscuits for dinner and they were half sand. Chickens eat sand so I guess I can.

Jack just got back from hunting, he killed one pheasant so Pet, we are going to have fried pheasant for supper. No, he is going to stew it, he doesn't know how to cook anything, can't even fry meat. He cooks everything without salt and it isn't fit to eat and he thinks he is a good cook. Now I will try to keep the sand from blowing in the stewed pheasant, Tra la la

Well at last Hardesty has come. He arrived Friday evening at 4:00 P.M. and without a letter for anyone. Now I want you to know that I don't think that is treating me right at all. He did not wait until Livingston came and of course I am certain that he has lots of mail but I should have had at least sixteen letters and didn't get one. It may not be your fault but I think that if you would write lots of letters I would get one once in a while.

Saturday, September 3
Now mamma, before you get this letter you will see Hardesty but I will tell you what we are going to do and he can tell you too. We are within six miles of North Pine River and North Pine River is twenty miles from Fort St. John. Now we are going to take our boat up to Pine River and up Pine River as far as the water will let us go and

build a log house and go into winter quarters, trap and hunt and prospect for gold this winter and make out of it all we can.

The Shaw boys are going with us but on their own hook. That is as much as I can tell you now of our future. We will be close to Fort St. John for the winter so send all your mail there as you have been doing.

Hardesty has his things all packed up and is waiting for a man to come down from St. John on a raft. He is going down to Peace River Landing with him. Our party is dwindling away one by one. I don't think there is anything the matter with Hardesty except a genuine case of homesickness. He calls it reumatism but I don't think so or he could not walk to St. John, a distance of twenty-six miles in one day.

If they are going to send a man to take Hardesty's place, I would like to have John Cantlon. He would be all right here and the country would agree with him. It would cost about $100 to fit him out and pay his way up to Pine River. We have enough provisions to last us about two and a half years or more.

Saturday evening and we are stuck here until Monday now as the Englishman and the man that Hardesty is going down the river with has not come from St. John yet, so Hardesty will not leave us today. Mamma, I wish you and the kids were up here to spend the winter with me but it gets too cold, 52 below zero.

Sunday, September 4, 2:00 P.M.
Hardesty has just left for Peace River Landing on a raft with a man by the name of Watson and is the man that took that picture I sent you. He had been to St. John with his brother doing freighting. Hardesty took a cry when he bid us goodbye. I was making biscuits, had a pot of beans cooking and stewing a kettle of dried apples when he left.

I sent a letter with him to you and one to Tivnen, would have sent this one but did not have it finished and did not care for anyone to see it first but you. That leaves the outfit to Peters and I. We had a settlement and divided the money up equal with what Hardesty left us and we both have $226.04 apiece. Hardesty took a hundred dollars with him besides all of his clothes that were bought in the outfit.

I have had no word from you since the 16th of May. I am going to St. John the last of the week for the mail and some traps. The Brick Brothers with their boat are on their way up from Peace River Landing. They have a store at St. John and I expect they will have some mail for me. So keep on writing all winter and I will get some of them sometime. It is getting cold up here and we have only three weeks until it will be freezing weather so we must hustle and get our shack built. I will send this letter out by the first chance. TRA la la.

Wednesday, September 7
I have been too busy to write any until now and now I haven't anything to do but write. The two Shaw boys and Peters and I left Struck Creek on Monday at 9:00 A.M. and arrived at Pine River at 4:00 P.M. We found there was not much water in it but quite a stream if it wants to be. We camped in the mouth of it for the night and Tuesday took a look around the diggens to see what kind of a place we were getting into.

I found it one of the prettiest places I have ever seen and we at once made up our minds to winter on a high water island in the forks of Pine and Peace Rivers. Our camp is right on the point of the island and in a thick forest of pine trees and up above the water twenty feet. The Peace River is about one fourth of a mile wide and the south side of the river has been burned off by a forest fire. There are big gravel bars everywhere in the water and about fifteen acres of land between us and the water.

Today we finished unloading our cargo and carrying it up on top of the hill and have got it up on a scaffold high and dry. We will commence in a day or so to build a shack to live in. The Pine River runs nearly the same direction as the Peace. The south side of the Peace is all burned off and nothing but old dead snags left and we can see all over it from our camp. On the north side of Pine River the hills are bare with just a few bunches of trees. In back of us to the hills is a thick pine forest and looks like a jungle I guess, though I never saw one and it is full of bears (and I will have some of them too Myrty).

Thursday, September 8
Well dear girls and boys, I guess it is time I was bringing this small note to a close. I am going to St. John tomorrow to see if I can get a letter from you and try and send this one out. If I don't get a letter this time I won't have but about one more chance to hear from you until some time next April. Brick Bros. have not gone up the river yet and they are on their way up for the last time this winter and will have lots of mail.

After that it will only be a chance if I get any mail from you until next spring. So I won't know a thing about you unless I get some mail tomorrow or when Brick Bros. come. It almost sets me wild sometimes thinking about it. It has been so long since I have heard from you and if I don't get word tomorrow it will be longer. I would be all right if I knew you were all well and all right.

Harry, I have just got done setting up a grindstone. I made the shaft handle and put it in a frame and it is all set up and ready for grinding. We will commence Monday to build our shack.

It is very nice weather, just like the fall of the year. The leaves are all turned yellow and are falling off, there is frost every night.

This leaves me in the best of health feeling like a fighting cock and will be perfectly contented to get a lot of letters and good news from you. I am praying all the time that none of you are sick or in want.

Harry and Presh, once more let me ask you to be good to your mother and sister, I know you will won't you. Keep away from the gambling dens for it will ruin you as long as you live. You have me to look at for an example. Save your money, give it to mamma, she will take care of it for you and if you will do this we will come out all right in a year or so in spite of the devil. I am going to make some money up here and every bit of it will be saved.

Myrty you sweet daughter, I would like awfully bad to see you but you and I will have to stand it until next fall I spect. I hope you have got a good position and when I do come home we will tell each other how much we think of each other. And mamma I know how much I love you. I have found it out by being away from you so long. I know that there is none that can fill your place and it is a good way to test it by being absent for a while. So now I am going to do my best and come home and buy a farm and raise duck and geese. I will quit now and live in hopes that I will hear from you tomorrow. Many many kisses and sixteen to you all and a few big squeezes. I am your

Klondyke Explorer, bear hunter
and gold digger
Papa

8

Pine River Camp, British Columbia, N.W.T.

Sunday morning, September 25, 1898 – Just after killing three ducks.
My Dear Sweet Daughter,

I will now commence to answer your ever welcome letter, your big letter, your typewritten letter, your best letter of all, your letter that mentioned so often of getting all my letters, your letter that I read over so often that I know it by heart, your letter of which was the first print I have seen for four months, your letter which saved me from forgetting how to read print, your letter that was an answer to my prayers that nothing would harm you and that sickness would stay away, your letter written August 1, 1898.

You mention in this letter that you are getting all of my letters and that the last one you got was the one I wrote July 6. Well if that is the last letter you got from me, you won't get some that I have written since, until I arrive home next fall and about six months after. I wrote that letter of the 6th while we were in camp at the mouth of Swan River on the lake. We were there three days. There is I think, sixteen or nineteen letters between me and you that I have written since then, some of them have forty pages but I suppose you will get them all.

First I will tell you what we are doing, how we are situated and how we will spend the winter. I suppose before you get this though,

Hardesty will tell you part of it but he left us before we went into winter quarters.

After Hardesty left us, our party of eight men on the one boat split up and our party and the Shaw party (they are the two men that started with us from Athabasca Landing) came on up the river to the mouth of North Pine River about six miles and have gone into winter quarters. The other party of three (the Grimstons by name) stopped where we left them and went into winter quarters at the mouth of Struck Creek where the Indians struck on us. (I named the creek that name.)

Well, we have got the prettiest place to live in the whole N.W.T. It is on an island and the pine trees are so thick back of us that you have to go edgeways to get through them and at night it is sixteen times blacker than a car load of black cats. It looks awful scarey in there but I'm not afraid. We have our house built and it is right on the edge of the woods and on a bank twenty feet high and the front part faces the east and looks out on an open space of the Peace and Pine Rivers of about a half a mile square. We can see anybody go by if they go by. Our house is sixteen by eighteen and made out of pine logs daubed up with mud, have one door and two windows, a fireplace and a chimney made out of sticks and daubed up with mud. It is the little old cabin in the woods.

The two Shaw boys have theirs built a little north of us and is the same size so there are four Klondykers of us camped for the winter at the mouth of North Pine River and the Peace River.

If you come to see me send your card first as we are very stylish and don't receive callers without a card. Dash attends to the front door and if you don't give him a card he will give you a nab in the leg and bring some butter and eggs too or I will forget how they taste. We have not moved into the house yet on account of the mud not being dry and the weather is so nice that we are living in our tents.

It is fall here, the leaves are all yellow and nearly all fallen off. Have had some big freezes. If the letter I wrote the sixth of July is the last letter you got from me, there is sixteen or nineteen more between me and you, some with forty pages.

I have thirty-six steel traps and am going to trap this winter, think I can make some money. We are going to give this place a good test for gold — going to sink some shafts thirty feet. We have hopes of finding gold around here as there is gold in small quantities every place we prospect. So now don't be surprised if we find it in large quantities.

We have pheasant and duck every meal. A pheasant is as big as a prairie chicken. We are getting kind of tired of them but it is so much fun to hunt them and it saves the bacon pile too you know (as we have got only five hundred pounds). Dash has learned to stance a pheasant, he is a pointer. If the last letter you got from me is dated the 6th of July there is sixteen or nineteen more between me and you, some with forty pages.

We have not killed a bear or moose yet — have not had time and they are back on top of the hills now. Yesterday I cut a cord of wood and corded it up. It is for this winter when it gets fifty below zero. We are going to cut ten cords. Well I have told you all about our surroundings. I will answer your letter but not until after dinner. Jack is calling me. We have three roast ducks and vegetable soup for dinner. Tra la la.

Well I ate so much duck I can hardly waddle, quack, quack. I don't know how to sit down. Well dear daughter, it's better to be among the bear and moose than to have no company at all, and so far as getting lonesome, if you were up here in this wild and uncivilized country you would die of lonesomeness. Of course there is lots to see and do up here but then there are no people, no shops, no 364, no electric lights, no bands to hear of Saturday nights, no Myrty to look at, if one doesn't fight it out of his thoughts he almost starts for home and it takes a man with a will to stay up here.

But I am up here on a mission and will do what I started for if it kills me. I am up here for yours and the boys and mammas benefit and I must — I will use every effort to make it win. I have made up my mind thoroughly to stay with it for eighteen months and I am very hopeful that I will be rewarded as well as you and the men that sent me here.

Myrty at age 20

Nothing will be left undone. Every nook and crevice will be turned upside down in search of what I came for and if there is small quantities of gold everywhere up here, which is true, there must be large quantities of the yaller stuff and I believe before next fall there will be as much excitement here as there was at Dawson

City. Someone will stumble on it and who knows but what it might be me.

Well now don't get mad at what I wrote in my last letter to you about gadding around for I was mad. I couldn't get any letters from you and I was so lonesome that I had to tell you to stop gadding and think of your papa once in a while, but since I got your last letter that wound is all healed up. But I would like to have them come a little thicker and not have so many circuses. I just bet that you and Berthy did have a circus.

I wrote that letter you got last from me on the sixth of July while we were camped in the mouth of Swan River on the lake. If that is the last one you got from me, there is sixteen or nineteen more between you and me, some with forty pages.

You always did have lots of fun and I like to see you have fun only don't forget your dad between acts. What Scotts was it that you all went to — Jim Scotts, Mayor Scotts or Nigger Scotts — you didn't say. You say you and Henry Cline have quit again — that makes sixteen times — you had better stay quit now. He has red hair anyhow. I expect it was grand for you and Henry Cline to go boat riding on that tadpole pond. You ought to bring him up to Slave Lake and you could get all the rowing you would want for eighty miles.

Did you mean me or Henry when you said that everybody stopped you and asked when you heard from your pa. I wrote you a letter on the sixth of July while we were camped in the mouth of Swan River on the lake and you say in your last letter that was the last letter you got from me. If that is the last letter you got from me there are sixteen or nineteen more between me and you, some with forty pages. You just put a card in your hat — "Heard from pa on the sixth of July."

What letter of mine did you have published in the Gazzette and why didn't you send me the clipping out of the paper? Now I want you to get all them and send them to me, just the clipping for if you send the whole paper I won't get it. Half of the papers don't go any farther than Edmonton.

Tell Mrs. Belmer that there is no fence up here or grapevines to holler at her through, but there are lots of pine trees and brush.

Just the same, I often think of the fun we used to have jabbering at one another through the grapevines.

Well you and Henry Cline and the summer kitchen on the shores of Mattoon certainly do have a time. Well you just have as much fun as you want to but don't forget what I told you and don't forget your piano and above all don't forget your school. Get that perfect first and get a position and then just have all the fun you want. You don't have any trouble getting a position if you are perfect in your schooling but you must not let a day go by that you don't practice and get it just the same as you know the alphabet. You will get the position all right. Mr. Katz will get you one or Mr. Tivnen but you must be good in your studies.

If Harry made $72.00 in one month you just tell him to give you $5.00 of it and if he won't just take it anyhow.

On the Fourth of July I was on the lake rowing all day. We made it to the mouth of Swan River and a heavy wind came up which lasted three days so we camped there and I thought I would write you a letter while we were there so on the sixth of July I wrote you and you say in your last letter that was the last letter you got from me. Well if that was the last letter you got from me there are sixteen or nineteen more letters between me and you — some with forty pages.

Well I will quit for today as I don't know when I will get a chance to send this out. I suppose I will have a week to write it in anyhow, I most generally have a month. So goodnight. Tra la la.

Monday evening, September 26
I just got back from hunting. I only killed one pheasant so I am going to have pheasant for breakfast. I was working all day on the house — going over it and daubing up the sun cracks and making Dash a dog house. His house will be air tight. The days are getting shorter — sun sets at 5:00 P.M. and rises at 6:00 A.M. Good healthy nights to sleep. After a while the night will be eighteen hours. Won't we get lots of sleep then?

I was looking over my memorandum book today and the first thing I saw when I opened it was July 6th — camped in the mouth of Swan River on account of high wind. I wrote you a letter while we were camped there. You say in your last letter that is the last letter you got from me. Well if that is the last letter you got from me, there are sixteen or nineteen more between me and you — some with forty pages.

I have eaten so much fish that I have fins growing out on top of my feet and duck — well my toes are webbed together from eating so much. I expect that I will get out on a log and drum like a pheasant before long for we have pheasant every meal.

Tuesday evening, September 27

Well if you could just see me. I have been daubing Dash's dog house today and I am just about as dauby as the dog house but you bet he has to have a good warm house. You don't know how much company he is to me. He can almost talk. Of mornings when he gets up he will yawn and gape about a dozen times. I guess he learns it from Peters   he gapes about forty times the first thing in the morning. Sometimes he forgets that he has just gaped and he will start to gape again and get about half way through and then will happen to think, "Why, I just did gape once." That is the way Dash does and he will turn his head sideways at me as much as to say, "That is the way Peters does."

It has been trying to rain all day and now it is raining and it is one those cold rains   yes and the rain is wet. You bet I stick to the beans and bacon, they are mighty good up here. A change from pheasant to bacon is something that our neighbors don't all have. We have neighbors every one hundred miles.

I don't say now that you haven't been getting my letters but I do say that all of your letters except the last one are too small by thirty-seven pages and the lines are too far apart and if you knew how lonesome I was up here you would write me everything you know. Something about the street fair if you please. Jack says supper so excuse me.

Well after a large portion of fried bacon, some rolled oats and stewed dried apples and molasses made out of sugar I will say some more but not much this evening for it will be dark soon.

I hope I will have a bag of gold when I come home. I won't wait for you to let me in, I will knock the door down with the bag. The way you write in your last letter you must be through with your school for you say that mamma talked to Katz about a place in his store for you. You do say that you have finished bookkeeping and that Mr. Blood and Cakendalpherrastorekidneyandlights liked you but I can't get you to say a word about shorthand. If you get a position, don't get married. It seems like that is a mania there with the typewriters.

I suppose Hardesty is just about across the lake by this time. He must be as far as Swan River anyhow. I suppose he thought of the three days we were in camp there on account of high wind and could not sail. You say that is the last letter you got from me. Well if that is the last letter you got from me there is sixteen or nineteen more between me and you — some with forty pages and a whole lot of sketches. Good night, I am going to bed directly.

Wednesday evening, just about two hours before sundown. (We haven't got a clock.)
This morning I baked four apricot pies and cooked a pot of beans and chopped a half cord of wood. I can just make as good pies as anything that wears petticoats and they taste just like pies — in fact I believe they taste better than pie up here. But I had a notion to get homesick after they were all baked for they looked like mamma's pies setting on the table. But then I said to myself, "I mustn't" so I went out and fitted a pick in one of our picks and wondered how much gold it would fetch out of these miserable hills for me. But I had the pie for dinner all the samey.

Yes, if you get a position with Blood and Cakendalpherrastorekidneyandlights and get $6.00 per week that won't be bad for a start. Now little girl you must just study hard all the time and get your studies perfect and watch your chance and you will get a position at $50.00 per month. Don't think that after you get a position that you are through but just keep on learning it over and over so you won't forget it.

I am going to supper now and it will be too dark after supper to write and we are saving our candles. Tra la la.

Thursday, September 29, about 1:00 o'clock, anyway just after dinner.
Well I am mad, disappointed, lonesome and don't feel very well myself. You know I have told you about the Shaw boys being with us and that we got them to go with us from Athabasca Landing and as we have been together ever since clear up to where we are now and both parties of us got our houses built and just ready to move into them and as Hardesty had to go home to see mamma and that only leaving four in our crowd. Now this morning Dave Shaw said, "I have been thinking of something all last night". I said, "What is it Dave?" He said, "I have been thinking of building a raft and getting out of this bloody country".

Mind you, that was the first hint they had given me and it struck me like a cannon ball. I thought they were not in earnest about it but after breakfast they gathered up an ax and some tools and did actually go up the river and found some logs and are building a raft and are going home just as fast as the water will take them and I don't care if they both get eaten up by the bears.

The reason they are going home is that they have only enough grub to last them until April and have just 40¢ in money. They haven't got sense enough to see farther than their nose. They went to work and built a house, took two weeks and then found out they would have to go home this fall. Let them go, I don't care. I guess me and Dash and old man Peters can live all right.

Peters went down the river to where the Grimstons are in camp to see if they wouldn't come up here to where we are and take the house. I put up a sign on the house, 'House to rent". If they come up there will be five of us.

I will get a chance to send this letter out by the Shaws and this will be the last you will hear from me I expect for a long time unless someone goes by that is going out but it kills me to think that I won't get but about two more letters from you and then it will be frozen up as solid as Greenland. Yes, I got yours of August 1st but you must keep on writing, there is talk of the government putting on a mail carrier all winter.

Mr. Brick Bros. are due by here any day. I am watching for them so I can get the mail and then I won't have to go to St. John. The regular mail man is due the first of the month but he goes on the land trail fifteen miles north of us. I will have to go up to St. John anyhow unless the Hudson Bay man sends it down by someone that would be coming down the river.

This morning everything was just white with frost — ice half inch thick in the bucket. It is coming in another month and I will put on my snow shoes and slide down this hill to pass the time away.

Now I will have until about tomorrow evening to finish this letter so I will have to write some to all of you and some to Mr. White and send it in this letter. Explain to them that I started this fashion to economize as there are no stamps to be had up here and I don't want my supply to run out.

We haven't started to prospect for gold but are going to sink some shafts the first of the week. Tell Mr. White that I have just as good hopes of finding gold as I did when I left Mattoon and that if anything turns up favorable he will know of it immediately.

Keep this part to yourselves as no one but the White folks are to read this part of the letter. Tell him that there is gold on any of the gravel bars in the river. Of course it is flour gold but it is a sure sign that there is a lead someplace where this fine gold comes from. I am led to believe sometimes that it is washed down from the head of Peace River. But then comes another obstacle that knocks that idea in the head and that is that the little creeks and branches that empty into the river contain the same kind of gold.

We are going to sink some shafts between the main banks of the river and where the bed of the river was one day and is grown up with trees now. Tell him that we can't go any farther this winter than we are now and that we will prospect this place for miles around and if we are not lucky in finding anything we will go farther next summer.

Well talk about being lonesome — this is the lonesomest day I ever did go through. The Shaw boys are up the river building a raft and Peters is down the river at the Grimstons. No one at camp but me and Dash and a pine squirrel. Why, every time a leaf falls on the house it sounds like a tree fell.

When you write, tell me if Hardesty wrote that he was coming home. Tell me what he said about the trip and if he gave you the letter I sent by him and what the people said about him corning home and all about it. I expect stock in the Mattoon Mining and Investment Company went down on his arrival. But it is worth just as much with him in Mattoon as if he were up here on Pine River and will be run on as good a principle and will be pushed ahead as though he never was along. Children should stay at home anyhow — no place up here for children unless their parents are along. Excuse me Myrty, I want to write some to Harry and answer his letter.

You rascal, why didn't you write me a big letter? Your letters are like Myrty's, the lines are too far apart, looks as though you didn't have much to say or else you wanted to spread it all over two sheets and call it a big letter but it beats Nan and Presh's too, yes and mamma's. I am much obliged for the papers. Since reading those papers I hear the war is over, don't know how true it is. Send me some more papers and register them. Tell me all about the Mattoon street fair.

Harry, let me warn you to be awful careful out on the road. Don't be careless, be very careful, you can't be too careful. I remember that I used to be careful but twice in my life I came pretty near getting killed, once going by Hillsborough my head just missed the water spout, it touched my hair as I went by, another quarter of an inch and it would have knocked my brains out. The other time was going by Tower Hill, the spout hit my arm. I never said anything about it to anyone until now so you can't be too careful. Be careful when you go to get on the engine and off of it. Now don't think this is all bash but always think before you act.

Have you got a regular engine and how are you getting along? Do you have any trouble with any of the officers or the men on the road? And Harry, see that my insurance is kept up and my dues paid, be sure and pay my dues, it isn't much. I believe if White told me right, I am exempt from all dues except grand dues. See him and ask him all about it and ask him how much I owe now and you pay it the first thing you do. I want to be a full member when I come home. I will pay you all back and more too.

Friday morning
Everything is a hustle in our camp this morning. The Shaw boys are getting ready to leave in the morning. We bought part of their outfit, all of the flour and fruit, bought it to speculate on. Flour is worth $14.00 per hundred up here and we bought their 650 pounds for $42.50 so you see we made about $55.00 on that one article. Bought 40 pounds of rolled oats for $1.00 and it is worth $5.00. We will make about $100 on what we bought from them. If we trade it to the Indians for fur we will make three times that much.

Keep this part of the letter to yourself. They had to sell it cheap in order to have money to get out of the country. We have a stock of goods now that is large enough to start a store and every pound of it is worth its weight in gold.

Now one more thing I want to ask of you Harry and that is, don't go to the gambling places. If it wasn't for the gambling see where I would be instead of pulling on a bloody boat until you could knock my eyes off with a club. I ought to have a nice farm and a big brick house for us to live in and all the reason I haven't got it is that I spent my money gambling. I am ashamed to even think of it but it is so and no mistake.

Now if you keep away from such places you will have a farm by the time you are as old as I am. Now Harry, you know this is a fact. Then take it to heed and don't do it because your father did. Break that old saying, 'A chip off the old block'. Do you get along all right with everybody? You could write me a big letter if you would take time and if you would answer all the things I have asked you it would be interesting to me up here.

Let me remind you to take good care of your mother and sister. Spend your money on them and it will be a credit to you and make them feel proud of you. If you are making $72.00 a month see what you can give them and you'll still have a lot left. Save all the money you can until I come home and we will buy a little farm and bid goodbye to the miserable past life of ours. Well I must stop now and finish Myrty's letter as I have only 'til morning to write and I must say a very few words to mamma and Presh.

Well old stickin I will finish your letter. We have rented the house the Shaws built. The Grimstons came up and looked at it and concluded to take it if we would throw in the firewood. Of course firewood is quite an object up here, there are only fifty thousand acres right back of our cabin but we don't chop it for them. They are going to move up right away so that won't be so bad after all. There will be five of us and three dogs camped in the mouth of Pine River for the winter.

It seems like I have been up here for a year but it has only been about three months since I was on the lake and it seems like a year since I wrote you a letter on the 6th of July while camped in the mouth of Swan River. You said in your letter of August 1 that was the last letter you got from me. Well if that was the last letter you got from me there are sixteen or nineteen more between me and you, some with forty pages and sketches. Now girl, sit right down and write me a big letter and don't spread it allover a dozen sheets of paper and say that is a big letter but put the lines close together and nothing less than forty pages is go up here. I must stop now and write some to mamma and Presh.

This leaves me all right in every particular only a little bit lonesome. I do hope that this will find you in good health and good spirits and with a good position and just having lots of fun and a good time in general. This is my prayer for you and I feel that it will be answered.

My prayers were answered before I got your last letter for I prayed every night before I went to bed in my tent that the good Lord would take care of you and keep sickness away. Stand it until next fall girl and you will be awful glad to see me and I will bring you a nice present. Write me lots and often, one like the last one of August 1st. Many kisses and hugs. I kiss your picture all the time.

From your Klondyke papa Jim

NORTH PINE RIVER CAMP, BRITISH COLUMBIA, N.W.T.
September 30, 1898

Dear Mamma,

You old stickum in the mud, why didn't you write me some in Myrty's letter? Not a word from you, to serve you right I ought to send an order to Myrty to chain you up anyhow. Now don't let me die up here of lonesomeness for the want of reading matter. I know you don't want me to come out of this N.W.T. looking like Rip Van Winkle. I will excuse you this one time and that is all, if it occurs again Rip is a sure go.

Well Mamma, we have a nice place to live this winter, got our house done but haven't moved in yet, the mud isn't dry yet. We will move in the first of the week and the Grimstons are going to move up the first of the week and take the Shaw building. Then our nearest neighbor will be twenty miles. They are camped five miles this side of St. John and there are three of them. The next nearest neighbor is thirty-five miles below us, a man and a woman. I will go to Sunday school with the bears and moose and the wolves.

I am going to sink some shafts around here (have not found that heart yet) and prospect this place thoroughly. If there is a striking in this country by anyone, you see we are in the country and have that advantage over everybody that has to come six hundred miles and pull a boat. I am hopeful and in good spirits, good health and got an outfit that will last us three years. I feel all right only get pretty lonesome some times.

6:00 P.M.

I have been in the house all afternoon making a table. Have it all done except putting the shelves on. It will be a table and cupboard combined when I get it finished and it is a daisy. I am sitting by it now and writing by a candle. Peters is baking bread and the two Shaw boys are sitting around gabbing. I have a fire in the fireplace.

This log cabin doesn't look so snotty, I tell you and when our neighbors move up here it won't be so lonesome. I might as well own up that it is. I wish you and the kids could be here with me, it would be a treat to you and talk about health, anyone can eat bark off the trees up here.

Today has been one of those cold cloudy days, a regular blue day, it snowed a little to make it more miserable. But it is time for it to snow, let her come, I am fixed for it now.

It is going to be a trying task for us to go through this trip until next fall unless you folks write me lots of letters and big ones and I do hope you and the kids will get along all right. They certainly ought to make enough money, the three of them, to make a nice living, and I hope Harry and Presh will hold their jobs and give you their wages and when I come home I am going to buy a little farm.

Mamma, see that my dues are paid up in the Brotherhood. It is only $2.00 per year. I want to be a full member when I come home for if this trip turns out to be a failure I can be reinstated and get my rights back on the road.

But I will make this trip a success if any man on earth can. I have got the stuff in me to stay with it. If we don't find anything around here this winter or between now and April we are going on up to the head of Findlay River and across from there to the Liard River and Pelly Banks. Those are the plans we have laid out. Some have gone in there this fall but only a few.

As a general thing the people that come in here don't bring enough grub to last them but one year and as there is only five months that a man can track a boat, they only get as far as St. John or Hudson Hope and then have to go out back home before the lake freezes up and then their whole year is lost and their grub eaten up. We don't have to do that you see for we have got grub enough to last three years and while I am up this far

I might as well see what there is in it.

Now after this letter I expect you won't get letters from me as often as you have been for there won't be as many people going out and it will take longer to go out. But I will have one written all the time and the first son of a gun comes along I can send it out and you must keep on writing. I will get them in the spring if I don't get them this winter.

Tell Mr. White that I will write him and send it in your letter unless I find a gold bank forty feet thick. Then I will send him a telegraph. I have to be saving with my stamps as there is none up here to buy. I can't see what is the matter with Tivnen. I can't get a word from him or any of them.

There I was lighting my pipe with the candle and of course there was a drip of tallow had to splatter on the paper. I didn't do it a purpose, it was natural.

Well I guess I have said all I know and more too. It is getting late and I want to write some to Pet. I guess I will have to stop anyhow, if I write much more it will take two stamps. I hate to stop writing for I love to write but I have run out of something to say and of course will have to stop unless I just make marks ----- that is something like Harry's and Myrty's letter, just something to smear over a couple of sheets of paper and then call it a letter and I suppose walk up to the post office as big as the gander and walk in and say, "Give me a stamp, I want to mail a letter,"

But Myrty done elegant, the last letter 1 got from her was written on August 1st. Now don't think the next letter you write you'll say, "1 bet he will get enough reading matter this time", for 1 will fool you. 1 don't care if it takes three men to pull it in a boat and call it an outfit going to Klondyke. 1 have got seven months to read it in.

1 guess 1 will close by the usual way, hoping this will find you all well as 1 am myself. Write often, lots of squeezes, lots of letters, lots of gold, lots of fun, lots of yanking on a boat up to your neck in water, lots of big letters like you wrote August 1st. Hoping you will get my letters with forty pages, 1 quit until the next one and now a thousand kisses from your Klondyke Jim.

Well Pet, smart alec, all 1 have from you since 1 left home is a big grin. 1 guess you hate to say, "Dear Father" is the reason you don't write. Yes, 1 didn't get a letter from you August 1st or any other old August, on Swan River either. What is the matter with you? 1 think you might say something if only, "Dear Father, 1 set myself down to articulate a few words of a great importance to you but as 1 am very busy doing nothing

1 haven't got much time to say much more that would interest you much," or something like that.

You could write me a big letter if you wanted to. You have been going to ever since 1 came up here and that is getting stale now and don't go any more, so sir, I will expect a few scratches from you anyhow pretty soon so I will say goodbye to you sir, hoping that you will get all my sixteen or nineteen letters I wrote since July 6th.

Jim Dad

9

British Columbia, N.W.T.

Sunday evening, October 9, 1898
My dear wife and children and brothers and sister,

I will now commence to write you all a big letter — for one reason to save postage stamps. I will answer Hat's, Neva's and Nora's and some to George. In fact we will call it a family affair. Oh yes, and Ollie and Bertha. You may think I am in a hurry to write you a letter of several pages, but as one of our near neighbors is going out of the country in a few days this will be a first class opportunity to send out this letter and it might be the last chance for some time as winter is right here with us.

Already we have had three inches of snow and the ground is frozen hard. This man that is going out is one of the Grimstons. He lives in Toronto, Canada and is going out on some kind of business and will return in April and go on in the direction of the Klondyke. He is going out with a party by pack horses. That will leave only four of us here in camp for the winter.

First I will tell you what I have been doing today to pass the time away. Sunday is an awful long lonesome day up here with the bears and moose and wolves and I have to figure out through the week how I will spend Sunday.

I always think of something to do but today I came pretty near running out of what to do so I started in the morning by cleaning up the house, washing the dishes and dish rags, scouring the table and the pots. Just what you do of mornings, a general cleanup.

After I got through it was about 10:00 o'clock by the sun (we haven't any clock), then I came to the conclusion that I would do some baking. First I put a large size piece of bear meat in the oven to roast for dinner, then I stewed some apricots and made four pies and baked biscuits and I want you to know I had a dinner for your whiskers and it was good enough for a king to set down to.

I had good luck with everything, the biscuits were just elegant with bear gravy, the pies, well they were out of sight, that is, one of them was after we got through. I wanted everything to turn out as it did on account of Peters, he thinks he can cook, and pan my gizzard, I can't eat his cooking at all.

First I will say that he is a darned fool, he is childish, he don't cook a thing but what he will say just like this, "Well that's all right, that's good, no one could kick on that bread, that fried meat, that hominy and everything he cooks is all right and I'll be darned if it is fit to eat.

He doesn't put salt in his vittles, no pepper, he makes tea and coffee that doesn't color the water. Throw a couple grains of coffee in the river a half a mile up and go below and dip up a cup full of the precious liquid and then say "Isn't that good?" I got so darned mad at him bragging that I says, "Yes, that's good for anyone that was raised on a bottle."

You talk about me making a fuss when I eat, he eats just like a hog and smacks just as loud. He won't eat meat for breakfast, some toast and rolled oats and some colored water is his breakfast so I just go ahead and cook what I want and how I want it cooked and he can eat it or let it alone. He certainly is the darndest bore I ever was with.

We all killed the bear and right on the sand bar in front of our house on Thursday evening. "We" the devil! The dogs killed it. It was a cub bear about as big as two big coons. One of the Grimstons crippled it and the dogs finished it. Dash had a hand in it just the same, he did the clown act, bit it on the legs. It was his first bear fight. I was eating dinner and didn't go to the fight but stood in the door and looked on. We took half of it and Grimstons the other half. So that is why I had roast bear for dinner today.

There is lots of game around here but at this time of year it is all back from the river in the hills and bears are getting ready to go into their dens for the winter. As soon as it gets a little colder they go into their dens and stay there all winter and all they live on is they suck their fore paw. I am anxious to kill one before they hole up for the winter. I want a big one.

We have company this evening, the Grimstons. Their house is not finished yet, no fireplace. We have ours all fixed and are as comfortable as if we were in a brick house. I made a table and cupboard and stand table three feet square and I made me a big arm chair and it is a daisy. One can make anything if he has the tools and we have a whole kit of tools.

I made the chair out of reed willow. It is just as the willows grow and I am surprised because I didn't think I could make a chair as nice as that. I could get $5.00 for it easy in Mattoon. All agreed that it gives me great credit except Peters, and he did not say anything.

A few nights before we were all saying that we were going to make each of us an easy chair, so Peters said, "Well, I will wait until you all make a chair and then I'll make me one." Now we will see what kind of a one he will make. He thinks that no one can make anything but him. But he envies me this chair. I don't believe he will make any at all. Some time ago he made a camp stool and it is six inches too low for the table. I wish you could see him eating at the table on his camp stool. You can just see the top of his head. That's just the way he is, he will eat off that camp stool all winter just because someone made something nicer.

He is one of these kind of fellows that when he tries to make anything he either gets one piece too short or too long or spoils it altogether and when he uses a tool or handful of nails, there is where he leaves them. Ask Hardesty, he can tell you how he does, he spoils more material than he uses and nails are worth 40¢ per pound up here.

We have just got done arguing about a shot gun, he says to our company and me just now, that he could take a shot gun and shoot through a two inch board forty feet off so I says, "Now Jack, you know that there is no shot gun that will shoot that hard." "Well I know that they will", he said. So I says, "Tomorrow I am going to measure off forty feet and shoot at a two inch board and show you that it won't." He changed the subject right away so I will tell you tomorrow all about it.

That's just the kind of man he is in all his talk and would turn anyone against him. But I am determined to run this outfit and put up with him anyhow. He would be awful glad if I would get sick and if I do I won't go home without taking the outfit with me. Well once more I will let Peters be and talk about something else.

It is getting late so I guess I will go to bed and write some every day. Tomorrow I am going to sink a shaft and look for gold about a half mile from camp on one of the high water islands. The river ran there one day but now it is thick forest but as good a chance for gold as could be. Anyhow, I will put down a hole twenty-five feet and see what is at the bottom of the hole. So I will say goodnight and write some tomorrow. I will be two weeks writing this letter and it won't do to say too much in one night. Tra la la.

Monday evening, October 10
Well I have been working all day prospecting. I have a hole down fifteen feet, am going twenty-five feet and if there is no signs of gold I will try some place else. We are going to prospect up Pine River at least twenty-five miles. I expect you are all anxious about me, if I am ever going to find any gold. Now if you are you must not worry but give me time. It is just like this.

There is only five months that you can travel with an outfit up here and then you have to look for winter quarters and build a house that you won't freeze in. And it takes a month to build the house and you have to build it before it freezes on account of the mud drying. If the mud freezes before it gets dry then the first day it thaws a little it will all falloff so this was as far as we could get and get a house put up and we just got it done in time for the ground has been frozen three inches already.

But we are only a hundred fifty miles from where we tried to get to this season, so we will start from here next May and it will take us some time in April to make that hundred fifty miles unless we find gold around here so now you see just how it is.

We should have made farther than this and would have if the Indians hadn't struck on us and Hardesty hadn't got homesick. We should have made as far as Hudson Hope, that's eighty miles from here but as it is, we will have to be contented. We are comfortably fixed for the winter, we are just elegantly fixed and got lots of wood right around us and stacked up in ricks, ten cords of it.

Our house is warm, ten inches of solid wall, have a good warm bed, two double blankets and a sleeping bag. We have a nice big fireplace, burns three foot wood, have a stove and all our outfit is stored away on a rack in the back part of the house. Our beds are swung underneath and it is just like a hammock.

Well I didn't try the shotgun today, I worked too late but I will let you know the results so goodnight for this eve. We have company, the Grimstons. Tra la la. I must help to entertain them.

Tuesday evening just after supper.
Well I didn't try the shotgun today either but I will tomorrow sure. This has been a lovely day, nice and warm. I haven't much to write about today and as we are going to have company after a bit, the Grimstons, I won't say much this evening. I would give the world, not the Klondyke, if George was up here and Cantlon you rascal, you missed one big corner in your life by not coming. It would do you good to live this kind of life for a couple of years. You would be able to take a bull by its tail and throw it over the fence. But it is a queer country, nothing like you think it is. It is uncivilized, nothing to look at but the high hills and what I call a jungle all around, full of bears and wolves and moose. Just suits me and I know it would you.

And George, it will seem kind of funny along in January to see the days about four hours long. Good healthy nights to sleep, you can get all of that you want. It is rather lonesome I will admit but yet there is something about it that is fascinating. There are no Indians close around us but they will be around this winter trading bear skins for something to eat.

But one can take his gun and go up on the hill and kill pheasant, grouse and bear and moose if he wants to and that passes the time away and one can look for gold which is interesting but still I long to see my ma and black eyed girl and my big strapping boys and all of you but we will have to put up with it until this time next year anyhow, for I am determined to find gold if I have to go to the north pole.

Well tra la la, our company has come and I will have to stop writing and smoke the pipe of peace. All five of us right now are setting around the fire and smoking. Goodnight, we will now listen to some of Peters lies.

Wednesday, October 12

Bertha, you just ought to be up here now and take a slide down some of these hills. Well I remember one time in Ohio, myself, your pa and John Hinkle sliding down a hill and your pa went right on down the hill but part of his pants stopped short on a snag. There are no snags on some of these hills.

It would be a treat to you to take a trip through this part of the world. It is healthy and the air is so pure. Come up and I will teach you how to eat corn bread and bacon. But I suppose you are thinking of matrimony very strong and couldn't think of leaving the haunts of your intended long enough to pay your uncle a visit.

You just ought to come up here too Nora, awful good place here to climb trees and break your leg but there are no cherries on the trees and no fruit of any kind. Just trees, rocks, hills, rivers and gold. It is a long ways to go a visiting here and the nearest neighbor is about forty feet, three of them. The next nearest neighbor is thirty miles.

Well I do get lonesome but when I do I take the gun and my old right hand banner, Dash, and take a stroll up in the hills, look for gold, kill some pheasants and I forget all about being lonesome. I have made up my mind long ago to stand it and make this trip or bust a gut. We will love one another all the more when I come back. You must take good care of your health and not get sick. You bet I think lots about the war and if I was there I would have gone sure. I am glad to hear that you have a good wheat crop and I guess that you will get a good price for it.

Now school marm I don't want you to criticize my spelling or writing either, for I don't get enough letters or papers from any of you to keep me in practice and if you all don't write to me oftener I will forget how to read, write or spell either. I won't forget how to spell my name for while the mud was soft that I put on the outside of our cabin, I stamped my name over the window. The mud is dry now and my name is there for keeps.

Well it seems that I have forgotten how to spell lots of words. Now gun, I don't know which is right gun or gunn. I guess I will have to make signs if I forget how to spell or else learn to talk Indian. If you come to a word and can't read it or get any sense out of it just say "Mine-stock-tane". That means in Indian language, "I don't understand, skip it". And if anyone bothers you while you are trying to make out what I am trying to write, you say "Mush", that means get out.

Well I was awful glad to get the small letter from you and Bertha and will have to beg you both to pardon for not answering them sooner. I have no excuse to offer only when I do write to mamma and the kids that my letters are so big that I haven't got anything left to say to anybody.

You and Magg talk about riding up Pike's Peak on an ass, well you just ought to be here to ride up one of these hills. It would take more than an ass to climb one of these hills. I don't believe a mule could do it. Our hills are mountains here. From the top of it you can see the Rocky Mountains eighty miles away.

Say little rascal rascal rascal rasc ras ra r rr, if I am not mistaken the last letter I wrote to you I directed it to mamma. Beg pardon.

Well the mail has not come yet and it is two weeks due. I have been looking for mail two ways, one from the regular mail man, Livingston and one from Brick Bros. who was to be along in their boat two weeks ago. I guess they will not come, the water is too cold to track now and Livingston is due the first of every month and he has not come yet. But I heard that he will not be here this trip until the middle of this month and that is Saturday, so miss, I will expect sixteen or nineteen letters from you, some with forty pages.

Well little girl, I hope that you are getting my letters of forty pages by this time. If I don't get any from you it would be some consolation to know that you are getting my letters but I would give a whole lot to get a letter from you dated October the 12th, right this evening, to know what you have been doing the last month, the last two weeks, the last week, the last day or two, the last day, today, this evening at 6:00 P.M. October 12, 1898.

Yes, if I could just know if you are getting along all right, that you are having a good time and aren't sick I would not feel so lonesome. But I won't know what you are doing on the 12th of October '98 until some time in the spring. All I can do is to keep on praying that my daughter is all right and I believe that my prayers will be heard.

I can imagine that I can see you sitting at a desk with books as big as a table in front of you and a pen behind your ear thinking about your papa in B.C. Well, I hope so anyhow, if you just kind of control yourself and don't get too awful anxious about your beaux, I know you will get a good position and when your Klondyke pap comes home he will have something for you.

That picture you sent me, well I know that no papa has as nice a daughter as I have. I look at it every day. I want you to look just like that picture when I come home, and don't you forget what I told you.

I suppose the street fair was a grand success and did you play for anybody? We didn't have any street fair up here but we killed a bear. Well we are going to have company in about an hour, the Grimstons. Then I will have to stop and entertain. They are putting on their chimney and they are coming down after supper to spend the evening.

I wish you would take a fool notion Neva and come up here. It would do you good. You said you had the fever to come and a trip through here with Dessie would make a new girl out of her. Dessie, you come anyhow and I will show you how to cook. I will give you roast duck for dinner and fried pheasant for supper and bacon for breakfast and on Sunday a great big hunk of roast bear, yes and cornbread. You would soon get fat and you could go hunting with me and Dash and if we saw a grizzly we would both climb a tree.

Now Neva, you asked me to be a good boy, now you can't do anything up here but be good. Of course I can't go to Sunday School but I can get out on a log and play the fiddle to the pine squirrels and the bothersome birds. The Grimstons have come so I will have to stop and entertain awhile. Goodnight, goodnight. Now for a smoke and who can tell the biggest bear stories. Tra la la.

Thursday, October 13
Well I tried the shotgun today and it didn't shoot through an inch pine board forty feet away and once more I made Peters out a liar.

We had company tonight or rather I had company for I am all by myself for a few days. Peters and one of the Grimstons took a canoe and three days grub and have gone up Pine River hunting. Well as I was saying, says I, I had company, the other two men spent the evening and I began to think they was going to spend the night. I wanted to write tonight and they have just gone home and it must be 11:00 P.M.

I suppose you aren't running an engine yet. Myrty says in her letter of Aug. 1st that you made $72.00 last month. That's good. Save your money now and don't start out like your dad, just because you make lots, spend lots. If you have to spend it spend it on your mother and sister, fix her up so you will be proud of her. Every pay day spend $10.00 on buying Myrty something nice for she is a dear good sister of yours and you must take good care of her and keep her in nice clothes.

How are all of the old boys getting along anyhow? Are there any changes in any of them? I suppose there is on account of Kirby's death and Bennett's discharge. Is Ben Bazle still night foreman and how Is Paul and Bates and Luffersen, are they in their same old places? I will expect forty sheets from you soon. I wish you could be right here too with me.

You didn't say where the dipper was located out there at the same time I wrote about it, I would like to have known. Now at about 12:00 midnight the seven stars are located a little bit northeast at about an angle of about forty-five or fifty degrees.

If anyone deserves to get rich it is them that comes up here and I feel and have hopes that I will be fortunate. I don't hardly expect to find a gold mine where we are now but by this time next fall I expect to be pretty close to the Klondyke and in the gold regions. Anyhow I will do my best. I will hang on like a bull pup. There is gold here but not in paying quantities unless I had machinery to work it.

Say Hat, I want you to get someone to shoot George's picture. I have got all but his and I want it. Our neighbors has a Kodak and they have taken several pictures of us in different places and shapes on our trip and they are going to give me one of each of them but they have to send them back home before they can develop them so it will be some time before I get them. They are going to take a picture of our cabin and all that is in it and me making pies.

Well as it is after midnight and these blamed timber wolves are howling so I guess I will go to bed. Hat, do you know that I got a letter from Myrty written Aug. 1st, Well I did and it was a whopper too. Tra la la.

Friday, Oct. 14
Dick, Madge, Fred, Hugh, Jeff, Dan and Pap, if you could be with me tomorrow morning about 4:00 A.M. you could have some fun. Today I was up Pine River about three miles. I saw where three moose had crossed and gone back in the hills, fresh tracks, now won't I go after them moose in the A.M. Well I guess yes, I'll have moose meat for dinner Sunday. I would like to have you all along to drive them up to me so I could get them all at once. It is raining a little now and that is all the better, a moose looks like a hump back mule until you go to eat him and then it looks like meat.

Well as I am all by myself for a few days it kind of sounds lonesome around here. Haven't got no crickets, no clock to tick and all the noise there is is what the fire makes and the blamed wolves. Sometimes I just wish I could see the 364 go by about four hundred miles an hour. Just make a little blue streak. I wonder if I can tell an engine whistle from a house a fire when I come home. Well If I am going to get a moose I had better go to bed, it must be 11:00 anyhow, haven't got any clock, no watch, no almanac, no sense, no letters only one from Myrty written Aug. lst, so tra la la, I am going to bed and dream about moose and bear.

This is Saturday the 15th
Me, the devil, I didn't kill the bear or moose either. I was certain of a moose, I tracked it three miles and the last track was headed for Dawson City and I expect the darned moose is there by this time. I killed three pheasants and came home.

Well mamma we had a little snow last night, seems kind of queer to have some in October. It isn't nothing when you get used to it though. I have been working since dinner making a latch and door knob for our door, that completes everything in the way of furniture now except a wash stand. I made a rack for our goods and two bunks combined, made a kitchen table and cupboard, made a table, stand table three foot square and a stand to put the water bucket on. Put up the stove, cut a hole through the roof for the pipe, made a latch and knobs for the door, made a stool, made me a big arm chair and cut six cords of wood while Peters, all he had done was put the fireplace in and helped to cut the logs for the house. If he don't cut his six cords of wood he will cut it when mine is burnt up or he will freeze for I won't cut a stick after mine is burnt. Well I will have to stop now, I am going to have company, the Grimstons. I will write tomorrow, it is the lonesome day for me. Goodnight with a big smack.

Sunday, Oct. 16, 1:00 o'clock P.M. by the sun
"There," says the old woman, "I have just this yer minute got time to set down." I have been fussing around all morning, first washed my dirty clothes and then arranged the pictures and looking glass and

things on the walls. Well Myrty, all the pictures I have is two jokers that come out of a deck of cards and one blank card, it is all white. I nailed them up by the looking glass in a triangular position.

I have got two old magazines and one book, the title of which is "The Courting of Dinah Shadd" and my Bible on the table and a newspaper of May 1st and it looks some like a Y.M.C.A. Oh you bet I have got some taste about me, the way I sweep the floor, I made me a broom in the shape of a rake. I rake it all over every morning and sprinkle it well to keep the dust down. It looks like an onion bed after I get through with it. If you come to see me I want you to clean your feet on the grass before you come in on my dirt floor. And you mustn't rub against the wall, I don't want the gloss rubbed all off my mud, so I don't. One good thing about our floor, don't have to scrub it. Oh I guess we'll live all right.

Did I tell you I got your letter of Aug. 1st? The Hudson Bay man gave it to me as he went by on his way to St. John.

Well I think we are going to have some weather, it has been cold all day. When I hung my clothes out today, in a minute they was froze stiff. How is that for October? This lonesome day is gone at last and I'm not sorry. I can pass the time away all right through the week but Sunday somehow is a sticker. Well girl, I am going to bed, it is 11:00 by the moon. I had company this evening, the Grimstons and they are stayers. They want to set up all night and sleep in the day time. Goodnight after I take a bath.

Monday the 17th about 1:00 o'clock
I have had dinner. It is snowing just as hard as it can come down. Can't see twenty feet. I never saw it snow as hard in my life, it is not cold but looks very much like winter. Now if it will only snow six inches and then turn warm I am going to kill that bear and moose too.

Say folks, if I don't say anything that interests you say so, I feel as if I was going to run out of something to say pretty soon and I don't know how soon I will get a chance to send this letter out.

The Grimston that is going home says now that he may not go much before Christmas. Be a joke if I would have to keep on writing on this one letter until Christmas. I would run out of something to say sure then.

Peters and the Grimstons has not come back yet from hunting. Kind of think that they have got some big game or they would be back. They only went for three days. They went Thursday. Be a joke if the river freezes up and they can't get their canoe home. There they come now, talk about the devil and he will sure appear. They didn't kill anything but some pheasants.

Oh yes Myrty, I found another book to put on the table. Now it does look like a Y.M.C.A. It is a Bible of some kind. I will send you a leaf of it, see if you can read it, you ought to, it looks like short hand. Well I will quit for today, we are going to have company this evening, the Grimstons so tra la la.

Tuesday evening
I will try and say something today but I don't know what it will be. Oh yes, on Thursday morning one of the Grimstons, their partner Mr. Spencier and myself are going to take the canoe and go to St. John after the mail. We will go up one day and come back the next. Have been waiting for three weeks for the Brick Bros. to go by to get mail from them but they have not come yet and I don't think they will now any more this winter as the water is too cold to track a boat in. This is all today. I don't know if we will have company this evening or not, they haven't said anything about it yet. I just got done reading your letter over Myrty, the one you wrote Aug. lst. Forty eleven kisses to you all, goodnight.

Wednesday, Oct. 19
Well dear boys and girls, we will play like we were going to finish this letter tonight. We are going up to St. John in the morning and I will finish this letter and take it along and maybe I will get a chance to send it out by someone. Now if I don't get a chance to send it we will not call it finished and I will keep on writing some until I do get a chance to mail it. And if I do send it from St. John tomorrow I will write some there telling you if I got any letters, what letters and who they are from.

Miss Myrty, I had better get some letters from you tomorrow or you'll catch it. The last letter I had from you was written Aug. 1st.

Well I don't know what to write about this evening unless I tell you I am well and hope these few lines will find you all enjoying the same. I was busy all day setting traps and hunting. I killed three pheasants and that is all I saw. I found a regular fox den today, I have some traps set there. I don't know what kind of fox they are but it is a fox village.

We are going to whipsaw lumber enough to make a boat and a canoe this winter and that will take us quite a while to make them and will hope to pass the time away. The balance of the time we can put in hunting and prospecting and setting around telling yarns. Well I didn't find any gold in the hole I dug so I will try another place.

When you write, tell me what letters you have got from me, tell me what was the last letter you got and tell me all the news, everything. This letter, understand, has to be sent to all the folks. Let George read it and then send it to Neva and tell her to send it to Nora and Nora let Jeff and Dan read it, then send it to Dick and then to Hat.

You see I have saved fifteen stamps, that is 45¢. I have to do this for there are no stamps up here to be had, only what I brought along with me. Dear Hat, Neva, Nora, George, Jeff, Dan, Ollie, Bertha, Dick, Madge, Fred, Kate, Hugh, Dessie, Pap, Uncle John, boy you had better write to me or I will get a big stick. I can put my arms on the table all I please up here.

Mamma, tell Mr. White that I haven't anything of importance to write him now but as soon as I do I will write him. Tell him I send my best wishes to him and his family. Remember me to all inquiring friends and now I will bring this to a close hoping you are all all right and getting along nice. Send your papers registered and direct everything in care of Hudson Bay Company, Fort St. John via Edmonton, Alberta, Canada instead of McDougall and Secord. I make this change on account of after we get beyond St. John, McDougall and Secord aren't known. Well goodbye for this time, I must go to bed so as to get up before daylight and make St.

John tomorrow. (It gets dark at 5:00 P.M. now). Many kisses to you all. Write often and big letters like the one Myrty wrote Aug. 1st. Best wishes to all.

I am your Klondyke Jim

Thursday evening, October 20
Well we have just arrived in this beautiful city of cabins just after the crow goes to rest and to find a big disappointment waiting for me. That isn't anything though, I get them right along. Livingston, the mail man has not arrived yet. They are looking for Livingston and Brick Bros. and the preacher and all three will be here by and by. Brick has to come for he hasn't got his winter supplies yet so I suppose in a week's time he will have more mail than I can read. But I'll have to make another trip to St. John. Will get what mail Brick brings up as he goes by Hinkle town. Then he goes back again and I will send another letter out. This is all only it is nice going to St. John. Be good children, a few more kisses to all. Fifty extra ones to Mamma and Myrty. Best. KJ

Hamilton was awful glad to see me last night. He is the Hudson Bay man. He had his Indian to get us some supper. We have moose meat, bacon and bread and you ought to have seen us go for it. Of course walking thirty miles makes a fellow eat. After supper I played the fiddle and he the banjo and we sang and played all the old songs I ever knew, such as Nelly Grey, Swaney River, Gathering of the Shells at the Seashore, Twinkle Little Star and then I played him and the Indians a jig and the way they did hoe it down was a sight.

KJ

10

Pine River Camp in the Fall

I love thee, I love thee, how fondly how well
Let the years that are coming my constancy tell
I think of thee daily — my night thoughts are yours
In fairy like vision thy hands presses mine
And even though absent, you dwell in my heart
Of all that is dear to me, dearest thou art.
(That means you and the kids)

October, Thursday 27, 1898

North Pine River Camp, B.C.
My very dear ones, mamma and the kids,

    I will commence to write you another letter though the last one I wrote probably has not left St. John but as there will be a chance to send this letter out yet before the river freezes up I will try and interest you for a few days. First, all I can talk about will be the little incidents that has happened around camp since I finished writing my last letter to you, and of which I took to St. John to mail with the hopes of getting several letters from you all and did not get a single letter from anyone.
    For behold, the mail man, Mr. Livingston, had not arrived and is pretty near one month behind, all on account of he had to get married. Of course these things must be, mail or no mail,

disappointment or not, he must get married and have a little honeymoon for we all do, you know.

I can't say if he has come yet or not and won't know until some one of us goes to St. John or some one per chance be coming down Peace River. Thought Mr. Hamilton, the Hudson Bay man would send the mail down to us.

One of our neighbors is going to St. John as soon as the weather gets warmer, if it ever will anymore this winter. Canadian winter is here with us sure enough and with all its beauties. I don't hardly think it has set in for keeps. Think we will have a week or ten days yet of nice weather but can't tell at the present. We have five inches of snow. It is not very cold but looks for all just like winter.

These are the places of nature whose vast walls have pinnacled in clouds their snowy scalps and throned eternity in icy halls of cold sublimity.

That sounds like Byron or Shakespeare, I rather think Byron, if I get too high for you don't kick for it is all I have to do here is to make poetry and slide down these hills when I go hunting. Well as I said, winter is here sure enough. On Tuesday it snowed hard all day, about five inches and since then it has been cloudy and just so cold, not warm enough to melt the snow. Peace River is not froze up yet but there is lots of slush ice going down and will be the cause of no more boats coming up, I am afraid unless it should turn warm for ten days. There is two boats a month due that has not showed up yet — the Brick Bros. and the other, the preacher. Three with Livingston the mail man, but he goes the trail with horses. I have been waiting and watching patiently for Brick Bros and the preacher so as to stop them and get the mail, if any, but my hopes are gone in that direction for mail, all depends on Livingston now. I have no word from anyone since I got Myrty's letter of August 1st and I am over anxious to know about you, if you are all right.

Well I will have to tell you everything that happened around camp and if it don't interest you just mark it n.g. On Friday 21st I was at St. John and left you a letter to be taken out by Livingston or anyone that would be going out and I or we (the Grimstons) left at 11:00 A.M. in a canoe for Pine River camp. We arrived at the log cabin at 6:00 P.M. by the sun I guess for it sets at about 5:00 P.M. and it was just dark. Well Myrty I didn't have half as much fun as I did when I came down before on a raft for a canoe rides over the waves and rapids and ripples nicer than a raft but once more if you had of seen me bobbin' over those rapids on a raft you never would be any good.

I had a very nice time while at St. John. Mr. Hamilton is a jolly fellow. He is six feet tall, about thirty three years old and single, he has a fiddle and banjo, can't play much himself but is a good clog dancer so I give him some of my best and the way he did shake them long pendlums was a sight.

We did some target shooting, I had my Colts rifle along and he had his carbine, both #38. He give us our supper and breakfast and bed, didn't charge a cent, altogether a tip top fellow. He is coming down to visit us some time this winter.

On Saturday 22 I baked five pies, two raisin and three apricot, and I washed and I want you Harry and Pet, to know that we had some fun in the evening. At 8:00 o'clock by the moon, Dash commenced to bark and run out of his house just a raring. There are some timber wolves just across Pine River most every evening and he always barks at most everything that he sees moving. I always know when someone is going up or down the river in a boat for he will bark every time.

But this time it wasn't wolves or boats either. I was at Grimstons cabin when he barked. First I says, "Dash sees the wolves again", but it was a different bark from any of his warnings so I went out. I says, "Go get them" and you ought to see him try to get them. He was about forty feet from our cabin and was just making all kinds of a fuss and just like he was about to eat something up.

I says, "Get them" to him again and he got it and it got him. My first thought was that it was a lynx for there are quite a good many around, then I thought of a wild cat so one of the Grimstons grabbed his gun and got his two dogs. I went to the house and got my gun, mind you Peters was at home reading all this time and he don't like Dash and as I run to the cabin to get the gun he comes to the door and hollers to Dash to get out. I says to Dash, "Get them" and Dash was standing by a big tree barking. I couldn't get my gun cover off the gun for a bit and one of the Grimstons got ahead of me and shot. But as I hollered to Dash as Peters was trying to make him quit barking, something give a big snort, I hollered, "A moose" for it went just like a cow a snorting.

Grimston shot again and down came a bear, it tried to hug him but he was too smart for Mr. Bear. Now all of this happened right by our cabin, then say there is no excitement up here, say there is not fun, well I guess yes.

As Grimston shot the bear, he got the skin, I got half of the bear and him half. He and I have a bargain, the one that shoots the bear gets the skin so that is the way it is now.

As soon as the sun comes out and the snow begins to melt, I'll get a bear, that is me and Dash will for I will not go out by myself.

Peters looked like a damn fool after the fun was all over. I didn't say a word to him and he kept on talking. I didn't pay any attention to him and then he looked like a damn, damn fool. That is just the kind of a chicken he is. A man that no one liked. He won't eat bear meat, he don't eat pies, he don't eat cakes, he don't put any salt in anything he cooks so I cook to suit myself and of course I get to eat all of the pies and cakes and good things for he can't bake pies and cakes either and I am awful glad that he don't like all of these things. I judge from the way he cooks and the things he eats that he was raised on a bottle or a sugar tit, tea and crackers.

On Sunday 23, the lonesome day, of course I had fried bear steak for breakfast, Peters didn't taste it and you bet I was glad for I want it to last as long as possible for I might not get another one for a long time. For dinner I had roast bear and rice pudding. I cooked some rice then I took some condensed milk and stewed some raisins and put milk, raisins and rice in the bread pan, put it in the oven and baked it for a while.

Well now if that roast bear and rice pudding and raisin pie didn't go, take care Liza Jane, ma pass the pudding. Peters ate some of the pudding, didn't say if it was good or not and I didn't care what he said, I was too busy. Well that was what I call one of them dinners that I have seen you have when we have company only I didn't have any float. But would have had if I could have found some bird eggs.

On Sunday too it commenced to snow and snowed some in the evening. On Monday I took the gun and my pard Dash, and went hunting, killed one pheasant and one duck but didn't get the duck, the river (Pine River) was frozen over in one place and where I shot the duck the water was swift so Dash went after the duck and just as he made a grab for it he broke through the ice and duck, dog and all went under the ice. Well I didn't care for the duck but I began to get uneasy about my old pal but he let the duck go and got out all right so I didn't have any duck that day.

On Tuesday the 25th I got up at daylight to go a moose hunting with one of the Grimstons. There was three inches of snow and still snowing so he wouldn't go. Dash and I went up Pine River three miles and then up on top of the hills which are just about out of sight and took a circle around east and home but didn't see anything or any tracks, either moose or bear. They didn't run that night.

It snowed until after dinner, then it quit by 9:00 o'clock by the moon and then it commenced and snowed all night. We had company that night, the Grimstons, we had a good talking about our hardships coming up the river after which we had a game of hearts.

On Wednesday I went hunting, five inches of snow now, killed two pheasants, Dash got after a fox which was a hot trail and he run it for miles. I couldn't get him away from it, he got lost from me and went home about 11:00 o'clock by the sun, although I couldn't see the sun.

When I got home, Peters had cut half his finger off with an ax — damn fool — done it splitting wood by holding the stick with one hand and striking with the ax with the other one. I have to wash the dishes all the time now. I bet he done it on purpose. One of the Grimstons went hunting, his given name is Digby, he killed one pheasant, his brother Sell was sick all day and their other partner, Spencier by name, cut his whiskers off. He had let them grow long.

On Thursday the 27th I stayed around the cabin all day, baked some ginger cakes. I took one cup of sugar molasses, half cup of lard, teaspoon of soda, tablespoonful of ginger, a little salt, one cup full of hot water and enough flour to make a dough. I want you to know they weren't so snotty. Try it once Myrty and I'll bet you will like them.

Peters tried one and he said they was too hot for his little tender mouth, complained late that night that his mouth still burned. Next morning his mouth was still burning and by night the next day his tongue was all full of blisters just by eating one little ginger cake the day before. I get to eat all of the ginger cakes and they are nearly all gone and I am going to bake another soon. The Grimstons thought they were awful good.

Oh yes Myrty, I must tell you a joke on myself, I like to have forgot it. On Thursday the 20th, the day Sell and Spencier and I went to St. John, he wanted to start early and I am the first up every morning (the nights are fourteen hours long). So this morning I wakened up in the night, looked out through the window and it looked like it was getting daylight and I heard the whiskey jacks chirping. They are a bird and look like jay birds only bigger and can holler as many different ways as a poll parrot. In fact they go just like a parrot. So I got up right quick (thinking it was late or that I over slept) put on my pants and shoes, built a fire, put on the tea kettle and then went to the door and opened it and there was as pretty aurora borealis (or northern lights) as ever you saw, joke on the daylight. It was as light as day and looked like the world was coming to an end (although I never saw a world come to an end) joke on the whiskey jacks too. I felt like someone sent for and couldn't go — don't act a fool, you would do the same thing.

I got your letter of August 1st. If that is the last letter you got from me July 6th, why there is sixteen or nineteen more letters between me and you, some with forty pages and some sketches of the river. Yes I got your letter of Aug. 1.

Friday, October 28
I have been tinkering around all day not doing much of anything. I went out a little while in the afternoon, killed one pheasant. They are the easiest thing to kill outside of a louse, there is. Dash has just

enough pointer in him to like to hunt them and he gets everyone that is in reach of his smeller. When he gets after them on their trail they will just fly up in a bush or fly a little ways and light on the ground and all you have to do is to say, "Will you walk into my parlor?" and if they don't walk, shoot them. They are just the size of a prairie chicken and look like one only they get up on a log, stick their bill in the log and drum with their wings, it sounds just like thunder. In taste, they are just like a half grown chicken.

If the sun keeps on it will get so far in the south that it won't make a shadow and the moon — it is trying itself, might as well not shine at all as to come up for an hour and then set again. I guess it is trying to catch itself. I will quit for tonight and see what will happen tomorrow. Goodnight with kisses for all. Tra la la.

This is Saturday, October 29
And I want you to know that it has been snowing just as hard as it can come down since dinner. I went hunting this morning. I have lots of fun with these Englishmen. They are a queer set in their talk and actions and everything they do. In the first place they try to be aristocratic and are just the same as any of us Klondykers. Someone staked them or they wouldn't be here.

I must talk about them some now and give you an idea how they are, it may be interesting to you. I know it will tickle the kids. In the first place they talk like all Englishmen. You can't do a thing for them but they will say, "Oh thank you, thank you very much." Now mind you, everything you do or say you will do, there is a thanks, always. Well that part is all right, it is politeness of course but here is one of their ways and it is a corker. I laughed 'til I couldn't stand up and am laughing yet.

This morning Sell came into our cabin, I was just getting ready to go hunting. Well yesterday he went down to their old camp (Struck Creek) to get some things that they hadn't brought up yet and there is a trail that goes down to their old camp on top of the high hill that runs all along the river and is a good place to kill pheasants all back on the level.

So he says, "Jim, are you going gunning this morning?" I says, "Yes, I am going a hunting." He says, "Would you mind going with my brother, Digby and I?" I says, "No, I would like to go with you very much." So he says, "All right," I says, "How soon will you be ready to go?" "Oh", he said, "after breakfast about 10:00 or 11:00 o'clock."

Well, that settled it right there, he had just crawled out of bed and had come in our cabin to get warm. He says, "As I was journeying down to our old haunts yesterday, I came to a rivulet and discovered where a ferocious beast had killed a fox and devoured its carcass." He says, "My brother Digby wants to go down that way and see if we can dispatch the animal and would like to have you go along." So I says, "Well I will take the gun and go on over the hill and kill some pheasants and go on down to the canyon," (for that is all you could call it) "and wait for you."

Well I went on and hunted 'til noon by the sun, built a fire to keep from freezing to death and waited a couple of hours and "my brother Digby and I" didn't come so I went down to the rivulet to see if I could see any tigers or lions or elephants or ferocious beasts. You bet I kept a sharp lookout for I did not have my old pal, Dash with me. Something mashed one of his toes and it was too sore so I left him at home. I had my gun cocked and was ready for bears, lions, tigers or anything.

Well I got down to the bottom after sliding half of the way and found the head of a fisher (fisher is an animal about half as big as a fox) and where a timber wolf had dug it out of the snow and tried to make a meal out of the bone. Well, I sat down and says, "All the damn fools aren't dead yet."

That fisher had died last summer of consumption or old age and Sell was so excited on seeing that head there that he didn't know himself from a musket. I shoot at the same ferocious beast every day or so standing in the cabin door just for fun so that ended the hunt. Well, "I and my brother Digby" was afraid to go up on top of the hill so they went down along the river and that way I missed them. Oh I have lots of fun.

You ought to see them, they always set from two to three batches of bread before they get one. They will set their yeast and it won't raise so they throw that one away, try it again and the next time they will forget to attend to it, throw that batch away, the darned fools will run out of flour and yeast before spring, and I have told them how to make bread forty times.

Well I will stop now by telling you that Dash's toe nail came off today while I was hunting. He got after a wolf and the nail came off. That makes two of the nails off one foot. The other one he lost by running through the fire that time. So as we are going to have company directly, the Grimstons, I will stop for tonight and tell you what I do tomorrow. I won't go to Sunday school is one thing I won't do. Several kisses. Tra la la

Sunday 30th, Just after dinner.
This morning is one of those Sunday mornings. Puts me in mind of that we have in Mattoon in the winter time, where it snowed all night the night before and in the morning the sun came out as bright as can be, everything shining. There is six inches of snow this morning and the sun is shining bright all day but not thawing any and it is not very cold either. Everything is complete for a winter day in Mattoon but the sleigh bells. If I had some sleigh bells I would put them on Dash and take a walk just to hear them jingle. I suppose you have nice weather there and have not thought of winter yet.

The only thing that is worrying me is to know what I am to get for a Christmas gift and who will get me a nice present. I guess I will tell you what I have been doing this morning and what I had for dinner. I had enough you bet. The first thing after breakfast I put on a pot of beans and a great big hunk of sow belly. Now beans for dinner on Sunday — who ever heard of such a thing. Well then I went into the pastry business. I put on some apricots and some raisins to stew, I made four apricot pies first, then I made another batch of ginger cakes. As before — about a half a bushel of them. Why, if I didn't bake a half a bushel at a time Myrty, I would have to bake them every day, and Peters don't eat them either.

Peters happened to kill a duck after shooting three times to get it, so the oven was vacant and I put the duck to baking. Then I put on some rice and cooked it a while, took some condensed milk and the stewed raisins and some nutmeg and put it in the oven to bake.

I had a general baking all around, so I had beans, roast duck, apricot pie, ginger cakes, and rice pudding and gravy for dinner. There, can you beat that ma, pass the duck gravy. Don't forget to speak to Menk for me a place as general cook in his establishment.

Now I am getting lonesome and can't write any more so I will wait until tomorrow. I am going to my traps and hunting tomorrow. Good afternoon to you all. I can see Myrty getting ready to go to League. Tra la la.

Monday the 31st
Well dear folks — snow, it don't do anything else but snow, we have ten inches of it now, but it stopped at 7:00 P.M. and is as clear as a whistle and I am waiting for the moon to come up to get a chance to do some shooting. Dash just this minute got back from chasing a wolf that went up Pine River. Digby shot at it but n.g.

Dash is so fat that he can't run fast but he does his best. Now there is no dog, I don't believe, that I ever saw that is as easy to learn and catch on to anything as my old pal Dash. Here is what he knows so far. I ask him if he wants his supper and he will give a kind of a halfway bark. I say, "Are you hungry?" Then he gives one loud bark. Then I say, "Are we old pals?" before I give him his supper and he reaches out his paw. That is all you have to say to him and now if you stand a bit before you give him his supper and not say a word he will reach out his paw — "Yes, I am your pal."

Then at night he stays in the cabin until I go to bed. I say, "Dash, don't you want to go to bed too?" He will give two barks (yes, yes). I open the door and as he goes out he reaches out his paw to give me goodnight. I get ready to go out hunting, I have the guns hanging up on the side of the cabin, I say, "Now what in the name of sense do you want, there are no mice there." He growls, I say, "Oh do you want me to go out and kill some pheasants?" He will bark until you tell him to quit.

Lots of times he will get on the trail of a pheasant and the pheasant hasn't been on the ground at all. I say, "Dash, hadn't you better look up in the trees some, he might be in a tree?" He will stop and look all around in the trees and if the pheasant isn't there close, he will give one bark just to let me know where it is. He likes to hear the crack of the rifle. I taught him to do this by pointing the gun up in a tree and very often kill pheasants in a tree. Well as soon as you shoot, he gets the bird, brings it to you and I wish Harry, you could see him as he brings the bird to you. You would never be any good any more. He brings the bird about six feet right down beside you. He don't wait a second until he is right out after another one. I taught him this trick coming up Slave River killing ducks.

I say, "Dash we are about out of wood, hadn't you better go get a stick?" He don't do a thing only go out and bring a stick ten feet long. I can put a loaf of bread or a piece of meat or anything down on the floor, he never touches it. No money could buy Dash and he belongs to Myrty and Myrty shall have him if I have good luck with him and nothing happens to him.

I started hunting this morning and go about a mile and got caught in a snow storm, had to come back. Pine River is frozen over solid, Peace River is pretty near and then all navigation will be stopped except by dog trains until next April. I am going to make a dog sled and break Dash to pull me on the ice to St. John after the mail. Come on Pet and we will take a ride. He is big enough to pull both of us. He will be pretty near as big as Andrews big dog. Well I must quit now for we are going to have company (the Grimstons) and of course it doesn't show good manners to read or write when you have company. I got your letter Myrty of Aug. 1st. Tra la la.

Tuesday the 1st day of November
And it has been a nice warm day. That is what we call a warm day. The snow melted some today. The thermometer stood this morning at 15° above zero. I suppose you are all getting ready to elect Bill Byers sheriff tomorrow. Well tell him I vote for him, that when he finds out what his majority is to just add one more vote.

I went hunting today, killed one pheasant. I guess I'm not going to get to kill any big game. For some cause the big game has all gone away from close around here. I don't know where the moose has gone and the bear are all gone to their dens I guess. It is the time they hole up now and don't come out 'til spring. But I may run onto some of their dens, if I do I will have some fun.

We had a little excitement just at sundown as I was coming from hunting. Sell and Spencier was shooting at a wolf but did not touch a hair on it. Well I will quit for this evening. I had bread pudding and whiskey dip for dinner. Haven't got any letters from you Since Aug. 1st and I got one from Myrty then. Tra la la.

Wednesday 2nd
I am going to have some fun tomorrow Myrty. I made a sleigh today for Dash. I have got shafts to it, have to make the harness yet and then I am going to have some fun — me and Dash. I am going to break him in sometime tomorrow. Now I know what he will want to do first and that is to take hold of the sleigh with his teeth or else run off with the sleigh wanting me to catch him but I will fool him for I am going to put a bridle on him. He will like the sport as much as I will I know. He is very fond of me.

Well it is considerable colder today. The thermometer stood this morning at 30 above zero. It is about 8:00 P.M. now. Does Bill Byers know yet if he is elected or not? I can see them all standing around the polls, drug stores, saloons and corners hollering for Bill Byers.

I have no chance of getting to St. John now for some time as the walking is bad. As soon as Peace River freezes up so it will bear a man, then I am going for I know there is mail there for me, no one can go up or down on Peace River now with a boat and there will be no Brick Bros. or preacher until the river is frozen and then they will come with dog teams so I don't know when to look for a letter from you. Not until someone goes to St. John or someone comes from there.

I am all by myself this evening. Peters is visiting the Grimstons. Mamma you can't guess what I am doing to pass the time away, that is, part of the time I am working on it. I will let you guess and will tell you at the end of the letter, no fair looking. Now all of you guess and see how near you come to it, what it is will be written on a piece of paper so you can't see it and on the outside will say, 'don't open this until you read all of the letter' and keep on guessing.

Get Miss Stump and Mrs. Kinser to guess and George and Anna and Frakes and Irish Jim and everybody guess. Call in the neighbors and have a guessing party. Now Myrty, no fair looking.

To the one that guesses the right answer I will bring a relic of British Columbia, so now guess ahead all of you. I will just say this much, you can't make it in one day or one week, and it is something you all have seen lots and lots of times. It is very useful, it is ornamental, it is something that lots of people go crazy over, it is made out of material in B.C. It is neither white or black, it is in thirty two pieces, eight of the pieces are all different.

It can't walk or talk and when it's done it's work everybody says well done. It is something that lots and lots of people don't know anything about and it is something that lots of people make a great deal of fuss about. I will pay the one that guesses the right answer. Well Pet, get yourself working on the guessing business. Get Godwin and Jim Frock to guessing, let Bill White guess, let everybody guess. I will stop writing for this evening and do some work on what I want you to guess on. Some kisses to all. Goodnight.

Thursday the 3rd
Well I worked last night 'til eleven on one piece and then didn't half finish it. Are you still guessing? I never made it before in my life. I never saw anyone else make it. I will make it and make it right if it takes me all winter in the log cabin on Pine River to do it. One can make anything if he has nothing much to do and is in an uncivilized country. It is pastime and he will do his best and I think he becomes naturalized to make anything he undertakes.

If I had the material I would undertake to make a piano. Each fellow has two days to guess in and each fellow has but one guess that he must settle on at 6:00 P.M. On the second day, you can open the little package that has the answer in and if anyone has guessed it correct he or she will get a nice present. If nobody guesses the correct answer, all of you go soak your head. If anybody guesses the correct answer, the balance go soak your head anyhow.

It is cold up here but nice weather. The sun is shining most of the time but is not thawing a bit. We have six inches of snow. Fun, I guess I did have fun today. I have got the sleigh and harness made and hitched up Dash and he went like the devil. Tried to run off and he would have succeeded if the sleigh hadn't got caught on a stump. He is all right and will like the sport as well as I will after I get him broke. Come up Myrty and take a ride with your horse dog. I don't know how he will like a woman, he never saw one, 'spect he will take you for a bear and eat you up. Well I must quit and do some work, it won't do to write all of the time. It makes me lonesome. Tra la la.

Friday the 4th
Today has been a nice day only it is cold, sun shown all day but didn't thaw a bit. Myrty, your horse dog is broke to work in the harness. I hitched him today, took him down on the ice and had a great time. At first he wanted to show off and take a hold of the shafts with his teeth and pull the sled that way, but I soon broke him of that. I was out about an hour with him and before I quit he went along in a trot before me just like he had always been used to it or like an old work horse.

I got on the sled and you ought to see him stick his toe nails in the ice and pull. He is all right and will be able to pull you when I come home. Now if you can get your fellow to give you a nice little sleigh for a Christmas gift you will be fixed all right. It will be quite a novelty to go up Broadway in Mattoon with a girl and a horse dog pulling you. Dash is an awful pretty dog. He has short hair, a long tail, long ears and is white and black spotted and is or will be as big as Andrews big dog. He is a great companion, don't know what I would do without him.

Well are you still guessing? I made a part of it today. Get Jim Guildoff to guess and Mr. and Mrs. Belmer. It only takes one to make it and would be a good job for a convict to make while he is serving his twenty years in the pen. It is the most tedious job I ever undertook but I will accomplish it.

Tomorrow is bake day. I don't know what I will get up but one thing certain, another half bushel of ginger cakes goes anyhow and some pies. I guess I will make apple pies sprinkled with nutmeg so I will quit for this evening and get to work. I want to try and finish this, this winter anyhow. Good night mamma, goodnight Myrty, bye bye Pet and Harry, I will see you later.

Saturday the 5th
I don't have much to write about today, I went hunting a little while and set four traps. I didn't bake today. Somehow I didn't feel like it so I says, 'I'll bake tomorrow'. It is cold and clear today. As I haven't got anything to write about I will quit and write tomorrow as it is Sunday. Goodnight.

Sunday the 6th
Well are you guessing Pet, no fair looking. Now mamma don't let any of them look until the end of the second day at 6:00 P.M. Well I can't bake today because it is Sunday and I have got to go to Sunday School anyhow. So I set around all day and read a book the title which was 'My First Violin'.

In the evening I had a game of chess with Spencier. I beat him four straight games, didn't lose a game. Peters did the cooking today. I just thought I would make him cook all three meals today and I wouldn't do nothing as I have done all the cooking ever since I have been in this country. Well he had roast pheasant and rice-I-don't-know-what for dinner, he called it rice pudding. It was just rice and nutmeg without the pud and about five raisins and a half. He uses raisins about like he does when he makes coffee. Takes four grains of coffee, if one of the grains is a little small he will split one grain and take four grains and a half.

Oh he is a damn fool, that is all there is about it. I wish you could see some of his capers when he is cooking. Just like a danged fool or a lunatic. He opens the oven door fifty times if he does once and then he will run to the table to get something and all at once he will make a leap to the stove for the oven and if the oven door don't come immediately, down comes the stove. I says to him, "Are you baking on a bet or a race Jack?" I never was with a man that I despise as I do this man Peters. But we get along all right because he knows he has to do the right thing or get kicked out.

How I am longing for John Cantlon or George. Well I guess I will quit for today for I am lonesome. Haven't got no letters yet from any of you since I got Myrty's letter of Aug. 1st. Myrty did you get any of them letters with forty pages that was in between me and you since you got that one from me that I wrote while I was in the mouth of Swan River on the lake written July 6? If you haven't, won't you have a time reading them sixteen or nineteen letters if they should happen to come all at once. Yes, I got your letter typewritten of Aug. 1st. Forty kisses.

Monday the 7th
It is snowing this morning. I cut up a tree 'til dinner and hauled it up to the cabin on the sled with Dash. He goes right along and has learned to stop when I holler whoa. After dinner I baked four pies and a half bushel of ginger cakes. Peters baked some crackers in the forenoon, I wish you could see them, they are too long, he don't like lard.

Well boys, Dash got after a mother wolf at 4:00 o'clock, him and Grimstons dog Dan, and by jingo they caught it. It was the prettiest race I ever saw, Dash was in the lead. They ran a quarter of a mile in sight, then up into the woods and nailed the wolf to the cross. Dash got bit behind the ear. When I got there the wolf was dead and the two dogs standing over it saying, "I have won the victory." I must quit, we are going to have company, the Grimstons. So I will get the chess set ready for Spencier will want to beat me. Several kisses.

Tuesday morning, November 8th
To say I am mad is putting it in mild form, I am just damned mad and I don't believe there is one single one of you that cares a darn about me, I believe you are glad that I am out of the way. Last night there was a man that come from St. John. He brought the

mail down and is looking for some of his horses. He brought eight letters, all of them for Grimstons, I didn't get a darned letter and if you cared anything about me you would write often enough that I would get one letter every time that someone came by which is about once a month.

The preacher brought this mail up. He came up with horses on the trail. Livingston and Brick are to come yet and if I don't get a letter from some one of you, then I am going to Klondyke and you may never hear from me in about ten years. If you don't care enough to write to me you don't care enough to get letters from me. I suppose mamma is married by this time and don't care enough for such a worthless fellow as me to write to me. She didn't write any the last letter I got from Myrty of Aug. 1st.

This morning it is 15° below zero and still zeroing. How is that for cold in November? Well I will finish this letter today and this man will take it back to St. John to mail it. He is a Klondyker and is in camp at St. John.

Now as this may be the last letter I will have a chance to send out, I will tell you what we have partly decided to do. This much we will do sure and that is — in March we are going to leave here for Hudson Hope on the ice. Mr. Hamilton the Hudson Bay man is going to haul us and our outfit that far. It is eight miles from here. From there we don't know yet what direction we will take but it will be to the Nelson and Liard Rivers or in the Omenica country. I can't tell until next spring. But this much we will do, leave here the last of March before the ice breaks up for Hudson Hope. Get your map and you can see where it is. It is fifty miles above St. John on the Peace River and is at the foot of the Rocky Mountains.

We have or I have great hopes of finding something rich next summer. It is up in there some place and all I have to do is to find it. I have talked to three different parties who have been on Findlay River and made as high as thirty dollars per day on the sand bars. But of course they soon worked out what was on the bar. But if gold is that plentiful up there, there is a lead to it some place and I am going to try to find it. I will have all of next summer to do it in and now you can see why I want John Cantlon. If I only had him instead of Peters I would be fixed. But however, there is where this outfit is going and I will do my best.

I want you to tell Tivnen and Katz about this letter, in fact tell all of the stockholders, you can read to them as much of the letter as you like and you can tell Tivnen and Katz and all the rest of them but Bill White that I have not got one single word from any of them since I have left Edmonton, except Bill White and I have gotten four letters from him and they could just as well have written that many as Mr. White.

Well it is 17° below zero and the sun is shining bright. Peace River is just raging. The ice is crowding down it and such a noise. By morning it will all be frozen up so we can walk over it. I am baking bread today and cooking beans and the man is out looking for his horses. He will be here with us tonight.

Digby hung his clothes up by the fireplace last night and they all came over here to our house and the clothes caught fire and burned up, seven pair of winter socks, all his underwear and two shirts and some handkerchiefs. Now he will have to wear a white shirt and necktie this winter. They haven't got as much sense as Peters.

Well children I will have to bring this letter to a close as it is 5:00 P.M. now and this man is going back early in the morning and as this letter goes to you it leaves me in good health, good hopes, quite a good deal lonesome because I can't get any letters from you. It also leaves me six hundred miles from civilization and am compelled to stay here six months or else walk that six hundred miles out.

It also leaves it 10° below zero with it yet to get 40° more in the six months I have to stay here. Put it 50° below zero in Mattoon and you would freeze up, stove and all. I will have one more chance to send a letter out to you after this one. Pretty soon Sell is going home and when he goes I will send you another letter, after that it may be some time before you get another one and it might not. Anyhow I will write every time I have a chance to send a letter.

If you don't love me enough to write me you can rest easy about me, everything is all right and if you knew how bad I wanted to hear from you and with probably six months staring me in the face before I do hear from you. It does seem like if you had written often that I would have got a letter every time anyone came up here.

Myrty, you little rascal, and you said forty eleven times that, yes you got my letters. If I had a hold of you I would squeeze forty eleven letters out of you. Don't forget to practice on the piano for you know when I come home it will be two years without ever hearing a piano. I suppose you are flying high with a pen behind your ear and think you are some pumpkins.

I am anxious to hear all about Hardesty, what he said when he came home, what you said, how many questions you all asked him, how many questions he answered, what he said about me, what he said about Peters, what he said about the trip and country and all about it. Tell everybody that I am all right and can eat the bark off the pine trees. Well once more goodbye, I will quit now. I may write a few words in the A.M. before he goes.

Sell and Digby are going with him. I may get some letters when they come back. Bye bye mamma, bye bye Myrty, bye bye Pet, bye bye Harry, many kisses to you all. Your dad, Klondyke Jim.

Wednesday morning.
Just at daylight. Well Digby and Sell are gone on to St. John and this man is ready to go. I haven't any word to add only I would like to hear from you once in a while. Many kisses to you all. Hope I will get a letter tomorrow when Digby and Sell come back.

Jim K.

11

Pine River Camp in the Winter

November 12, 1898

Dear Mamma and Children,

Well here I am again writing to you and I just got done writing a letter to you of thirty seven pages. As Sell Grimston is going out home in a day or two, I will write again for it might be the last opportunity I will have for a long time.

Sell and Digby have just got back from St. John where they went on Wednesday. Didn't bring me any letters, not a darned stinking letter did they bring me. And I feel like I am forsaken, not a word from home since Myrty's letter of August 1st. And not much show for a letter now until next summer. I am strong, I will have to stand it I guess.

The letter of forty pages I left you when I went to St. John about a month ago has been there ever since until Thursday morning. That morning a man left for Edmonton and he took the letter of thirty-seven pages that I sent up to St. John with Sell and Digby and the one of forty pages, that is if he could carry them. I guess you will have reading matter enough when you get the two letters at the same time.

Oh my, if I could get that much news from home at once I would give $50.00 to the mail man. Livingston has not arrived at St. John yet and what's more I don't think the son of a seacock will arrive.

He got married two months ago and of course he is two months behind. I guess the devil is so weak by this time that he can't walk, hence he's not coming. At any rate he might have turned it over to someone else or hired someone in his place or else he strapped his bride onto a pack horse and come that way.

Brick Brothers will not be up until six weeks and the Hudson Bay Co. sends a man up to St. John every Christmas so now it lays between the Brick Bros. and the Hudson Bay Co. whether I get any letters from you until next summer. Unless Livingston gets strong enough to walk in the meantime. Surely if you folks had of written more letters I would have had some of them. One thing is certain, I would have got a letter every time anyone had come to St. John and that has been two times that parties have come in and I got no letters.

And then Myrty, the little black eyed, black haired rascal, the prettiest girl on God's green earth, had the nerve to tell me in her letter of Aug. 1st, eighty-five or thirty times, yes you were getting all my letters and that you had answered all of them and that something must be wrong that I wasn't getting them and that I had better see about it. Oh you rascal, if I had a hold of you I would shake a good time out of you. Yes, I got your letter written Aug. 1st. Sixteen or nineteen of mine are between me and you since July 6th when I was camped in the mouth of Swan River on the lake.

I want you to know it tries one's nerves to be in this country and this place with the thermometer registering at 17° below zero and still to get 50° below and no, not a word from home and no show for any for six months more but them that has a will and a constitution could go through with it, hence Hardesty's departure to see his ma. Well I am after gold and ma will have to wait a while I guess.

I have three dozen traps set this morning. I went to them and by jingo I caught a martin and a white weasel. Good luck, that is what I call good luck. The martin skin is worth $6.00 and the weasel is worth $1.35. So that is $7.00 worth of skins I have already. Now if I can get a silver fox tomorrow, they are worth $75.00, black fox are a $100.00. It is great sport. I will not get any bear now until March. They are holed up now for the winter. They come out in March and then I will get them. There are lots of them, thousands of them, mostly black bear, good many brown bear and some few grizzlys.

I am going to do my best on the trapping this winter and try and make a few dollars that way. You must excuse me if I don't write you thirty-seven pages this letter for I don't think I will have time and I don't think I can find enough to say to fill it up. Now I am going to stop for tonight as it is late and tomorrow I will stay home from Sunday School and write all day. Good night. I am going to bed.

Sunday about 1:00 P.M.
Have just had dinner and will try and pass some of this lonesome day writing to you. I have been busy all morning baking. I baked three apple pies, a pan of corn bread, cooked a pheasant and had rice for dinner. I put in the whole forenoon in that way. I get along pretty good week days but Sunday is a corker.

This is what I am thinking about right now. What if all of you were dead or some of you dead and me a writing to you as though I knew you were not, when I don't and won't know for six months maybe. I tell you that is enough to make one lonesome. Here I am up here in the best of health, nothing whatever the matter, only I don't know if you are in Mattoon or Africa. Don't know if you have got a divorce and married someone else or not. Don't know if you are all dead and have been trying to get me word of it or not.

All that I know is that I am six hundred miles from the nearest railroad, three thousand miles from Mattoon, frozen in until next March and in good health. I knew it would be this way if you didn't write often and that is why in all of my letters I told you to write often, that I knew if you did, every time someone came in from Edmonton to St. John I would get a letter. But no, I have missed two fellows that have come in and have had not a word from anyone since Myrty's letter of August 1st. And just think, suppose I have to wait until next spring before I hear from you.

One would say, well a man didn't care much for his family that could do that, stay away that long without coming home to see them but I can't come, I am frozen in and there is but one way that I could get to you and that is to walk six hundred miles, carry my bed and enough grub, nearly impossible. Well all I can do is to pray God that he will protect you all from sickness and any harm, which I do every night when I go to bed. He has been good to me so far, why not to you.

Today it has turned warm and the snow has melted but tomorrow it might be 20~ below zero. This country is visited this time of year by Chinook winds and will melt two feet of snow in one day.

I hope you will get the last two letters I sent you. I told you in them what we intend to do in the spring but I will tell you again in this letter. In March we will leave this camp, will get the Hudson Bay man, Mr. Hamilton, to haul our outfit on the ice to Hudson Hope. That is fifty miles over the hills by pack horses or thirty miles through a canyon and rapids, impossible to get through, only on the ice.

On the other side of the Portage we will build a boat or go by horses and pack. Don't know which way we will go from there yet. But it will be either to the Omenica Country or up the Findlay River, then across to one of the Black Rivers. There are two of them called the north and south forks and empties into the Liard River. It is allowing to what reports we hear in the spring which way we will go. Quite a good many went to the Liard River this last summer and we will hear from them in the spring.

We have an outfit that will last us two years yet in everything. Will prospect all the time wherever we go for there is gold here in small quantities everywhere you prospect and some one will strike it rich one of these days. Dawson predicted the gold in the Klondyke. He also predicted a rich strike in this country. He predicted thirty years ago that there was lots of gold in the Klondyke and they were all of this time finding it.

Well anyhow, I will do my best to find it in the next year. I have great hopes and have had if we ever get to the mountains and that will only take us six days in March to reach there. Tell Mr. White and Cantlon that I am in the same opinion, same hopes and far more in a better condition as I was the day before I left Mattoon and also that Cantlon should be with me. He would get far in this country.

I don't look to find any gold around here that would pay more than $2.00 per day although we are not done yet prospecting around here. There is some mining going on all along Peace River. Three miners are camped twenty-five miles below us and are this side of St. John and are working on a bar making $2.00 per day and five or six miners are working on a big bar at St. John making from $2.00 to $3.00 per day. They are putting in the time and making a grub stake so as to go on farther in the spring.

I have just now had my picture taken (three of them) by Sell with a Kodak. He has to take them home first to have them developed, then he will send them to me. He also has some more that he took when coming up the river on the boat in camp and with the Indians that struck on us. I will send them all to you when I get them. These last three are taken with me and Dash standing at the door of the cabin with Digby and Spencer at one side and crazy Peters inside of the cabin wouldn't have his picture taken. In the first one Sell coaxed him to come out. He is the biggest damn fool that anybody ever saw.

I suppose you all guessed the right answer to what I was making — a set of chess.

Sell leaves in the morning for St. John, then over the trail for Edmonton with pack horses — him and another man and he will take this letter with him to Edmonton and mail it. Now I haven't got any more to write about.

I want to impress on Harry's mind very strongly to keep my dues up in the Brotherhood, it isn't much, only $2.00 per year and I want to be a full fledged member when I come home. I suppose Harry has a regular engine by this time and is making lots of money. Remember what I told you in one of my former letters, to take good care of your mamma and sister, keep away from the bad places, spend your loose change on Myrty, make her look nice in clothes, she is nice every other way.

And Presh, you must do the same and both of you break that old saying all to the devil, that he is a chip off the old block. And Myrty, you dear little angel, you must help to take good care of mamma and don't forget that piano. I reckon you are engaged behind someone's desk. And mamma, all you have to do is to work real hard to see that these kids of ours does all of this that I have asked them to do.

I don't know when I can have a chance to send you another letter out, it may be a long time and it may be only a short time. Anyhow I will send a letter out every time I have a chance. One thing certain, I have lots of time to write one and will always have one ready. It is now just sundown and I will quit, hoping this will as well as all other letters I have written, reach you and I hope that you have gotten those sixteen or nineteen letters I have written. Remember me to all of my friends and relatives. Hoping that this will find you all in the best of health and doing well. Many, many kisses to you all I remain as ever your

Klondyke papa Jim
Here's a pheasant feather right out of the tail.

• • •

PINE RIVER CAMP, B.C. N.W.T.

Tuesday, November 21, 1898
[actual calendar date was November 22 — Ed.]
My dear wife and children if I have any.

I take the liberty and opportunity and gall to write to you again. That is, I will start to write but don't know when I will have a chance to send it out, and I don't know how soon it will reach you but suppose it will be welcomed when it does arrive at its destination. I have no word from anybody since Myrty's letter of August the 1st and it isn't fair to make me do all the writing. I have written as many as a dozen big letters to you since I have any word from you, and it begins to look all one sided. You make me do all the work. I commence this letter now with no hopes of sending it out until Dec. 22 and it will be a memorandum of each day from the 15th of November until I have a chance to send it out.

On the 20th of December Mr. Hamilton sends a man from St. John with the mail by dog train to Dunvagen arriving at Dunvagen on the 24th of December. On the 20th of December Mr. Daniel, the Hudson Bay man at Slave Lake post sends a man with the mail to Dunvagen arriving there on the 24th of December. The two men meet there, the man from St. John starts back from Dunvagen on Christmas day the 25th (I guess it is the 25th, I don't know, I am pretty much uncivilized) and will be by Nig Hinkles log cabin about New Year's Day (that's the first of January). So that will be my only chance to send this letter out. If I do you will know it I guess. Well now I have told you how it happened or how it is going to happen so I will start in with my letter by referring back to the 15th as that is the day I sent you the last letter by Sell Grimston.

First I guess I will tell you about the weather. Cold, well I guess yes. It is so cold here that there is blue fuzz flying in the air all of the time. Why, I went for a bucket of water, (it is three hundred yards) and when I got back to the cabin it was frozen to the bottom and I couldn't throw it out until I built a fire all around the bucket. Then I had to go and get another bucket full and I thought I would fool the north pole this time so I ran my best and poured what little I could pour into the pot and set it on fire. I had about a quart, the balance was ice.

Dash sleeps in the cabin now and he walks the floor about half the night just like I have seen old men (and women too) do to keep warm. He is awful glad when it is morning so I will build a fire. He will come over to my bed but don't say a word (he looks awful hard though) for me to get up. He always shakes hands with me without me asking him to.

Have taught him a new trick since the last I wrote you of his capabilities. I feed him out of doors and of course have to shut the door while he eats, but have taught him when he is through eating to ask me to let him in. He will come to the door and bark once and if I don't let him in right away he will bark again just once. I taught him this trick by telling him to speak if he wants in.

Well now about the weather. On Tuesday the 15th, nice warm day. On Wednesday the 16th, nice warm day. Peters got back from St. John, didn't bring me a darned letter. On Thursday the 17th, three inches of snow — snowed all day. Thermometer at 7:00 P.M.

stood at zero (look out now for a corker). Saturday the 19th the thermometer stood from 3° to 10° below zero all day. Went to my traps, caught two white weasels, fell down forty times. We wore moccasins and in dry snow they're as slick as greased lightening and I slipped on the side of the mountain and you ought to see me hike down that incline, never stopped until I got to the bottom. Now I didn't want to go that way at all and I couldn't get back so I had to go that way. Dash thought I was playing so he took down the hill after me and Dash and I and the gun and the two weasels all landed up in a heap at the bottom. I hurt my knee and my hip by bumping over the rough places. Such is life in these large north pole countries.

Sunday the 20th
22° below zero at 8:00 P.M. and still zeroing. Forgot that yesterday was Saturday and had to wash today. Now Myrty, nobody saw me I guess.

Monday the 21st at 7:00 A.M.
32° below zero, stood all day from 18° to 32° below zero.

Tuesday the 22nd at 7:00 A.M.
36° below zero. It hasn't got much more room to zero. The thermometer only registers 60° below. I guess after that they will send the north pole down here, well let her come, I was here first. Wait a minute until I thaw the ink out. You ought to see the inside of our cabin. Every hole and corner is covered with a thick frost except right by the fireplace. It looks like some pictures I have seen before of some winter scene in some cave. If it keeps on I will make a good Eskimo. My bed is warmer than the house or fire either so when I get so cold I can't stand it any longer I hike off to bed.

I crawl into the sleeping bag, then I put on top of that two double blankets, put on a pair of German socks and say come on North Pole. These nights are so long up here that I am afraid I will get bed sores or corns wearing the German socks.

Pine River Camp in the Winter / 135

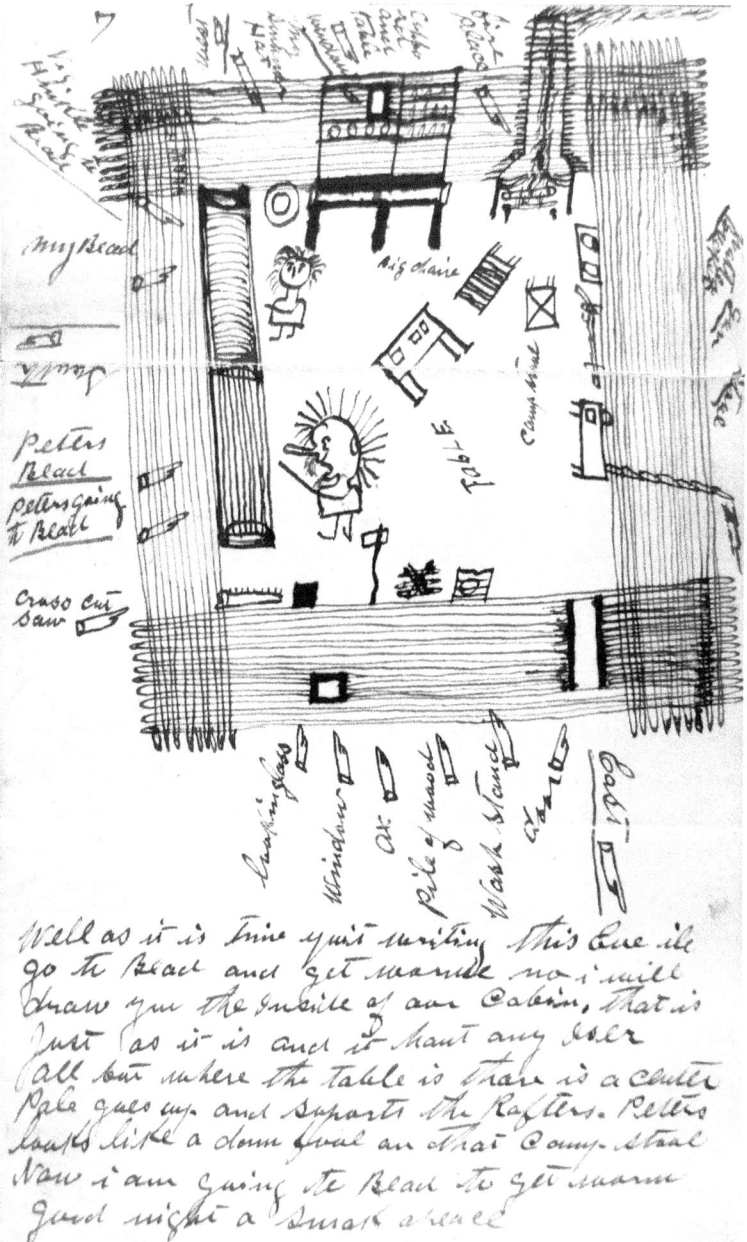

Well as it is fine yours writing this one ile go to Bead and get warm no i will draw you the inside of our Cabin. that is Just as it is and it haint any door all but where the table is there is a center Pole gues up and suparts the Rafters. Peters looks like a down fual an that Camp stoal Now i am going te Bead to get warm good night a Smart a rence

Inside the cabin

Sun rises about 8:30 and sets at 4:00. Sixteen hours of solid comfort. Call it that if you want to but I call it sixteen hours of endurance. Well it won't do to write too much at one time or I won't get stamps to send it so I will quit for tonight and write some each day until the dog train comes along. Good-night, I am going to bed and let my whiskers get white.

Wednesday the 23rd at 7:00 A.M.
80° BELOW ZERO. GEE WHILICANS THIS CABIN IS COLD THIS MORNING. The sun is shining bright but it is too cold to go out, except Peters, he has to go out to chop wood. He is out this very minute hacking away at it and I am sitting around the fire enjoying it. You can call it enjoyment but my left side is pretty near frozen. I have my wood cut, cut it when it was nice and warm. Him being smarter than anybody has to cut his wood at 80° below zero, the darned fool will freeze. All I have to do is to go out to my wood pile and carry it in. I have nine cords chopped that I haven't touched yet. I'm saving that for when the north pole comes down to see us. Peters just came in from cutting wood, puffing and snorting with icicles on his whiskers and says this is the nicest day out and he crouched up to the fire as close as he could get and grunted and snorted. Ask Hardesty how he goes.

Pretty soon he took off his moccasins to warm his feet. I says, "What's the matter, are your feet too warm that you have to take off your moccasins to cool them off?" I wish you could hear him grunt. Every breath he takes he goes aaahhhh. Make a man go crazy to be with him. I make all sorts of fun of him and he hasn't got sense enough to know it. Even Dash actually makes fun of him for every morning Dash will yawn and stretch a dozen times and squeal and grunt.

Well it is about 8:30 P.M. by the moon and seven stars and it is a little bit warmer. It is 22° below zero now. Not quite as much fuzz flying in the air. I suppose that by the time you get this letter winter will be over with you and you won't remember anything about these dates I am giving you. But you ought to get this letter by the 22nd of January if it goes out on the 22nd of December and about that time I suppose you will be having some zero down there and we will be having things a popping up here.

It is a good thing that Hardesty went home. He, when he was here in the summer, was frozen to death all the time. He couldn't no more stand this climate than a honey bee. He had on his heavy Klondyke under clothes when he left us and he would hug up to the camp fires like a sick kitten.

I had a game of chess just now. There my ink froze up on me again, if it keeps on I will have to write this letter with a lead pencil. I just got done playing three games of chess with Spencier. I beat two games out of three. He plays as slow as Doc Howard or Ben Jenkins.

Well as it is time to quit writing this evening I'll go to bed and get warm. No, I will draw you the inside of our cabin. That is just as it is all but where the table is. There is a center pole goes up and supports the rafters. Peters looks like a damn fool on that camp stool. Now I am going to bed and get warm. Good night, a smack a piece.

Thursday the 24th at 7:00 A.M.
26° below zero but it is cloudy and we are going to have a change of some kind. 1:00 P.M. by the I don't know what, it is snowing. This is one of those days. It is too cold to snow and it is too cold to rain so I guess it will what, unless the clouds begin to fall in big chunks. Just the same it is snowing a real fine snow and it is only 10° below zero now at 7:00 P.M. Only had about five hours daylight today on account of being cloudy. I suppose we will have to dig ourselves out of here in the morning. Let her flicker, I have a shovel. This is all for today, I don't have to go to bed to get warm this time but I am going to bed just the same. Goodnight.

Friday the 25th
7:00 A.M. 2° above zero and a foot of snow. Now that is more like it. I thought the north pole wasn't ready to come yet. I can't see anyone to ask them if this is winter yet but I rather think that this

must be an unusually early winter, that is, I mean that it is unusually cold for this time of year.

Well I went to all my traps today and rebaited them and straightened them up out of the snow. It has been too cold for game to run but Digby came in with a cross fox. I think I will have something in my traps in the morning for it is warm tonight.

It is 7:00 P.M. and it is 12° above zero. Peters says he has found a rabbit patch and he is going to it in the A.M. There has been no rabbits here for seven years and this is the seventh year. They disappear for seven years, something like a locust only they don't split open on the back. But rabbits up here turn white as snow in the winter time. So do weasels and so do snow birds.

Mamma, on page nine, ten, eleven and twelve I will write you and the kids something confidential and I think it best that you say nothing about it just at the present unless you might tell George and Anna or if you hear any talk or know anything about what I am going to say, you can then use this, what I say to whatever advantage you see best. I will begin and give you the whole details.

I suppose you have often wondered why I talk about Peters the way I do and I have kept it from you until now for a reason of my own. When he was in Mattoon, you know, and we decided on him as one of the men to go with this party, and when he left there to go home they gave him a draft for $600.00 so he could buy the horses on his way home. Well we didn't buy horses you know, so when we left they gave Hardesty and me $50.00 each in money and a draft for $200.00 each, that making $500.00 between the two of us or $250.00 each. Well the company paid for the goods that was bought at Chicago amounting to $650.00 or thereabouts.

When or while we were at Edmonton, the company still owing us $642.00, sent the draft payable to Peters, Hinkle and Hardesty and all three had to sign the draft. But the company sent the draft in a letter addressed to Peters, so we all three signed the draft and went to the bank to get the money. We got the money and Peters stuck it down in his pocket along with the other $600.00 he brought from Mattoon. Hardesty and I didn't say anything at the time but

I thought a damn sight so I expected he would wait until we got in camp and then divide it up all equal. But it went on from day to day just that way.

Now stop for a minute and think about it. Hardesty and I owned one third of one-half of all of this and Peters carrying our money as though we were not capable of carrying our own property and as though we had to have a guardian and he was our guardian. Well Hardesty and I got to talking about it to ourselves thinking that surely he would take a twinkle to himself and divide the money but not a hint came from Peters.

So we let it go from day to day and I finally said to Hardesty that we would make him divide the money, that I was no lunatic and didn't need a guardian. So one evening after we had quit work and gone into camp after supper I says, "Peters, we want that money divided up". He says, "Well all right", but was awful fidgety. So Hardesty got out his money, what he had left, it was 113.00. I got out mine which was $7.00. (I had paid for our living and freight on goods which was $75.00. Peters got out his pile which was only $612.00. (Imagine my thoughts but I didn't say anything). He should have had about $1,100.00. So we divided the three piles up equal making $244.00 per man, making Peters short in his accounts nearly $400.00. I figured it all up and showed Hardesty but didn't say anything to Peters, not yet. Now the place we made him divide the money was after we had traveled up the Athabasca River five days, making over a month that he carried the money, or carried our money. Well of course I lost confidence in Peters and Hardesty and I took to watching him.

Now mind you, I kept a book of all the money that was paid out and what was bought with it even to five cents worth of dog meat for Dash. So coming up Peace River while in camp at Dunvagen, Peters and I had some words and I accused him of being short $386.00. He denied it of course and said that he could show up and I says, "You bet you will have to show up, I am the man that will make you show up." So afterwards he got a letter from Clark or Montague or it might have been Tivnen, anyhow one day he was in an awful hurry to write to one of them. After he had the letter written he says, "Now there if that don't satisfy you" — meaning whoever he was writing to, "you can go unsatisfied". He says, "I guess that statement will satisfy them".

Now stop and think him sending a statement to the Mattoon Mining and Investment Co. and myself and Hardesty a third partner of the one half and not let either of us see what kind of a statement he sent. (That is why I wrote to Tivnen for a duplicate of Peter's statement). Looks as though Hardesty and I were working for Peters on a salary but he will be damnedly fooled before I am through with him. I watch every move he makes, I set down every cent he spends and what it is for. I won't let him waste a thing about the outfit and I give him to understand that things will and shall be kept straight from now on until we get back.

Of course he doesn't like me and of course I don't like him although we are on fairly speaking terms and that is all. But there is a storm a brewing. He will do something before long and then I will tell him that he is a first class SB and if he makes one break I will throw him out of the cabin and out of the company and take charge of the whole thing myself.

He has forfeited his rights anyhow to any rights in the company long ago and I am only keeping him on probation. Every stockholders interest shall be taken care of and to my best abilities. We have a two year outfit now or more and I am going to use it in trying to find gold, which if I do, each stockholder will benefit in proportion to his stock.

Now you know why I talk about him so in my letters to you and I don't tell any lies about him to you. He certainly is the craziest fool I was ever with and it makes the trip very disagreeable to be with one in this country that you can't trust or one that you don't like. Hardesty can tell you the same as I have told you if he will. Well I have explained it all to you so now you know how it is.

Tomorrow is Saturday and Myrty, I am going to bake another half bushel of beans while Peters goes to the rabbit patch as he calls it and I have to wash tomorrow too. I wash on Saturday, only when I forget it then I wash on Sunday School going day. So I guess I have said enough tonight so will stop now and perform on the violin. Forty eleven kisses.

Well this is Saturday evening by the moon and it is as clear as a crystal. This morning until noon it snowed and now we have fifteen inches of snow and the thermometer stands at 12° above zero, more like it. Pet, bring up your sled and you can have all the fun you want. Bring Clarence with you.

I went out a little while this afternoon with the gun and Dash but the snow was so deep I couldn't walk and Dash — you ought to have seen him. He couldn't make out what it all meant. The first deep snow he has ever seen. He thought I was playing all of the time.

Well I baked up the half bushel basket of beans in the forenoon and washed. Peters, he has been cutting wood all day, would rather cut wood in fifteen inches of snow than if there was no snow at all. He couldn't tell a hawk from a hand saw.

Tomorrow is Sunday. I don't know what to do after Sunday School. One good thing, the days aren't very long. If the sun keeps on it won't get up over the hills on the south side of Peace River. I haven't much to write about today, we haven't had any visitors since the man was down from St. John. We're looking for Mr. Hamilton down any day to bring the mail.

Haven't got any word from anyone since Myrty's letter of August 1st. I would give $50.00 right now if I could get a big letter from all of you. It is the hardest part about this trip to do without word from home. It would be a pleasure trip now to start with fifteen inches of snow, at 8:00 o'clock in the evening and walk to St. John twenty-five miles just to get one letter from you. Wouldn't think anything about it. And just think, we'll have to wait until the 27th of December and maybe not get any, then that will be five months since I have heard from you.

Did I say gold? Yes gold is what I am after and up here in this country one can't get gold and letters both at the same time. I suppose in the spring I will get letters by the dog train full. Well I will quit for the night and play a game of chess with Spencier. Oh did any of you guess the answer to my last conundrum? When you write tell me who guessed the right answer. Goodnight.

Sunday the 27th
Well it is snowing. It is 20° above zero. We have snow to sell, do you want to buy any Harry? I have been setting around all day reading, playing the fiddle and playing with Dash. Peters doesn't like Dash but I give him to understand that I think more of Dash than I do of him and that Dash will sleep in the cabin whenever it is too cold and when I say so and that Dash shall have all he wants to eat (he is fat as butter) and that Dash is not to be mistreated by him and that when he abuses Dash that he will have me to lick or get licked himself. And that Dash is my own property (he has an idea that Dash is as much his dog as mine but I will fool him) and that he can have Dash to hunt with providing I don't want him at the time and that he does not mistreat him while on the hunt and that is the reason I play with Dash.

Well mamma and the kids, I will draw you a picture of the cabin and all the surroundings, Pine River, Peace River, the pine forest, the hill and everything just as it is all around for two miles and just as it looks in the autumn when the leaves are all off. Look on the big sheet of paper, page 25 and you will find the picture, the name of everything with its number.

I don't claim to be an expert artist but this picture will show you just where we are camped for the winter and Myrty, if you should happen to call on me you will know when you come to the place, now don't forget to give your card to the janitor and don't try to go in without giving him the card or he will take a piece out of your pASSage.

I will quit for tonight and give you more tomorrow as I want to take a bath and I have to fix my pants. Goodnight.

Monday 28th
Now whenever any of you get to wondering where I am and what I am doing, look where number twenty nine is and you can just say, 'there he goes up the hill'. Now don't get a photo of this drawing and try to get rich off it or I will have you prosecuted for infringing on my patents. I laid this town site out myself, we haven't any mayor elected yet but we have one liar and three dogs.

Peters wanted to build our cabin over where number twenty-two is but I wouldn't have it that way. The timber over there is small, not more than three inches through and not good wood to burn while where we are there is pitch that is in the pine and besides if we had of built over there we would have got all of the west wind right in the face.

An old Indian has spoken for our cabin when we leave here. I told him he could have it, he lives ten miles up Peace River, just found that out lately. So I suppose when we pull up stakes, Pine River camp will be occupied by a lot of squaws and red faced Indians. It is about 8:00 P.M. by Bear Ave. and the thermometer stands at zero, think it is going to get cold again.

1. Our cabin on the corner of Bear and Pine Streets
2. Grimston's cabin on the corner of Wood and Pine Streets
3. Dash's dog house on Bear Street
4. Dan's dog house
5. Wood Street Park
6. Grimston's east window
7. Broken window light in the window
8. Door in our cabin opens to the east
9. Grimston's fireplace
10. Poplar tree leaning right over Grimston's house and they are scared to death every time there is a wind, can't cut it down or it would fall on the house
11. Wood Street
12. Patch of small bushes north of Grimston's
13. Our cook stove
14. Bank going down to Pine River 15 ft. high
15. Backwater between Peace River and the bank on the south side of our cabin
16. Big gravel bar five acres
17. Channel running when high water running from Pine River back of our house empties in the Peace River and is full of bear tracks
18. Hills on the south side of Peace River

Hinkle's Cabin, overview (details follow on pages 146–47)

19. Pine forest which has been burned off by a forest fire
20. Work bench.
21. High mountains on the east side of Pine River and there is no timber on them.
22. Small forest of poplar on the east side of Pine River and you have to go through it to get on the trail that goes up the high hill and is one of the places I go hunting.
23. Looks like a great big man ten feet long but it is only a high peak on the mountain.
24. Two big logs on the sand bar.
25. Bear Avenue and got its name by Dash treeing a bear there.
26. Our fireplace.
27. West window.

Pine River Camp in the Winter / 145

Grimston's Cabin, overview (details follow on pages 148–49)

28. Water Street and goes down past where we get water.
29. Up Street and is so slick now that the only way I can come down is to set down and let her flicker.
30. Tree that Dash treed the bear on.
31. Our east window.
32. High bank on the south side of our cabin.
33. Thick pine forest back west of our cabin and is full of bear.
34. The mountain west of us and is the highest place around here. On a clear day you can see the Rocky Mountains from there.
35. My chair.
36. Peters place with his little camp stool six inches too low. He made a big chair but it won't stand alone, has to lean it against the wall.

Hinkle's Cabin *(detail, left)*

15. Backwater between Peace River and the bank on the south side of our cabin
16. Big gravel bar five acres
18. Hills on the south side of the Peace River
19. Pine forest which has burned off by a forest fire
24. Two big logs on the sand bar.
32. High bank on the south side of our cabin.
41. Peace River
43. High Water Street.
44. Bear Track Avenue.
45. Is a skedaddle. Now Myrty, you know what that is, of course you do and Harry if you can't tell a hawk from a hand saw you won't know what 45 is.
49. Pile of drift wood on the south side of Peace River.
50. Second Island and got its name by any of us asking one another, "Where did you kill that pheasant?" and we would say, "On the second island," that is if we killed it there.
51. Third Island and got its name the same way.
54. & 55. Two small channels and makes island 50 and 51
56. An island in the middle of Peace River and is about two miles west of us.
57. ˜The sun just rising over the hill on the south side of the Peace river
58. ˜The sun setting just right there over pretty near where it raised, it only travels a quarter of a mile

Pine River Camp in the Winter / 147

Hinkle's Cabin *(detail, right)*

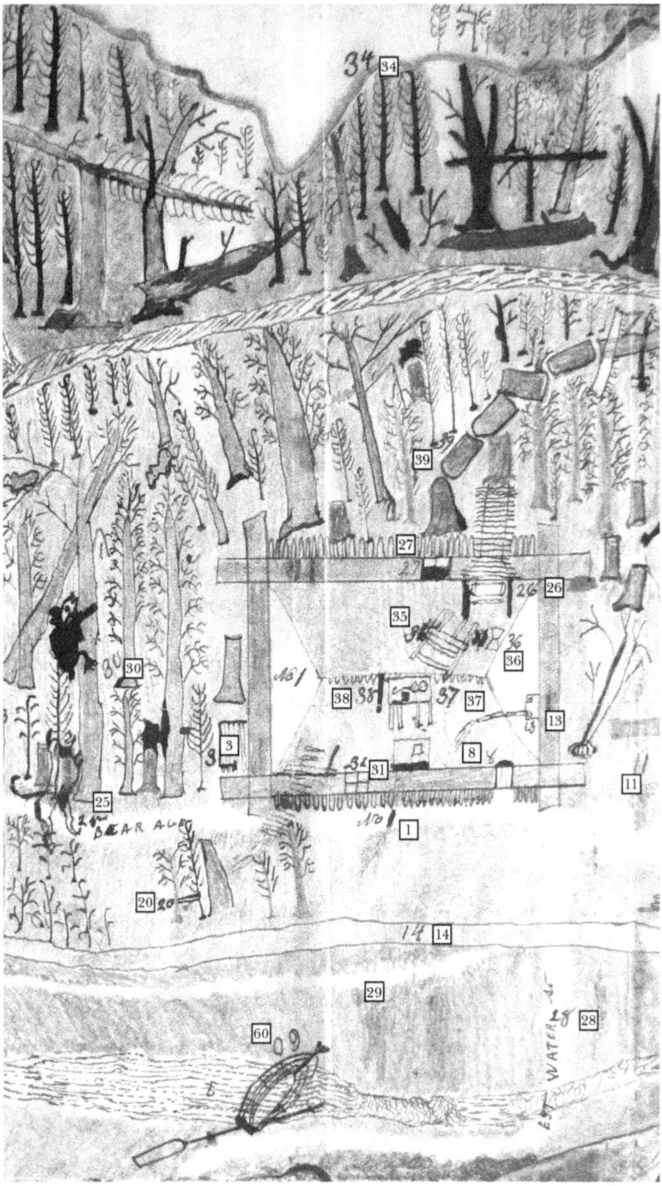

1. Our cabin on the corner of Bear and Pine Streets
3. Dash's dog house on Bear Street
8. Door in our cabin opens to the east
11. Wood Street
13. Our cook stove
14. Bank going down to Pine River 15 ft. high
20. Work bench.
25. Bear Avenue and got its name by Dash treeing a bear there.
26. Our fireplace.
27. West window.
28. Water Street and goes down past where we get water.
29. Up Street and is so slick now that the only way I can come down is to set down and let her flicker
30. Tree that Dash treed the bear on.
31. Our east window.
34. The mountain west of us and is the highest place around here. On a clear day you can see the Rocky Mountains from there.
35. My chair.
36. Peters place with his little camp stool six inches too low. He made a big chair but it won't stand alone, has to lean it against the wall.
37. Table sets against the center pole.
38. Center pole.
39. Tree I am sawing up for back logs.
60. Our boat and is frozen in the ice two feet thick.

148 / KLONDIKE TREK

GRIMSTON'S CABIN *(detail, left)*

2. Grimston's cabin on the corner of Wood and Pine Streets
4. Dan's dog house
5. Wood Street Park
6. Grimston's east window
7. Broken window light in the window
9. Grimston's fireplace
10. Poplar tree leaning right over Grimston's house and they are scared to death every time there is a wind, can't cut it down or it would fall on the house
17. Channel running when high water running from Pine River back of our house empties in the Peace River and is full of bear tracks
23. Looks like a great big man ten feet long but it is only a high peak on the mountain.
33. Thick pine forest back west of our cabin and is full of bear.
40. Pine River.
42. Pine Street.
61. Me taking a walk back in the woods and Dash playing with me. Now if you notice you will see a mistake in this part of the drawing. If you hold the picture looking to the west, I will be standing on my head and if you turn the picture around the other way, the trees will be standing on their heads.

Pine River Camp in the Winter / 149

GRIMSTON'S CABIN *(detail, right)*

12. Patch of small bushes north of Grimston's

21. High mountains on the east side of Pine River and there is no timber on them.

22. Small forest of poplar on the east side of Pine River and you have to go through it to get on the trail that goes up the high hill and is one of the places I go hunting.

48. Is me reading an old paper that is as yellow as saffron and I found it at Athabasca Landing.

52. Right Up Pine River On This First Island and got its name by me asking Peters where he killed that pheasant and Peters saying, "Right up Pine River on this first island."

53. Small channel cutting off the corner of the island we live on.

59. Peters rabbit patch.

Note: The sketches on pages 146–47 and 148–49 were originally glued together, and dovetail perfectly when aligned.

On the originals, glue is still visible at the left of the sketch on facing page where the sketch on the preceding pages overlapped it.

Likewise, the bottom edge of the sketch on 146–47 also had glue on it, indicating the presence of a possible extension, now lost.

It may be that Nos. 46 and 47 (missing) were on that addition.

37. Table sets against the center pole.
38. Center pole.
39. Tree I am sawing up for back logs.
40. Pine River.
41. Peace River.
42. Pine Street.
43. High Water Street.
44. Bear Track Avenue.
45. Is a skedaddle. Now Myrty, you know what that is, of course you do and Harry if you can't tell a hawk from a hand saw you won't know what 45 is.
46. Wolf Island, now there's a corker for you, number 46 is the plainest number on there.
47. Now, now, now.
48. Is me reading an old paper that is as yellow as saffron and I found it at Athabasca Landing.
49. Pile of drift wood on the south side of Peace River.
50. Second Island and got its name by any of us asking one another, "Where did you kill that pheasant?" and we would say, "On the second island," that is if we killed it there.
51. Third Island and got its name the same way.
52. Right Up Pine River On This First Island and got its name by me asking Peters where he killed that pheasant and Peters saying, "Right up Pine River on this first island."
53. Small channel cutting off the corner of the island we live on.
54. and 55. Two small channels and makes island 50 and 51.
56. An island in the middle of Peace River and is about two miles west of us.
57. The sun just rising over the hill on the south side of Peace River.
58. The sun setting just right over there pretty near where it raised, it only travels about a quarter of a mile.
59. Peters rabbit patch.
60. Our boat and is frozen in the ice two feet thick.

61. Me taking a walk back in the woods and Dash playing with me. Now if you notice you will see a mistake in this part of the drawing. If you hold the picture looking to the west, I will be standing on my head and if you turn the picture around the other way, the trees will be standing on their heads.

Tuesday the 29th
7:30 A.M. 10° below zero. Peters has gone to the rabbit patch and I am all alone and have got a great big pot of beans on and the blubbering of the pot is as lonesome as a cricket at a wake. Digby just came and borrowed the wash board.

Wednesday the 30th
Nice bright morning at 7:00 A.M. 12° below zero. I just got back from across Peace River, went over on the ice, went to see if there was any game prowling around over there, it is the first time I have been over there.

Thursday Dec. 1st
Well it didn't snow but turned colder. At 7:00 A.M. 12° below zero. Now don't wonder where I learned to be an artist for it is all I have to do up here among these snow covered hills to pass the time away and by that I have learned to be an artist. You see that the air is so clear up here that ones brain is so clear that he can learn to do anything. This is all for tonight, Goodnight.

Friday the 2nd. 7:00 A.M. 14° below zero.
I am going hunting today and set some traps. I am very much disappointed in the trapping business, seems as though the game has all left around here for some reason I don't know, haven't caught anything yet to amount to much. March and April are the two best months to trap in. In March the bear come out of their dens and in April the snow goes away and all the game is hunting something to eat.

Myrty at the typewriter and Peters rabbit hunting

8:00 P.M.
Set some traps for rabbits today, they are jack rabbits as big as dogs. Think we'll have rabbit for dinner Sunday. It is not so cold this evening, 3° below zero. Bye bye.

Saturday the 3rd just after dinner.
I just got done baking four pies and another half bushel basket of beans.

Well I suppose you will get tired of my pictures but you mustn't for it is pastime. It is like one in jail (although I never was in jail) have to do something to pass the time away. If you don't want to read my pictures, give them to Verge and Hazel. I will quit for tonight as tomorrow is Sunday.

Happy dreams to all of you. I dreamt last night that I was lacing up my shoes and I broke a shoe string and that was the first thing I did this morning was to break a shoe string. The night I caught two weasels in my traps I heard those traps go off in my sleep as plain as if I had been there, some kisses.

Sunday the 4th
What a lovely morning and it is only 2° below zero. My dear dear daughter, you have been in my mind all morning so if you don't care I will draw your picture, you think I can't do it, so I'll fool you. I am going to draw your picture sitting at the typewriter machine and now you just see if it doesn't look like you. I'll show you that I'm a natural born artist and have just found it out. Now there smarty, I told you I could. Now doesn't that look like you?

Oh I can draw anything. I will draw you a picture of Peters rabbit hunting. He is always talking about going to the rabbit patch so I will draw you a picture of himself after a rabbit. He is doing the cooking today and I am doing the eating and writing this letter. I will make his picture with a lead pencil. I guess it won't rub off. Now that's Mr. Peters after a rabbit and he couldn't shoot the rabbit so he threw the gun down and tried to catch the rabbit. I guess he didn't catch it for he never brings any home. He always shoots three times at anything he sees, once to see how his gun shoots, once to see if he can hit the thing he is aiming at and once so that people can't say he didn't shoot because he had no chance to shoot, and he told us ever since I and Hardesty knew him that he could throw up our hat and put five bullets in it before it fell to the ground. You would never be any good Myrty if you could see him cook.

Actually it is a circus to watch his didoes. He is always on the jump, first to the coffee pot, then to the skillet, then one bound over to the table after the spoon, drops the spoon nine times out of ten, then to the coffee pot again and forgets what he got the spoon for and commences to stir the coffee with the spoon. He is the darndest man to stir things you ever saw. Today he got dinner, he cooked some rice and made some dip for the rice. He set the cup that had the dip in it on the table and he left the lid to the coffee pot laying on the table.

Now he had been stirring the dip for a half hour so he rushed to the stove for the coffee pot, found there was no lid on it, leaped to the table after the lid but had to reach in the spoon box, grab a spoon and stir the dip again after it had been done for ten minutes. Now he had just put the rice in the oven before this, it hadn't got warmed yet, he happened to think about it and if you would have seen that leap for the oven, well sire, I thought I would bust.

I says, "What's the matter, do you see a wolf?" and I jumped for my gun but I saw him go down for the oven door and jerk it open and down came the stove pipe. I had a notion to run out and shoot the gun off and holler murder.

Well I didn't have rabbit for dinner today for I didn't get to the traps. Am going in the morning. This has been a nice day, only 2° below zero. The sun has shown all day.

Myrty I don't know what I will draw next. Oh I tell you, I am going to have you teaching the typewriter and one of your scholars come into your private room to ask if she could go home to go sleigh riding. So now look on page twenty-two and you will see cinderella asking you to let her go home. Goodnight, I will do some drawing. My next drawing will be a very difficult one but I have it in my mind and I will see what I can do. It will be Harry and his sweetheart

Pine River Camp in the Winter / 155

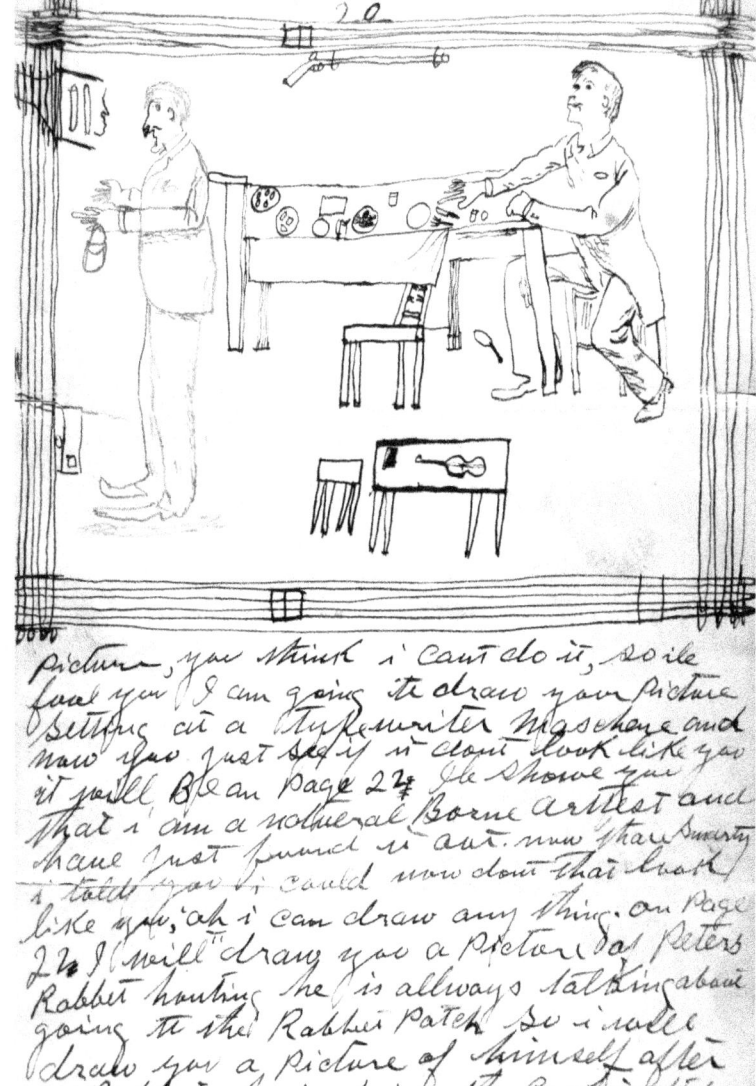

picture, you think i cant do it, so ile
fool you I am going to draw your picture
Setting at a Typewriter Magschene and
now you just say if it dont look like you
it will. BE on Page 2½ Ile showe you
that i am a nolueral Borne artlist and
have just found it out. now i have swerty
i tolde you i could now dont that look
like you, ah i can draw any thing. on Page
2 ½ I will draw you a Picture os Peters
Rabbet hunting he is allways talking about
going to the Rabbet Patch so i will
draw you a Picture of himself after
a Rabbet. he is doing the Cooking today
and i am doing the Eating and writing
this letter. I will mark his Picture
with a lead Pencal I guess it wont Rup of

Peters cooking

Harry and his sweetheart taking a rest after a long bicycle ride

taking a rest after a long bicycle ride. Look on page twenty-four. Goodnight.

Monday the 5th
Now that picture is not so snotty — it is made with a lead pencil. I didn't do a very good job on the bicycle but I haven't seen one for so long I have forgotten how they look. Take care Enoc, that gnat will sting you and the dog is hollering at you.

I went to Peters rabbit patch today but didn't see a thing. This has been a nice warm day and the sun shining all day. At 7:00 A.M. 10° below zero. Now that may sound strange to you after telling you that it has been a nice warm day. We don't think that is cold until it gets to thirty. That is all today. Goodnight.

Tuesday the 6th at 7:00 A.M. 30° above zero.
What do you think of that, this beats all the weather I ever saw. One week it is 30° below zero and the next week 30° above. Just to freezing now at 8:00 P.M. I will have to draw the sketch of our cabin over, I was holding it up to the fire to dry the ink and I got it too close and scorched the paper so now I will draw you another one and a better one and more of the country, that is it will be on a bigger sheet of paper and of course will reach out farther and I will have to add more scenes and more numbers. It will take me about three days to make it and I will do my best on it and if you ever get it you can take it up and have it photoed and frame it. Won't that be nice? That's all tonight. Tra la la.

Wednesday the 7th
Still warm, just down to zero all day. I have been busy all day sketching, I want to get it done before the mail man comes along. That's all for today, we only have five hours of sunshine up here. Good healthy nights to sleep. Goodnight.

Thursday the 8th at 7:00 A.M. 2° below zero.
Nice day, am going hunting. 1:00 P.M. Just got back, killed one pheasant and caught one weasel in trap. 10° above zero.

Friday the 9th
Just down to zero this morning. We are having some awful nice weather but I think the north pole will be down soon, always a storm after a calm. Well I haven't much to talk about today. It has just been eight months today since I saw you and it has been four months and nine days since I have heard from any of you.

Who knows what has happened in that last four months and nine days. I hope nothing to any of you. Goodnight.

Saturday evening Dec. 10
I just got back from hunting and as I was coming down the high hill over where Up Street is, I saw an outfit coming down Peace River. Well you ought to see me hike down that hill. I just let go all holds and set down and held my feet up and made a bob sled out of myself. The first thing I have seen that looked like civilization for five months. They're camped here tonight. They have some mail for some people that are camped along Peace River. Don't know if they have any for me or not. They said they would look after they got their tents up and got supper but I am awful afraid that they have nothing for me for they told me that Livingston had not got to St. John yet.

Well now I will get this letter ready and send it out by them. They are going right straight to Edmonton and this will be a good chance so I will finish it up tonight. I have all the pictures finished and it is going to be a big letter and I hope you will get it all right.

Let everybody that cares anything about me know of this letter and give them my best wishes. This leaves me in the very best of health and spirits, only a little bit lonesome on account of I have not heard from any of you for four months. I pray every day that nothing has happened to any of you.

Tell Mr. White that I will not write to him now as I have not got very many stamps and there is nothing to write about and you can tell him all about me and if you want to you can read him part of this letter or as much of it as you want to. I will write Tivnen a letter tonight and send it with this one of yours.

We have had two weeks of the nicest weather I ever saw. For two weeks the thermometer has stood at about zero but we are looking for the north pole down soon.

Now I will have another chance to send you another letter Christmas and you can call it a Christmas gift. I will send it out by the man or dog train that goes to Dunvagen on the 24th. So now I

of chile with lonesomness Ever
night i am busy writing this
letter and making this Picture
They are not as good as if
some Profesinal artist had
sceteched them. and this
Picture of our camp is just
as Natueral as life o clock
my best on it Every thing you
will find the Name and the
Number I feal as Jolly this
Eving as a young colt you see
this is the first company
we have had They are Camping
to Spend the Eving with
us after they get their Supper
it is a Sarvey party on there
way home they have been up
on the Parsnip River thare is
10 men 16 Horses three sleds
and two dogs of them. well
I supose By the time you get
this letter you will be
having some fero in mattoon
now is Hartlesty has he got
his old Run Back again and
has he got the Rehomytisim
yet. he is missing half of
his life By not being Up
here to Slide down these
Hills. oh yes i must finish up
the Picture I havent got it all
numbered as yet. No 60 is our
Boat and is frozen the Ice
two ft thick. No 61 is me takeing
a walk Back in the woods and
dash Playing with me. now if
you Notice you will see a
Mastake in this Part of the
drawing if you holes the
Picture hunting to the west
I will be Standing on my
head. and if you turns the
Picture around the other way
the treas will be Standing on
there head. I made this mastake By not noticing
which way i had the Paper when i shad me
and as i had the Picture half done before i
noticed it and havnt got time to make another

A whimsical sketch

guess I have told you all I know and more too, and the pictures I have sketched for you were made these long nights and it was pastime. I would have died with lonesomeness. Every night I am busy writing this letter and making these pictures. They are not as good as if some professional artist had sketched them and this picture of our camp is just as natural as life, I did my best on it.

I feel as jolly this evening as a young colt. You see this is the first company we have had. They are coming up to spend the evening with us after they get their supper. It is a survey party on their way home. They have been up on the Parsnip River. There are ten men, sixteen horses, three sleds and two dogs of them.

I suppose by the time you get this letter you will be having some zero weather in Mattoon. How is Hardesty, has he got his old run back again and has he got the rheumatism yet? He is missing half of his life by not being up here to slide down these hills.

We have had three of these men to visit us this Evening. Stayed until 9:00 o'clock, had quite a chat. Now you can look for another letter in just about a month from the time you get this one. After that I can't say when you will get one but will send one every time anyone will be going out. I hope this will find you all well and in good spirits and with Harry a good job and Presh and Myrty with a position. Don't forget to pay my dues in the B. of L.E.

It is not cold here now, just down to zero but we will have it soon. Let George know of this letter and all inquiring friends. Remember me to Mr. Katz, Montague and all of my friends. Write often and send me some papers, Mattoon papers, Cincinnati Enquirer and St. Louis Globe and be sure and register them or I won't get them. Send all letters to Ft. St. John via Edmonton, Alberta, Canada, care of Hudson Bay Co. I will quit now by sending you all a thousand kisses a piece and one over, you have that one Myrty. Myrty write me lots in the letter. Just tell me every little thing you know. Harry, don't spread your lines out so well, put them closer together, you will find that you can get more on a sheet of paper by putting the lines close together. Presh, if you can't find anything to say just send me a blank sheet of paper and sign your name to it. I haven't got a scratch of a pen from you yet or any other kind of a scratch. Mamma, you see that they do this thing right and write a little more yourself. Well I hate to say goodbye but this sheet of paper has run out. The night is about to run out and my candle is only an inch long and I will have to say goodbye.

From your Jim Papa Klondyker

• • •

CLARK AND SCOTT
Horace S. Clark — John F. Scott Attorneys-at-Law
Mattoon, Illinois

December 17, 1898

Jas. Hinkle & J.R. Peters,
Alberta, Canada
Gentlemen:—

We had a meeting of the Directors last night and Charlie was there. We were together a good while and learned all we could from your letters and from him, and so far as I know I believe our folks are all well satisfied and in fact gratified at what you have done. You have had a hard trip and worked most faithfully, and our general opinion is that your plan is a good one, to prospect around about where you are and spend the winter as well and as pleasantly as you can. We know you will have a good time part of the time but it will get very lonesome and dreary before the ice breaks.

I for one am very strongly in favor of sending someone up there to join you as early as he can get there to take Charlie's place, as he thinks he will not be able to return on account of his rheumatism. It would do you very much good to get full and personal reports from home, etc. I do not know how the other folks may feel about it. It has been hard getting us all together and we fear it will be hard for you to get any letters from us, and I write you hastily. We want you to write us anyway what time you think our other man ought to leave Edmonton if we conclude to send him, and how he ought to leave, whether he ought to arrange to get himself through or whether he ought to take horses or any kind of supplies for you.

Please write us fully and freely just as you feel about it, for you can rely upon us being your friends.

Very truly yours,
Horace S. Clark
[Dictated]

12

Christmas in Pine River Camp

PINE RIVER CAMP B.C., N.W.T.

Sunday evening, December 11th, 1898

Dear mamma and kids,

    I just sent you a letter out this morning (by a survey party that stopped here last evening on their way to Edmonton) with a sketch of our camp. Hope that you will get it all right. Now then I will commence right where I stopped on the last letter and write you a little every day and each day tell you what kind of weather it is and what I am doing. I will send this letter by the Hudson Bay man that leaves St. John about the 20th. He goes as far as Dunvagen and gets the mail and brings it back to St. John.

    This has been a nice day. Now at about 8:00 P.M. the thermometer stands at 20° above zero and it has clouded up and looks very much like we were going to have a gee whileper of a snow. In the morning I am going up to the island in Peace River to set some traps for beaver. Just found out there are three villages of them up there. They're worth from $15.00 to $25.00 a skin.

    There will be a party of three down from St. John tomorrow or the next day. They are coming down to get some bacon that they bought of Grimston and to see us about hauling us in March to Hudson Hope on the ice. That's all for tonight.

Monday the 12th
Well the three men didn't come today and I didn't go up to the island to set beaver traps either. You can, if you get my last letter and sketch, call that island two miles up Peace River. I think it is No. 56, call it Beaver Island. That is the place the beaver are and is where I will be a good deal of the time this winter.

If you get my last letter and this one and a few of them before my last letter you will have a memorandum and a sketch of Peace River and our camp and the whole thing for thirty-five miles and from the time the Indians struck on us until I finish this letter. So someday when you are all together, get all of the letters and sketches down and read them all over at once and it will sound like reading a novel.

It snowed a little last night and has been snowing a little all day. It is a little bit too cold to snow hard. Now it is about 6:00 P.M. and it is 12° above zero. Been going around in my shirtsleeves all afternoon. Oh but we will get paid up for all of this nice weather. Don't look for anything else but a load of north poles down in a few days. Let her flicker, we were here first this season.

I am going to have a big game of chess after a bit. Spencier plays a pretty good game and it keeps me a hiking to beat him sometimes. He generally gets one game out of three or sometimes I will get the first game, the second game will be a draw and I get the third game. But he has got enough conceit to believe he can beat me. But I don't think that way. So here he is now. Goodnight. Slip me a kiss Myrty.

Tuesday evening 13th
Two hours after dark and have just had supper. It is a little bit colder today. At 7:00 A.M. it was 12° below zero but the sun shown all day. Actually if old sol don't get up a bit higher we will only get to see the rear part of him. Well I beat Spencier two out of three last night and he didn't like it. I will take the conceit out of him. I don't like an Englishman anyhow.

The three men have not come from St. John today either, look for them tomorrow, and if they don't come tomorrow will look for them the next day and if they don't come the next day will look at them when they do come.

I won't have time to write you a very big letter this time and I won't have time to make you any pictures as we look for the Hudson Bay man to come along about the 18th, then goody goody he will be back about the last of the month and I'll have some letters letters letters. That isn't long to wait is it Myrty? I have waited for five months, ought to stand it for fifteen days more.

Where are you going Christmas Pet? Oh but Christmas will be past before you get this letter. I tell you mamma and kids, it tries one's nerves to not hear from you for five months and me a writing all the time every day to you. There could be such a thing as you all being dead and me still writing as though you weren't. Five months is a long while not to hear a word from any of you. But I feel that my prayers will be answered and that the last of this month I will get a great big pile of letters from you and that you are all well, fat and sassy.

If only I had something to read. Why didn't I bring a hundred magazines up here? Didn't have enough sense I guess. I started last night to read the Bible through. I read fourteen chapters last night and five chapters today and I find it quite interesting.

It is twelve days until Christmas, I suppose you are fixing to have a time. So am I going to commence in a few days to have a time on Christmas, me and Dash. I am going to have apricot pie and rice pudding with raisins in it and dip with whiskey in it and roast pheasant with gravy and a whole pot of beans with gravy. Well that's all for this evening, I will read a few more chapters. Goodnight.

Wednesday 14th
The three men have not come yet. At 7:00 A.M. it was 3° below zero. Today it has turned warmer and now at 5:00 P.M. it is 15° above zero. I went up the street this morning to my traps and when I got back about a mile I heard something squalling for God's sake so I hiked over that way as fast as I could tear and there I had a rabbit in one of my traps. Well actually Harry, it is as big as a mule and it is just as white as the snow, all but its ears, they are four inches

long. Going to have stewed wabbit, fried wabbit and baked wabbit. It will last us two days.

I haven't got much to tell you today. I am about run out of gab. But I guess there is enough in the last letter to make up for what I don't put in this one. If you get it don't forget to tell me if you got the last letter with the sketch. Well good night for this evening. No, here is a riddle Myrty, first before I say goodnight. I will tell you the answer to it because I would have to wait too long before I would get your answer and if you haven't already heard the riddle you can have some fun with someone else. The riddle is, why is a raven like a writing desk? The answer is — because there is a B in both.

Thursday 15th
Nice warm A.M. 10° above zero. I went up Pine River this morning hunting, killed two pheasants.

Well at last the men have come. They got here at 1:00 P.M. today and I never was so glad in all my life. They brought us a big hunk of fresh beef. Well I wish you could have seen me go for that steak. I could eat it raw or any old way. It is the first beef I have tasted since I left Edmonton.

One of the men's name is Cashman and is Mr. Brick's clerk. The other man's name is Lamb and is one of a party of five Klondykers who are camped at Halfway River which is thirty miles above St. John. He drove down on the ice to St. John to get a dressed beef and him and Cashman drove down here to our camp to see us about hauling us up to Hudson Hope on the ice in March. Mr. Cashman has just gone to bed. They brought their bed with them and they have just laid their bed down on the cabin floor by the center pole. Joke on the elephant if he steps on them.

Peters has gone to bed. Mr. Lamb is over at Grimston's and I and Dash are setting up by the fire. I am writing and Dash is thinking. He is thinking about going hunting tomorrow. I guess he is the blamedest dog to want to go hunting. Every morning he tells me, "Let's go hunting Jim." If I go to put my gloves or coat on, he will go up to where the gun is and grabs a stick in his mouth and just goes crazy. I say, "Do you want to go hunting?" and he is out and down Water Street and over half way up the street before I can get out of the cabin. That's all for tonight, I am going to bed.

Friday 16th
Well if this don't beat all the weather I ever saw to be right close to the north pole. This morning is as warm as in September and the snow is melting all away. Yes, and Pet if we didn't have some fun right in camp today, I wouldn't say so. Well U just had more fun. Peters came up just after I and Dash did the business. He shot his gun like a damn fool. Well I guess I had better tell you what happened.

I stepped to the door and right down where our boat is to the right about twenty feet (get your sketch) stood a wolf looking right up at me. Well Pet if you could have seen me hike after the gun, didn't say anything to Peters but he saw me make for the gun. He says, "What is it, where is it, what do you see, wait 'til I get my gun". He fell down trying to get his gun.

I didn't say a word, Dash got excited which he always does when he sees a gun. Well I got out to the edge of the bank and let him have it but shot too low and shot just the forefoot of the wolf. By that time Dash saw it and the way he did hike after that wolf and caught it over by the other bank close to Up Street. Well if that wasn't a scrap for your whiskers. Now you can imagine how long it would take a good big dog to kill a little bit smaller one but my old pal never let up until he shook the daylights out of the wolf. He is so fat that when he got done stopping the wolf's breath, he was looking around for his own breath but he looked up at me and as much as said UREKA. Well I just had more fun. I skinned it, the skin is four feet long, its tail is eighteen inches long and as big around as a stove pipe. Dash and I claim all the honor.

Well Mr. Cashman and Lamb left this morning just at daylight. Didn't make any bargain with them to haul us to the Hudson Hope, wanted too much.

6:00 P.M.
Still warm and snow melting and we have another visitor from St. John just arrived. He came down to see about hauling us to the

Hope. Now Mr. Lamb asked us 5¢ per pound to haul us, he has lots of money. This man will haul us for 2¢ per pound. He has no money and wants to do it so as to get a grub stake for next summer and I guess we will let him have it. Don't know yet, we may commence right away to move, take a couple loads up anyhow, hate to leave this nice little home but I am after gold and that is what I will have if there is any to be had.

You see if we get to Hudson Hope or to the other side of the Portage which is twelve miles the other side of the Hope, we will be just about a hundred miles farther in the spring than we would be if we stayed here until spring and it will be nice traveling on the ice. The worst part will be building a cabin after we get there. But we will be willing to live in anything in order to get up there. Well I guess I have said enough tonight so I will say goodnight and help to entertain this Klondyker.

Saturday morning the 17th
Well it thawed all night and is still above freezing this morning. I guess the snow will all go — the hills are bare now. Our visitor has just left us for his camp at St. John. His name is Travers, there are two brothers of them and they have just enough grub to last them until spring so they are going to haul us to the other side of the Portage — twelve miles the other side of Hudson Hope for $2.00 per hundred. We have 4500.

They have six horses, they will take two loads up and one of us will go with them. Then they come back and get the other load. It will take eight days to make the trip and we are going to move as soon as the ice and weather gets good. It will have to freeze up first and come some snow.

We will, I think, get away by the middle of January, it all depends on the weather. I am awful glad to make this move so soon, it will help to pass the time away and we will be one hundred miles closer to the gold fields in the spring and have all of the summer before us to prospect in. We will be right in the Rocky Mountains. It will put us three months more ahead than if we stayed here until spring and it is so much easier to travel on the ice.

I don't want to get away from St. John though until the mail gets in there but it will be there about the first of January. After that it will be a hard matter to get mail until in the summer unless I walk back to St. John which would be sixty-two miles to walk unless the government puts on a mail carrier which they have not done yet but are talking about doing. Well if we can't get any letters, it is gold that I am after but it would be a part of my business to get letters from you and know that you are all as happy as I am, barring lonesomeness.

Harry, do you know the difference between a baby and a sea gull? One makes its bed on the water and the other makes its water on the bed. Say Myrty, if I don't get a gee wholiper of a letter from you when this mail man comes back, you'll get your head thumped by me.

Well still they come — more visitors this evening. The preacher and three men just left us. Now a preacher in Pine River camp, wouldn't that cork you? But it is a fact, a real live preacher. He is taking the three men down to Dunvagen, then he is going on to Slave Lake Post and will be back in a month and will bring all the mail there is. So you see we will have two mail trains in the next month. Ought to get a gee wholiper of a pile of letters then.

We bought a quarter of a fresh beef at St. John and the preacher fetched it to us. Charged $2.00 for bringing it to us. We only had to pay 10¢ per pound for its fore quarter. It will last us all winter. Come up kids and mamma and take Christmas dinner with me. You can go back in the evening. Going to have something good, suet pudding with whiskey dip. Don't forget to give your card to the doorkeeper. Myrty we receive visitors in style.

Well I have some encouraging news for you. I will give it to you just as it is. On our way up here about fifty miles back from Peace River, we all stopped to prospect and went up this creek about a half mile. Peters found a piece of quartz about as big as a small egg which looked good. We kept it, didn't say anything to anybody. Today we analyzed it and found it to be awful rich. We got the gold out of it and weighed it and it runs $850.00 per ton. Now understand this is just a little piece of quartz that had broke off from the main lead and washed down the creek. It is up that creek some place so when we are coming out we will stop and find it and it has solved the problem of where all this fine gold we have been finding everywhere we prospect comes from.

I tell you we are full of hopes now of finding a good thing up here next summer. There is a man by the name of Nickols has a quartz claim up on Findlay River which pays a $1000.00 per ton. A quartz that pays $100.00 is considered good. The biggest stamp mill in the world is at Juneau and it only pays about $4.00 per ton.

Now don't get excited about this that I am telling you but just keep cool and I will exert every known scheme to get us a gold mine and Harry and Pet, just keep on working and take good care of mamma and Myrty. Don't waste a cent, spend all your money on them for I feel just like I was going to have more luck than forty men. There being fine gold all along Peace River on the sand bars is an evident fact. There is gold in this country and lots of it and all a man has to do is to pull his daylights out for about a year getting up here and then find it. Ah dog gone the big girl anyhow. If I am lucky and find a gold mine I will take you to Europe, Stirrup or someplace. I feel so good I can eat a pound of this raw beef and two pounds cooked for supper. Even Dash has been gay all day, I guess because I am.

Well I have just finished reading the first book in the Bible Genesis, fifty chapters. I read a while, write a while, cook a while and hunt a while, and play chess a while and I find the days and months are slipping by faster than I thought they would. Just eight days until Christmas and I can see you all talking about it and wondering where Dad is and what he will have for Christmas and that is just what I am thinking of you folks. You can just put it down that Dad will celebrate Christmas to the best of his ability in the way of eatables. Other luxuries I will have to do without unless Dash brings me something.

I am going to put one of these ribs out of this quarter of beef we got in Dash's stocking. All of you can just say, "Well Dad has got lots of things to eat on Christmas," for I am the lad that can get it up. Have got a rabbit and two pheasants saving up besides the quarter of beef. Going to have beef for breakfast, rabbit and gravy for dinner and stewed pheasant and dumplings for supper and along about 10:00 P.M. eat a little of all three. Going to have apricot pie with condensed cream, going to have a tub full of ginger cakes with tea, going to have rice pudding with raisins, going to have bread pudding with whiskey dip, going to have suet pudding by the belly full. So now you know just what I had for Christmas. Goodnight. I am going to play chess now.

Sunday morning before sunup Dec. 18th
This is the last day I will have to write in this letter as the Hudson Bay Lightning Express Knickerbocker dog train No. 36 will be along here at 3:00 P.M. today so I commence early this morning to be sure that I get it all in this letter that I am going to say. Enclosed please find Christmas gifts to all of you which I trust will be unthankfully received hoping that you will lose them soon on account of their immense value and trusting they will displease the eye on account of their magnificent beauty.

It is all I can send on account of the size of the envelope and the dog train No. 36 doesn't carry express in winter time. Of course this will be a little bit late but if you get it you can refer back. You just excuse me this time for not making you any pictures. I didn't have time. I suppose the dog train will layover here tonight and I will have to entertain the engineer.

Just after dinner and oh my, had roast beef and rice pudding. Well I will do my best to write some more for I am looking for the dog train express at 3:00 P.M. They may not stop only long enough to get the mail. We are anxious about the creek we found the quartz in. If wasn't so far would go back yet this winter but it is fifty miles back. Well it will be there for a long time and when we do come back will prospect every inch of that creek and there is not one chance in one thousand of any other man finding it.

Imagine our eyes when we assayed the little piece of quartz and found it full of gold — to just take the quartz as we found it and look at it, one would think it was just a piece of hard rock broke off of some big ledge of rock and wouldn't be worth a cent a ton.

There is gold in here and I am confident that we will find it, more so now since the last discovery.

Well you ought to get this letter by the 20th of January. I wish I could get a letter that quick but I am looking for fifty letters when this dog train comes back and that will make up. It is two hours after dark and we have had supper and the dog train has not arrived yet. I expect they have broke a side rod. I don't look for them now until about 10:00 A.M. They were to have left St. John this morning so the preacher said and preachers don't lie only when they go to bed.

This has been a nice day, just at above zero all day. I have been reading the Bible and writing all day. Read fourteen chapters in the Bible. I can't think of anymore to say tonight so I will quit and finish in the morning. 65,000,000 kisses a piece.

Monday morning the 19th
Snowed just a little last night and this morning. The temperature is 30° above zero with the sun shining. It is just sun up. The sun rises a few minutes before nine. So if it keeps on the school children will have to go to school in the dark up here. And dog train No. 36 has not made its appearance yet. Yes, I got your letter Myrty written Aug. 1st. How many of the sixteen or nineteen letters that are between me and you have you got yet, since the one the 6th of July that I wrote while camped in the mouth of Swan River on the lake? SMARTY, I would like to have a hold of you to shake some tar out of you.

Well if the dog train comes today and doesn't stop all night with us, I will have to say goodbye in short form some time today for I am leaving the letter open for anything I can think of. I expect the engineer got drunk or the fireman couldn't keep steam. They might have some of John Malones slack coal, anyhow something has delayed them. But they will be along about supper time. We will have the lunch counter ready for them. But I won't have raisin pie, just apricot, cold roast beef, ginger snaps and mustard. Twenty cents a cup for coffee, Pine River prices. If they don't want to pay it let them eat snow. I'm not up here for my health.

Since dinner it has got just as foggy as it can be and it is getting colder. 25° above zero now. We are going to have a big snow and then get a load of north poles.

3:00 P.M.
Here is the dog train so I will have to quit unless they stay over night. Oh well, I'm not in half a big a hurry as some people. They are going to stay all night. They are both Indians. One of them by name Anderson can talk our talk, the other one can only say uhg uhg, eat a saw log and sell canoes. They have two big husky dogs. The first thing Dash did was to jump on one and bite him right on the fire *[sic]*.

Well mamma and kids, the time is getting short to write what I have to say in this letter and gab is getting short but this leaves me in just the very best of health, not an ache or pain, weigh about 195 pounds, am in great hopes of making a small fortune out of this trip. Everything seems to be in my favor as strength and health are concerned and we will be in the mountains when the ice breaks up in the spring instead of here. We will have all of next summer and right in the gold fields to prospect in.

Besides we have this creek I spoke of when we come out. I have great hopes in that. You can tell Cantlon and he will have an idea to give you about it, that we found this piece of quartz about a half a mile up this creek from Peace River above high water mark and that both sides of the creek banks are two hundred feet high. Don't know how far it runs back from Peace River and that it was just a small piece of quartz broken off, looked like a ledge of quartz. We couldn't tell to look at it that there was a speck of gold in it but saved it because it was quartz and something you don't see very often up here for it is mostly sandstone. But Saturday we assayed it and it was just full of gold.

I hope this will find you all in good health and I hope this dog train will bring me some good news from you. I don't know when I can send out another letter to you but it will be whenever anybody goes out and if the government puts on a mail man I will have a chance to send a letter every two months and as often between as anyone will be going out.

Well we have just had supper and these redskins say they are going to start at 5:00 o'clock in the morning. That's three hours before daylight so I have got to hike a little and get this letter finished. Harry as soon as you get this letter go and get me a small calendar. Put it in with your letter. We have none and I am liable to forget whether it is Sunday, Monday, day or night or anything. Send me some Mattoon papers, some St. Louis Globes, as many as you can send and register them.

I will begin to finish this letter up and by the time I get wound up the sheet will be full I expect. Remember me to all my friends, let George know of this letter and all of the girls. Write me often and big ones and Myrty you did very well the last letter I got from you which was written August 1st. See if you can get the lines closer together and the words smaller and get foolscap paper. You can say more on that kind of paper than you can on smaller paper.

Tell me everything that has happened and what you have been doing, what everybody says about me, what kind of a street fair you had and just fill two or three envelopes full and Harry you can improve more. Your paper is big enough if you didn't spraddle the lines out so wide. Give me all the railroad news, all the changes in the officers of the road and the men and how is Irish Jim and Presh, send me an envelope full of grins if you can't find anything to say.

If you can't get any paper get Harry to let you write in between his lines, there is room enough. And mamma, I am looking for a gee wholiper of a letter from you only I hope there won't be anything in it about my Peggy or my girl, this girl, that girl, the other girl, the girlies girl girl. You make them bladder skites of kids write me big letters and you do the same.

If you knew what they are worth to me up here in this uncivilized country, you would tell me every time you went out to the wood shed to get a load of wood or every time you say, "Now Presh, you are not going up to town tonight." Actually, if you don't write more and oftener I will forget how to read. So now I will quit for this time as I have got the sheet full. I will say goodbye to you all with a Merry Christmas and a Happy New Years with many many kisses and hugs and prayers.

I am your Klondyker Jim papa

• • •

The Pine River Star
Published Daily, Illustrated
James Hinkle, Pro.
Terms:— Three Skins Per Year

Dec. 16, '98
Items of interest
Big excitement on Water Street today. The editor and Dash Hinkle killed a wolf.

Tommy and Whitefoot Grimston were three months old today.

The population of Pine River Camp is nine. Eight male and one female.

The city is Republican on majority. Dan Grimston being a husky is not allowed to vote. Tommy and Whitefoot Grimston under age and females not allowed to vote.

Saturday Dec. 17
Daily Market
Bacon 25¢ lb., flour $11.00 per hundred, sugar 25¢ lb., fresh beef 12 1/2¢, pheasants 3¢ or one load of shot, bear not to be found, corn meal 20¢ for fresh, that which is moldy 17¢ lb. Large rabbits the size of a mule are a drudge on the market on account of their flesh tastes like dog. Golden syrup $3.00 per gallon, butter, that which is unstinkable not to be had, that which you can smell forty rods 65¢ lb. without hair, with hair 60¢ lb., dried moose meat 20¢ lb.

Railroad items
All trains five days late, the Hudson Hope, Fort St. John and Dunvagen is ice bound for ten days.

The Pine River Star, James William Thomas Mc Mullen Hinkle, Editor

---

The fast dog mail train on the H.H.F.St.J.&D. R.R. will be through Dec. 19.

Reverend Robison D.D. of Ft. St. John passed through here with three long haired Klondykers on their way to Peace River Landing. They gave us a call but did not ask for anything to eat. Had not heard yet that we had ginger cakes.

Don't forget the ball Christmas Eve at Hinkles and Peters shack.

We have four hours and forty minutes sunshine every day now and eighteen hours and twenty nine minutes moonshine, the balance is twilight.

Monday Dec. 19
No. 36 dog mail train arrived at 4:00 P.M. by the sun. (The editor's watch won't run.) Five days, eight hours and fifty nine minutes late. They stopped overnight with us and had heard that we kept ginger cakes.

No rude characters will be allowed at the ball Christmas Eve.

Tuesday Dec. 20
Mr. Wasslebridge of St. John drove into Pine River Camp this A.M. One horse and sleigh. Calling on the Grimstons. Mr. Digby Grimston went gunning today. Killed one blind, blooming, bleeding pheasant.

Wednesday Dec. 21
Good thing, shortest day of the year, sun raises right over there and sets right over here.

Lost, strayed or stolen, one bay horse seven hands high with ears frozen off. Any information will be thankfully received by Mr. Wasslebridge.

Thursday, Dec. 22
Don't forget that there is a ball at the shack, corner of Pine and Bear Avenue Christmas Eve.

Friday, 23
Mrs. Jennie Grimston is on the sick list, Tommy Grimston has learned to talk. Dan Grimston was arrested today and was given six swift kicks for stealing one side of bacon.

Dock Grimston says that Mrs. Jennie Grimston is poisoned on bacon rind.

Saturday Dec. 24
Everybody is fitting for a great time this evening. There will be a Christmas tree in the woods tonight. Music will be furnished by Hinkle's string band at the hop this evening. James Hinkle,

first violin, Jim Hinkle, second violin, Nig Hinkle, cornet and Jim Memphis Hinkle, bass.

There will be no drinks sold at the hop tonight.

River water handy on Water Street.

After the ball is over, Christmas.

Mr. Ryan of Fish Creek (four miles above St. John) drove into town this evening. He says there is no excitement on Fish Creek. (No one there but himself and horse.)

Dec. 25, Sunday morning special.
No shooting crackers to be heard.

After the ball everybody looks tired.

A very delightful time at the ball last night.

Lasted until the wee hours. Mr. James Hinkle broke one fiddle string. (Fiddle strings are worth $3.10). At 4:00 P.M. the guests began to arrive. (It gets dark at 3:00.) Mr. Dan Grimston was the first to arrive. Nig Hinkle don't like a husky anyhow. Told him to go home and finish the bacon he stole first.

Everybody seemed to enjoy themselves.

Oh yes, the editor forgot to say Merry Christmas to you.

Wanted No. 1
Girl to do general housework, chop wood, make fires, carry water, address J.R. Peters, soap box under bed, No. 1, Pine and Bear Ave.

Wanted No. 2
One St. Louis Globe Democrat so won't forget how to read.

Wanted No. 3
People who visit us to stay not more than one meal and not to ask for ginger cakes.

Wanted
To know if Myrty Hinkle has received those 16 or 19 letters yet.

To know if Frank Norule of Mattoon, Ill. knows anything about some hams that were stolen twenty years ago.

Ice two feet thick in Peace River.

Good place in B.C. for Johnny Walker to put up ice.

The editor has killed sixty two pheasants this month.

Monday, Dec. 26, 1898
Mr. Digby Grimston's blooming knee is stiff where he stuck the ax in it.

WANTED

A seamstress, apply between the hours of 10:00 A.M. and 2:00 P.M. All other hours are dark.

Three good men to pull on tow line in the spring. To know why the devil can't skate. How in hell can he?

Bread pudding with whiskey dip, 13 skins per hunk. Apricot pie made with bear grease, 3 skins per pie, bear steak in season. Mush without milk, 10¢ per spoon, with milk, haven't got it.

Our English neighbor, Mr. Digby Grimston who has a stiff knee wanted to know of the editor if he knew any riddles and he gave him one that he couldn't answer.

A man and his wife and kid were out bicycle riding and all three fell down and skinned their knees. Where did they go to get cured? The man went to Africa where the NEEgrow is, the woman went to Jerusalem where the sheNEE is and the kid went to the butcher shop where the kidNEE is.

The Grimstons have four stoves going in a shack 14 by 16, it keeps them busy.

Saturday Dec. 31
First time the editor ever spent New Year's Eve so far away from no place.

January 1, 1899
Happy New Year to you all.

Dog train just arrived, came in disconnected, engineer and conductors ears and cheeks frozen. Brought the editor four letters. Please excuse the editor, he is too busy reading his mail.

Wednesday, 4
The editor and Mr. J.R. Peters are going to move to St. John.
Pine River Star has been sold out. Mattoon papers please copy.

Goodbye
James Hinkle
B.C., N.W.T.

• • •

From Hinkle's Journal

Tuesday, December 20, 1898   Nice day, 27° above zero, been around home all day, made a tail board for fiddle. At 6:00 P.M. a man and one horse and a sleigh from St. John arrived to get some things from Digby.

Wednesday, 21   Shortest day of the year, took all of my traps up, aren't catching anything. Digby and the man went down to Struck Creek and brought up a load of goods. Nice day, 25° above zero. Beat Spencier six straight games of chess.

Thursday, 22   Snowed one inch last night. The man's horse got loose and he hunted all forenoon for it and then went to St. John after another one. Shot at a wolf, I and Jack missed it, Dash caught it over on Peace River and it got away from him, Dash and Dan ran it three miles down Peace River. Digby killed two pheasants. At 6:00 P.M. 19° above zero.

Friday, 23   Awful windy and 32° above zero, set twelve traps up west of camp.

Saturday, 24 Nice day, 30° above zero. Went to traps, baked pies and cornbread, Digby cut his knee with ax setting traps. Mr. Ryan of Fish Creek arrived Christmas eve at 8:00 P.M. looking for his horses.

Sunday 25 40° above zero, snow all going off, sun shown all day, had roast rabbit, roast pheasant and bread pudding for dinner, very quiet here all day.

Monday 26 Snowing this morning, 20° above zero, Mr. Ryan left for Fish Creek this morning, went to my traps, writing letter home to folks, Peters is making a toboggan.

13

Move to Fort St. John

Pine River Camp B.C.

December 27, 1898

Dear Mamma and children,

    I will commence now to write you another letter but the Lord knows when I will get a chance to send it out but will have it ready when I do have a chance. I have no word from you or anyone since Myrty's letter written Aug. 1st, five months ago. The mail man that the Hudson Bay Co. sent to Dunvagen went by Monday 19th and will be back this week. I am looking for them Friday unless something delays them, or there comes a blizzard or something like that. Have to wait at Dunvagen for the other mail man that meets him there from Slave Lake Post. He said he would be back for New Years if everything went all right.

    This morning it commenced to snow and has been snowing all day up until 6:00 P.M. just as hard as it could come down and now it is about nine inches of snow but it has cleared off and the moon is shining bright and is only 12° above zero. This snow may delay him a little but he will be along in a few days and then I wonder if I will get any letters from you. And I wonder if it will be good news or bad.

    If I don't get word from you this time I will always think there is something wrong or you don't care enough about me to write me.

It seems as if you folks had of written oftener I would have heard from you before five months. There has been five mails in since August and I have only gotten one letter, one from Myrty written Aug. 1st and then the little devil had the nerve to say eighty-five or sixty times in her letter, yes they had got all of my letters and had answered all of them and that something was wrong and that I had better see about it. Oh if I had hold of you now this minute.

Wednesday 28th
It has quit snowing and has cleared off nice but is colder this morning. When I got up the thermometer stood at 1° below zero. Today is nice sunshine but has been at zero all day. The snow is thirteen inches deep and am afraid that it will delay the dog train.

Thursday 29
One big load of north poles arrived last night. 31° below zero but the sun is shining bright. Everything is popping this morning. Our man Mr. Travers, has not come to move us to Hudson Hope yet. Am looking for him every day. They will take two loads and Peters will go with them and then they come back after the balance which will be about a month or the first of February if we have weather suitable. That is all for today. Slip me a kiss.

Friday 30th
Well now kids, this is a cracker jack. Now now now now. I'll just be doggone if there isn't blue fuzz flying this morning. How cold do you think it is up here? You ought to see me right now, you would never be any good. I am sitting right in the fire and have got on the suit I had on in the picture I sent you. This morning at sunup it was 48° below zero.

You have heard the trees and limbs crack after a cold night when the sun came out. Well if you were here you would hear them crack all through the night, without the sun shining. Just one continuous cracking and popping all the time. The sun has been shining all day and now at about 2:00 P.M. it is 42° below zero. Am afraid that this will delay the dog train No. 36. They are due this evening but the snow is so deep and it is so cold that they can't make as good time but they will be here by Sunday evening.

Oh I wonder if I will get word from you. It is awful suspence to sit here in this little shack and have not heard a word from you for five months, to wait for them to come and then what if they don't bring me any letters. Myrty you have gone out and have thought your nose was freezing. Well if you were right here now all you would have to do would be to go just outside the door, turn around, come back in to the fire, feel up at your nose and it would be stiff. I froze both of my ears just going down after a bucket of water. I felt both of them stinging before I got back and didn't stop to rub them and sure enough both of them were stiff when I got in the house and they were sore for a week. You can freeze yourself here and you won't know it. You bet I don't go out anymore without putting on my Klondyke suit, can't freeze then.

Well, it is about 8:00 P.M. and the dog train has not come and they will not come tonight. I 'spect their biler has froze up. I just now looked and it is 40° below zero and will reach to 50° by morning. Well let her flicker, I was flickering here first this season. Can't scare me a little bit unless they send down the old north pole. Well that's all for tonight. I am publishing a paper, The Pine River Camp Star and I must go to work on it. I will send you a copy of it. Everything in the paper is truth. So you need not be afraid of spoiling your morals. Kiss me.

Saturday Dec. 31st, 1898
And this will be the last I will say to you this year and I haven't got much to say anyhow for Pet, it is too cold to talk. My ink froze up and my lead pencil froze up and I am afraid my voice will get in such big chunks that I can't send it to you. This morning just before sunup, about 9:00 A.M., it was 53° below zero.

There seems to be no air at all. The smoke out of the chimney goes right straight up a hundred feet above the trees and if I would start and run two hundred yards it would kill me, would lose my breath. But I'm not going to run, Dash wanted to go hunting today so I opened the door, he went out and you ought to see him hike back in to the fire again, didnt want to go half as bad as he thought he did.

We are comfortable though, can keep good and warm, but it takes lots of wood to do it. The back part of our cabin inside is hanging full of frost and would make a nice chromo. Well I must go to work on the Star. Goodnight, the dog train has not come yet.

Sunday morning, January 1st, 1899
Happy New Year to you all. It has moderated some, at 6:00 A.M. it was 43° below zero. It is awful lonesome, these cold days here, too cold to go hunting, have to sit in the shack twenty four hours every day.

3:00 P.M.
Dog train has just arrived with both of their ears and cheeks frozen. Brought me four letters. Goodbye, I am too busy to write anymore today.

Monday morning January 2nd
Well I am glad and I am the most disappointed man in the Klondyke, glad that I heard from you and disappointed in not getting letters of a later date and in the children, out of the four letters, three from you and one from George, NOT A SINGLE WORD FROM MYRTY, NOT A WORD FROM HARRY, NOT A WORD FROM PRESH. Not even a single word from either of them after waiting five months and then not a scratch of a pen from them.

I took a big cry after I read the letters that you wrote and right before Peters and the Grimstons and the two Indians that brought the mail. Dash came up to me, laid his head on my knee and wagged his tail, looked up at me as much as to say, "What is the matter Jim?" I told him I had no friends but him and the gun. If I was a girl or a boy and had a papa that thought as much of you as I do, I would write if my papa was in an uncivilized country. Yes, I would say a few words to him if nothing more than for humanities sake.

If you had to go through the hardships that I have already gone through all for your sakes, even if you don't love me I would write some little thing in my mamma's letter. Just a word or two would have been worth lots to me. Put yourselves away from civilization for five months shut up, you might say, the same as in prison, you would be awful glad to get to read something from someone you know and that isn't half of it. It will be five months more now and maybe a year before I even have a chance to get the same kind of a letter you wrote last.

There is one more mail yet to come in this winter some time next month but it is not certain. It is the preacher that went from Ft. St. John a few days ago. He may not come back. If he doesn't, there will be none until after the ice goes out in all the rivers and the lake in the spring and by that time we will be hundreds of miles from Pine River Camp which will cause another delay until way in the summer. Of course our mail will be forwarded from St. John to wherever we go but it takes time in this country to do it.

I will proceed to answer mamma's three letters now. The first one is dated August 21st, '98 and was mailed the 29th. The day you started to write this letter I was in camp about eighty miles below here for three days and was busy all day the same day writing you folks a letter. I sent you or Myrty a wild rose twig with the rose buds attached.

I was awful sorry to hear that you had been sick and Harry too. I suppose you had to eat a mess of green cucunbers. You said that you and Myrty went to the wreck and you would send me the piece about the wreck but you didn't do it. What is the matter with you people down there? You are the hardest set to make understand I ever knew and some of your letters are dated and some aren't.

What kind of a wreck was it that Clark had and who did he have it with and who was to blame? If it had not been for William Thornburg writing some in George's letter and telling me something about it, all I would have known about the wreck was that Clark cried like a child when he saw his fireman killed.

I have told you folks, I do believe in every letter I have written to you, that there was no papers brought up this far unless they be registered for the mail is so heavy that anyone corning from

Edmonton to St. John can't begin to carry the papers and letters unless it is in a boat and boats stop running up here the first of September until the ice goes out in the spring in April. All the mail is brought up to St. John from September to April is by dog trains or pack trains with horses and I know I have told you a dozen times to register all papers.

Instead of that you register the letters and send the papers by mail. It is not necessary to register a letter and it isn't necessary to put more than one two cent stamp on a letter unless it weighs over the weight, I have forgot but I think one ounce. I get letters from you with two, two cent stamps on that don't need it. I will get them just as quick with one two cent stamp as if they had a dozen two cent stamps on them unless they weigh over an ounce.

You say the boats just happened to miss your letter. There is another mistake you made. If one boat does miss a letter, which of course they do, the next boat would get them which is about every ten days. The Hudson Bay boats and the Brick Bros. and Mc Dougall and Secord boats leave Athabasca Landing about every ten days all through the summer and the stage with the mail goes from Edmonton twice a week to Athabasca Landing.

If you have written more letters than I have, which you say you have, then you have not got the half of my letters, I have written you and the kids fifty-one letters. Eleven of them had forty pages, six of them had thirty-five pages, and the balance not less than fifteen pages. The letter that Hardesty mailed for me at Edmonton was the smallest letter I have written you. You say that you are more anxious to hear from me than I am from you. Please just turn that around, it will fit the best the other way for there are four of you and only just me.

Yes, to be sure I like to hear from the children but that isn't to be for I never have got a line from Presh yet and only four letters from Harry and about the same from Myrty and I notice the last three letters I got, neither of them said one single word. If they had just written some place in each of the three letters, HELLO PAPA, I wouldn't have been crying all day like I have been. This has been the most miserable day I ever went through. I would ten times rather be caught in a storm on the lake out of sight of land than go through another day like this. And tomorrow will be just the same. I can't eat a thing today, it chokes me.

You say Myrty is not through her school yet. I can't and don't understand it at all. One letter I got from her or you said she would be through in June. Another one said she would not be through until July, another one said that she was offered a position in a dry goods store and now you say she is going to take examinations in a week. She commenced in March, '98 and isn't through in October, eight months. I don't pretend to understand it at all. You said she was sitting on the porch lonesome. I wonder if she thinks of her papa that makes her lonesome and that she would go into the piano every little bit. If I could hear a piano I would be scared to death.

You said Harry was going to write every day. Well if he does I will get a big letter some time next summer if he don't forget to mail it. If he don't take his rest when he can get it I know he won't be able to fire one of those engines. He had better take the switch engine until he gets strong again and take his rest and not run around when he should be in bed.

It is not necessary for me to know what you do with your money. I am confident that you won't spend it foolishly. I see by your invoice that you don't have much to spend in any way. I see Presh still hangs on to the red onion and when bicycles get so you have to spend $5.00 for repairs, it is time to throw the thing away and buy a $125.00 one and it will be a good idea to pay cash as you go.

I am not surprised about Guildoff being let out, that makes four of the old men let out since I left. You told me to write to White as soon as I could. I have written him five or six letters, besides I have written him several sheets and sent in your letters and explained the reason I did, that was because I would run out of stamps and there is none to be had up here in this country.

Yes, Mr. White deserves a letter from me and I am not the man to not write to him either for he is the only one out of the whole Mattoon Mining and Investment Co. that has written to me and you must read him my letters to you or part of them and tell him that I have not forgot him, neither will I ever forget him. If I was to find a claim tomorrow he would be the first man that I would have to take the claim next to me.

Now you ask me not to swear and to practice refinement. Well I do swear but don't know it when I do and as for refinement, that is pretty hard to do up here for they don't wear linen collars up here and I have no one to practice with but Dash and the Beaver Indians and they can't talk any more than one of these spruce back logs I have cut out back of our cabin and all the millionaires have to swear a little bit. If you could see my long hair you would say refinement.

What does Myrty call "in a few days" — twelve months for that is as soon as I can hear from her now. The last word I had from her was written Aug. 1st. You say you hope my health will keep good. I have not been sick one minute since I left home until today and I would just as soon have a spell of sickness as to feel the way I do now. That answers that letter.

The next one is the one you registered. The post mark says September 12 but your letter says Friday evening September 12, Dear Jim and that you had been thinking about me constantly for two days and are wondering if I am sick (yes heartsick) and that you were trying to dream about me.

You don't work that right. If you want to dream about anyone you must be thinking about him or talking about him sometime in the day and then forget all about it and you will be sure to dream about him that night. You said you got a letter from Harry. That is more than I got and you didn't say a word about Pap Hinkle. George said in his letter that pap had something like a paralytic stroke but was better and that has helped me to pass a miserable day.

I can just see Mrs. Mc Granhan saying "YESSIR, I hope Mr. Hinkle will come back rich." Well you can tell her that I will come back rich if it is up to get-able. Myrty told me that she had a chance for a position in a dry goods store at $6.00 per week and she told me that Harry would draw $72.00 that month. Now is that all the money they can give you — Harry $15.00 to $25.00 per month, Presh $16.00 per month. You people must get down to business today, not tomorrow but today. How will it look for a millionaire to come home and have to take you out of the poorhouse, that's not refinement, you all must economize, you only have to do it for two years, then I will come home and work for you.

You are too big to climb peach trees. Suppose you fall and bust a *****. You would be in an awful fix, then what is the matter with that big hunk of a boy Presh. I only wish I could take my claim but I can't take it until I can find it.

NOW I WOULD LIKE TO HAVE BEEN THERE BEHIND CUNNINGHAM. A MAN THAT WILL JUST WALK HOME without asking a young lady should have a swift kick and I'm not like one that wouldn't do it if I was there. WHY DID she not just go in the house and let him stand there?

Why didn't you tell me how you heard that Hardesty was coming home? I didn't know that Monty White's boat was seized until you told me. There are no newspapers up here, only the Pine River Camp Star and there are no telegraph or railroads except the dog R.R.

You said that it was three weeks since you had heard from me and that was an awful long time, how would you like to wait five months? I didn't get the B. of I.E. Suppose it is where all the other papers are unless you registered it. That answers that letter of

September Friday, 1898.
The last one you sent is dated September 30 and that you had received my letter the 28th that I gave to Hardesty to mail at Edmonton. Now I did not give him any letter to mail at Edmonton at all, but I gave him a letter to give to you personally when he left us at Struck Creek Camp. I did not put any stamp on it and I don't see why he would mail it in Edmonton when he was going right home and could have carried it to you. I THINK HE HAS GIVE HIMSELF AWAY. If I was his wife I would give him H---. I did tell you why he was corning home, he claimed to have the rheumatism but a man couldn't walk twenty-five miles to St. John in one day that had the rheumatism and that I thought it was a first class case of home sickness.

I would like to have paid you a visit during fair week but I was too busy and too far to come. You said that you would send the Commercial. I DID NOT GET IT. I suppose that it is with the balance of the B. of L.E. and other papers.

Well I had my part of the wood cut and corded up, nine cords, long before you wrote and told me to get it ready. I cut nine cords before it snowed once, have not used any of it until last week. I have enough cut to last me all winter. I get the wood one day, Peters gets it the next and so on.

Now here you come again about Hardesty going to St. John and didn't get me any mail and then wanted to know if I hadn't landed there and got lots of mail. Well I'll swear it don't do any good to send you maps of the country, you get everything backward, you must be Dutch. How could I get mail at St. John and land at Peace River Landing?

Now Peace River Landing is eighty-six miles northwest of Slave Lake Post and Dunvagen is sixty miles northwest of Peace River Landing and Pine River Camp is one hundred miles northwest of Dunvagen and Fort St. John is twenty-five miles northwest of Pine River Camp so you will see by what I am telling you that when we landed at Peace River Landing that Fort St. John is one hundred-eighty miles northwest of Peace River Landing and we are camped just one hundred-sixty miles northwest of Peace River Landing at the mouth of North Pine River, twenty-five miles from St. John.

Get your map I sent you and all four of you lay flat on your bellies on the floor with the map in front of you and learn it by heart and get an idea of some kind where I am, what country I am in and then you will take more interest in this trip.

I suppose you know that I am living under Queen Victoria and not Bill McKinley. Now follow the river right on up and you will see that Hudson Hope is forty miles northwest of St. John and it is at the foot of the Rocky Mountains and is where we are going when we leave here in February.

Then keep on following the river and you will see that at Hudson Hope it is thirty miles through the canyon by the river and twelve miles over the mountain to where we will go from

Hudson Hope. There we build a boat and keep on going up the river to the Omenica River.

I will tell you the balance when I get there.

You said you enjoyed the map I sent and so did Mr. White and Clark. Do you mean the sketches or the map of the country? If you copied the sketches you must have had a time, and did Somerlen publish the sketches in the paper? If he did I want you to send me it in a letter, just a letter and all the other articles if any, just like a letter you would send me in an envelope. Of course it may take two, two cent stamps.

Tell Mrs. Belmar that when I think of our quarrels over the back fence that I go back in the pine forest back of our cabin and look for a bear to quarrel with.

Yes, I got the pictures you sent me and I look at them every day. I suppose Weber is satisfied now he is with Mc Kee.

I don't see why you want to cry all day because it wasn't me coming home. I would think that you would want me to stay up here until I found a little fortune for us, after I have gone through what I have to get here.

I never would have give up my good job to come up here if I had not had a determination to try and get us something to make us independent. It takes one year to get up to where we are going with just as hard work as ever a man went through. Not one man out of ten could stand it and not one man out of fifty that sticks to it after they get started.

I suppose you folks have formed an opinion — well he is having a good time, he sees lots of sights, he gets his way paid and I suppose you all wished it was you. But you have not the least idea of what it is. As near as I can describe it to you is this, three of you get a rope one hundred feet long, hitch it to a log that you can just pull handy and then pull it six hundred miles in mud and water and mosquitoes and buffalo gnats and you will know what you have to go through to get to the Klondyke. Well that answers the last letter you sent written Sept. 30, '98 and I have got the headache and I am going to bed.

Tuesday, 31
Well I will try to write a little but I don't know what to say. I am as tired as if I had been at work all night. I will own up to you I have got the blues, the worst kind, and I know it won't do to get the blues up here but I can't help it. When you folks do write, you don't seem to want to encourage me and encouragement up here goes as far as the grub we eat.

Of course I am not at hard labor while I am in camp here this winter, but the suspense that is attached to it makes it worse than labor. It is too cold to go outside of the door, therefore I have to stay in this little place sixteen by eighteen foot twenty four hours every day, with nothing to do, nothing to read only the Bible you gave me and I will soon have it read through.

I wish those fellows would come and take us to Hudson Hope. I don't care if it is 100° below zero, anything for a change. We are looking for them, don't know when they will be here but not until it gets warmer I guess. When I got up this morning it was 30° below zero and got up to eighteen before the sun went down. Well I have not got my mind on writing so I will quit and wait until tomorrow. I will take Dash and take a walk.

He has been coaxing me all morning to go hunting. I will take him out and give him some fresh air. There is lots of it here.

Wednesday, 4
This has been a nice day, sun shining all day and only 12° below zero. This morning when I got up I heard a bell, a cow bell back in the forest back of our cabin. I went back there and it was some horses. I just took another cry, it sounded so lonesome to hear the bell tingling, made me think of when I was a boy on the farm. Don't know whose horses they are but I suppose they belong to some outfit that is camped around St. John. It sounds awful strange to hear a bell up here. I suppose when I come home I will get scared at such things.

I wouldn't be so lonesome if I had someone with me that I could talk to. Peters isn't any more company than one of these spruce back logs. I don't like him and he don't like me, so you might say all the company I have is Dash. The Grimstons are poor company, they are English people and of course they are distant from Americans.

If I could get big long letters from you and the kids about once a month or once every two months it wouldn't be so bad but I haven't got a letter from Harry since July and any from Myrty since Aug. 1st and none from Presh, it looks as though they have forsaken me. I don't get any letters from anybody you might say, they all promised to write to me and nobody but you and Mr. White and George and Hat has written. Tivnen, Katz, Clark, Montague, Corne or Cantlon or any of them has not written me a line yet.

It takes encouragement up here in this uncivilized country besides main strength. Of course I have got enough will power to go ahead and make a success out of this trip but it would be much nicer to get some encouraging words from those fellows where it only costs two cents to do it. Well I mustn't write too much or I can't get it in one envelope for I won't have a chance to send this out until March unless someone happens to be going out so I will say goodnight and write a little each day.

Thursday 5th
30° below zero, nice sunny day though. Am looking for the men to come after us today. 4:00 P.M. Here they come now goody goody, I am tickled to pieces. Anything for a change. They have had bad luck coming down, two of their horses slid and all broke through the ice and went under down the river. So now I guess they are only going to take us to St. John at present. But we will have a better chance then to get someone to take us on.

We may buy four horses and go on our own hook. We started with three loads at 1:00 P.M. today and went five miles, then we came back to stay all night and they and Peters start at daylight in the morning and will make St. John tomorrow. Then they come back for the balance and me. That's all today. Goodnight.

Friday, 6th
At 7:00 A.M. 30° below zero. I made a mistake on Thursday, it was today that we took three loads five miles. I am too busy to write

anymore today. Am boxing up goods and getting in shape to start early in the morning. Ta ta.

Saturday, 7th
Well they are gone and me and Dash are all alone. It is only at zero all day and looked like it would snow. I hate to give up this wood I have cut here but it can't be helped. We want to get to St. John so we will have a chance to get someone to take us to Hudson Hope or else buy horses and go on our own hook. We have no chance here to see anyone and we want to be traveling on the ice. It is much easier and besides we want to be at the mouth of the Omenica River by spring if possible.

We have decided now to go to the Omenica country unless we change our minds. They have struck it rich there. Get your map and you can see where the Omenica River empties into the Peace and you can see where the Omenica country is. That's all for today. I must kneed my bread.

Tuesday 10th
I will skip one day for I didn't have anything to say. It has finally quit snowing and has got colder. There is twenty inches of snow and at daylight this morning 8° below zero. Well it is just getting dark and the men have not come back yet. This snow will delay them, have to break a new trail, don't look for them until tomorrow evening. That's all today. I must go and get my kindling and wood. Ta ta.

Wednesday 11th
Well I have just this minute got done washing the supper dishes and will try to say a few lines. I am all alone yet, the men have not come yet for me and I looked for them sure today. Imagine yourself six hundred miles from civilization in a pine forest all by yourself. I would just as soon be by myself as to be with Peters but it is an awful lonesome job, even Dash is lonesome, he just coaxes me to go hunting, will go every little bit and bring my cap to me. But the snow is twenty-four inches deep and can't go hunting. I would not be one bit lonesome if I knew that you folks were all well and getting

along all right. But I know nothing of you since October 1st. That's all today. Goodnight.

Friday evening 13th, about 8:00 P.M.
By the dipper I have skipped two days. I didn't have much to say so I will write a little this evening. The men have not come yet for me but will be here tomorrow. Digby has come back from St. John and he said they started today and will be here tomorrow. They will have to rest their horses a day so will get away Monday. I have had an awful time trying to pass the time away this week. How would you like to live in a little cabin way out in a wild country where there is lots of bears with no one but you and your dog. There is something about it that is very solemn.

Well we are having nice weather — only 10° and 12° below zero all week and sun shining. But the snow is two foot deep. I am awful glad to get away from this place although it is a nice place to camp but I want to be moving. I don't know how soon we will get away from St. John but just as soon as we can.

I think we will buy three horses and keep on moving as long as the ice lasts, and I don't want to get away from St. John either until the next mail comes which is in March, for if we do we won't hear from you until next summer. But we must scheme and get in to the mountains by spring so we will have a summer to prospect in. I will send you a letter out every chance I get, so if I don't hear from you, you will hear from me occasionally. That's all for this evening. I will finish this letter at St. John. Goodnight.

Monday 16th
I am having a time. The men came Saturday about 3:00 P.M., their horses about give out so had to rest them over Sunday. We loaded up the sleighs Sunday eve and found out that we had more stuff than they could pull at one load so now they have one with half of it up about half-way to St. John where there is cabin, then they came back this evening and we start in the morning with the balance up to the cabin, camp there for two nights and do the same thing from there to St. John. Anything to get there, I don't care.

We pay them $25.00 to take us to St. John and board them, cheap enough. You ought to see inside of this cabin now, nothing left but some boxes and skillets which makes it all the more lonesome. But I don't care, anything for a change.

We are having nice winter weather, for the last ten days it has only been from 10° to 20° below zero and that is nice for this country. I can't write much now, am too busy moving, will finish at St. John and tell you how we got there so goodbye now until I get to St. John.

Tuesday 31st
You will notice that I have skipped from the 16th to the 31st. I will now write some and tell you what a time we had getting to St. John. We left Pine River camp Monday 16th and didn't get to St. John until the next Saturday evening. It snowed all the time, had to double every three or four miles. The snow was and is now four feet deep on the level. The horses could not get anything to eat but brush and bark off the trees so I fed them oatmeal every morning or we would not have got to St. John at all. Poor things, I felt so sorry for them. I would have fed them part of my pancakes if I had not have had oatmeal.

We are at St. John anyhow and have a very respectable cabin to live in. It is about as big as a hen house but has a floor in it. It will do to live in just the same. I won't put any Brussels carpet down for I don't expect much company. We pay the Hudson Bay Co. $20.00 per month for it. Now it is something like living, here. There is altogether thirty-eight white men in and around St. John and about a dozen Indians.

This morning when I got up it was 35° below zero. Pretty cold but it has not been that cold all through January. The winter is about gone. After February it begins to thaw up here. The winter has passed away awful quick to me. Day after tomorrow is Groundhog Day. Harry, you must go out and see if you can see your shadow.

Well all of us Klondykers are chuck full of hopes. We all are certain that there will be a big strike made up in this country this spring. Everything indicates that way and everybody is getting ready to get to Hudson Hope or to the mouth of the Omenica River just

198 / KLONDIKE TREK

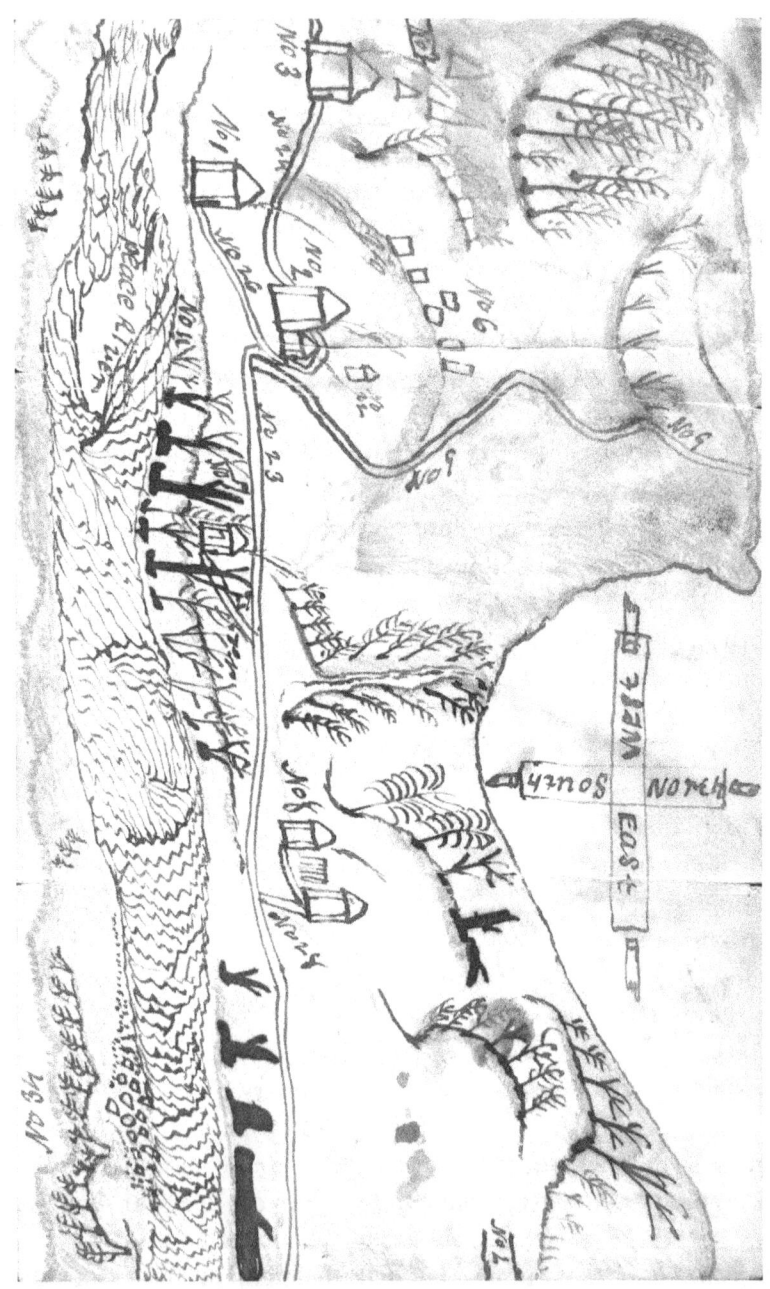

Fort St. John

as soon as the snow melts. I wouldn't take anything for my chances for I am certain if I keep my health that I will have a gold mine before the next summer is over.

That's all for today. I will not have a chance to send this letter to you until March. That is as soon as anyone is going out. The Hudson Bay sends a man out after the mail the 8th of March. There will be two mails in from Edmonton in February, the preacher that went out in December and another man that is coming in, in February so now I will quit for today and write more and finish this letter the last of February. Bye bye.

Feb. 2
Well did you all see your shadow this morning? I saw mine up here. At daylight it was 22° below zero and the sun shown all day. There is not much news to tell you. Everything around St. John is quiet. We are living high, there is a butcher shop here, a man drove thirty head of cattle in here in the fall and he is killing them every day, got them all killed but three, and he sells beef at 12 ½ ¢ a lb. It is the cheapest thing in this country, we get lots of it for nothing. I filed a saw for him today and he gave me all the beef I could carry to the shanty.

Well I haven't got much to say this evening. It is not so bad here as it was at Pine River, can go a visiting here and there is two good chess players here. This is the 7th of Feb., the month is flying, we have had some cold weather since the first.

Peters has gone up on top of the mountain to Suckerville to see some of them about taking us to Hudson Hope. We are going just as soon as the weather will permit.

Well three fourths of the Klondyker parties up here are stranded or you might say busted. Some of them have only enough grub to last them 'til spring. Some have enough to last them part of next summer and a good many haven't got anything and are going from camp to camp sponging a meal here and a meal there. Some of them are too lazy to get up of a morning, some few are energetic and try to work for what they beg but we are the only party up here that is well fixed, the only party out of fifty that have an outfit and we have yet an outfit that will last us all next summer, all of the next winter and summer after next, so you can say we are fixed. One party out of fifty that can stay two years yet. Of course half of the parties that are here will have to go out of the country as soon as they can get out, but there will be other parties come in, in the spring.

If we get to Hudson Hope by the middle of March, I will have a chance to trap through the month of April and I expect to make two or three hundred dollars yet before we go to prospecting. There is lots of game up there and I have thirty-six traps and April is the best month to. trap in. If I catch forty martin, that is $200.00, they are worth $5.00 here and $10.00 if I take them out, it don't take long to catch forty martin if you get where they are.

Some Indians brought in forty martin, fifteen beaver, two bear and a dozen coyotes three days ago and yesterday some brought in twenty-five martin. They bring them as far as fifty miles and trade them to the Hudson Bay for flour and bacon. That's all for today.

Friday morning, February 10th
Well as this month is flying away and is getting close to the time that we will pull out of here and as I have to write Mr. White soon, I will do some writing this morning. The Hudson Bay sends a man out after the mail the 8th of March. He goes to Dunvagen and meets another man that brings the mail there and then he comes back which will be about the 20th of March. So I must have my mail ready by the 8th of March. I don't want to get away from St. John until the mail comes in but if it gets weather so we can travel I will have to go, it is gold that I am after.

There is a party up at Suckerville that is going to take us to the other side of Portage, that means twelve miles the other side of Hudson Hope or past the canyon. If you get your map you will see that it is marked on the river at Hudson Hope, a big bend in the river just at Hudson Hope is the canyon and you will see that it says Cust House, that is the other side of the canyon and there we will stay until the ice goes out. We have bought a boat there from a

Klondyker that is camped here. So if we get out of here by the 15th of March, I will have the month of April to trap in.

From there we go to the mouth of the Omenica River and from there to the Omenica country where there has been a big strike made and over half of the Omenica country unexplored. They have taken $23,000,000 out of one small stream sixteen miles long in the Omenica district and they have taken $60,000,000 out of the whole Omenica district in thirty years so we expect to find something rich there. All Klondykers are headed there in the spring, them that has got grub enough.

This is the 12th
I have finished writing a letter to White so if you get this letter let Mr. White know of it. I told him to do the same if he got his letter. The weather is nice here now but not thawing any. It stays about zero through the day. This morning I heard the first bird singing which is a sign of spring coming. Let her come for I can't set still, so anxious to be going up in the mountains where the gold is. That's all today.

Monday morning the 13th
Well I will have to commence to wind up I guess as the time is getting close that I send this out and if I keep on writing I can't get it in one envelope. I hope the boys are doing all right and saving their money and making you a good living. Harry and Presh, you must not neglect your mother and sister, for remember, I am coming home rich if it is to be had up here in these high peaks. Save your money and if you have any to throwaway throw it away on your mother and sister, see that they don't want for anything.

I would like for both of you boys to get the Bible down every day and read the first, third, fourth and fifth chapters of the Book of Proverbs until you learn it by heart. Now don't think that I am sanctified but I give you this for good advice. Myrty, if they don't read those chapters you make them both sit down in a room and you read it to them. Now mamma, you make them all read those chapters. They are a good thing to go by and if you live up to them you will always come out on top.

Wednesday 15th
It has turned warm today, it was 30° above zero and snow melting fast. Today one of the men came down from Suckerville to see about taking us to the other side of the Portage. He will take us there for 3½ ¢ per pound or $3.50 per hundred and I guess we will engage him. He will take us as soon as the snow melts some and it freezes up again. It may be in a week and may not be for a month. Anyhow we will be on the move as soon as we can get away. That's all today.

Wednesday 22
I don't know if this was your birthday or was it the 12th or what is today, it is something, birthday, washday or something, anyhow I am thinking about you and I thought of you on the 12th but I can't remember if either one of those dates are your birthday or not.

Well we had four days of warm weather and the snow went away and settled altogether two feet but it has turned cold again. Yesterday morning it was 30° below zero. This morning it was 22° below and the man thinks it is all right for us to travel. If the weather doesn't change for a couple of days I expect we will pull out for Hudson Hope. We would like to have had it stay warm for two days longer and then come cold and it would have been nice traveling, as good as a pike. But as it is there is about a foot of hard snow on yet. It will bear a man up but not quite a horse.

The Hudson Bay man leaves with the mail the 3rd of March for Dunvagen, meets the other mail man there and returns about the 20th of March. I hope he will get back before we get away and I want to be on the move too whenever there is good ice. It is lots easier to travel on the ice than by water.

I don't think that I will be with Peters much longer for I expect to have to give him a swift kick and send him home or to some other seaport. There never was such a natural born liar as J.R. Peters is. I thought Dan Watson or Buck Town George could lie easy but Peters can beat them all. All the Klondykers are on to him and what new ones come along, it don't take them long to catch on. I get plumb ashamed of him and break it off in him often enough but he hasn't got sense enough to tumble.

He is no account to work, he is lazy, a liar, and a son of a B and can't help it, besides he is not honest. He will steal, he is not agreeable any way you take him and I won't be bothered with him. He don't know any more about gold than I do and not half as much, he is not saving, he don't take care of anything, he don't know what we have got in our outfit any more than Dash does and he is a man that will bear watching and don't you forget it — I am the man to watch him. I wish I had Cantlon or George Hinkle with me. We stand a splendid chance of finding something rich this summer if I had two good men so I could push along and get up two hundred miles farther but I will get there just the same.

Well it seems funny I commenced this letter in December and here you won't get it until the flowers are in bloom and I will be many miles from here if I have luck. By the time you should get this I will be within five hundred miles of Dawson City for we are going to the Omenica country which is about five hundred miles from Dawson City. Well I hope you will get this all right and I hope it will find you getting along nice and in as good spirits as I am and I hope I will get a whole lot of news from you before I get away from St. John.

Mamma, send for George when you get this and let him read this. I won't write to him separate this time. This will do for you all. Tell him I got his letter, the one that Thornburg wrote some in. I have to be saving with my stamps or else I will run out. Well this is all for today. I won't have but a few days more to write until I send this out. Goodnight.

Monday 27th
And only two more days of this month and we haven't got away yet. We thought a few days ago that we would have been gone before this but it didn't thaw enough and as it is, there is about a foot of snow and a hard crust on top which would cut the horses legs so we have to wait until it comes another thaw. For the last week it has

been cold, down to 40° below zero. I don't think now that we will get away before the 15th of March.

There are a great many Klondykers got the scurvy here. It is caused by not having fruit and vegetables and fresh meat to eat and the cold atmosphere and no exercise. There are no deaths but one man is about dead. There is no danger with proper food.

Harry, you and Presh ought to be here with me when we go to Hudson Hope. You would sure have a time killing bears and climbing trees. At Hudson Hope there is a canyon of thirty miles in the river and it is only twelve miles over the mountains or portage to the Cust's House. In that canyon there is lots of caves and places where bear hole up for the winter. They come out of their dens the last of March and we will be there just about when they come out and all you have to do is to have a gun and shoot and tear out for a tree if you don't kill them. I expect to trap there for a month.

We have just been discussing the prospect of traveling up the river. There are three parties that are ready to go now on the ice, our party and two more, but the first twelve miles up the river is bad. That is, there is a foot of snow and a crust on top with water underneath and then under that the old ice that did not melt the last thaw. After that is good ice all the way to Hudson Hope and we think we will start Monday if it stays this way. The man was down to see us about it today and is going to get his horses up to be ready anyhow.

Well mamma and kids, the way it looks now I will get out of here before the mail man gets back. Not knowing a thing about you since the first day of October, all I can say or do is to pray to the good Lord to keep you from harm, to feed you and take care of you and I don't want any of you to worry or fret about me. I am all right, I have not been sick a minute since I left you, I am in the best of health, weigh 185 lbs. and in good spirits, full of hopes and ambition and am all right in every respect. If I get out of here before the mail comes it will follow me on as far as Hudson Hope. Just as soon as it arrives in St. John, then I will have to come back over the Portage twelve miles after it. But that is nothing if I can only get word from you and good news. Now I have to finish this letter by Friday evening, the mail man leaves Saturday morning.

You will get this letter about the first of May and I will be to the mouth of the Omenica River, eighty-six miles above the Cust's House and maybe in possession of a million dollar gold mine, who can tell. Harry, Myrty, Presh do please write me a little of something, if you can't write me a whole letter get mamma to let you write crossways on her writing. I can read it. This is all for today, I have four more days to write in. Goodnight.

Tuesday 28th
The last day of February and I am glad of it. This morning it is snowing of course when I don't want it to. I expect it will come another foot of snow now and put us back again.

George, you old stick-in-the-mud, you are missing half of your life by not being along with me, all told it is a trying trip for anyone, it would force you to keep from getting home sick or get home sick, one or the other. I have to keep fighting it all of the time. But then you know when a Hinkle says he will do a thing he will do it or bust a gut.

I am after gold, it is a sure thing that it is up here, all I have to do is to find it, and I might think myself too smart or too much self conceit but I just think I am smart enough to find it. Anyhow, if I don't find it, it won't be because I didn't try and one thing sure, I will never give it up even if I do come home without it. I will come back again if I can get money enough to buy a grub stake.

Joe Bush, tell Thornburg that I appreciate the words he sent me in your letter, done me lots of good, him and you and Hat and Mr. White are all the ones that think anything of me. You four are the only ones outside of the family that have thought enough of me to write to me and I want you four to know, should I be fortunate enough to find a gold mine that you four will be the first ones that I will locate and don't forget it either.

It is like this, the law in this country allows one claim in each district. If I find a claim I will sure find a claim for you four first. Maybe there are some people that I can't spit on but maybe some people that I know will be glad to write to me. If they do I will make them enclose a stamp for an answer. Well though I had ought not to kick I wouldn't write to anyone I didn't like either.

Mamma, tell Mrs. Belmar that there is not a board fence in this whole country, my best wishes to her and family. Tell Mrs. Mc Granahan that I am dying for a spot on politics. Ask her how Bill Mc is by this time. How does she like the way he conducted himself in the last war, my best wishes to her and family. Ask Jake Stump if he has given up yet that I would make this trip, my best wishes to him and his family.

Best wishes to Mr. and Mrs. Kinser. Best wishes to Mr. and Mrs. Gilduff, tell Mrs. Flaharity that I am making the trip to Klondyke and have got the fever worser and worser. Best wishes to her and family. Harry, tell Blakely he had better take out some stock in the Mattoon Mining and Investment Co.

Tell John Cantlon if he was here to see the nuggets that the Klondykers have washed out in and around St. John on these sand bars and to hear the reports there are farther up the river that he would have the fidgits and couldn't set still to save his life. Some of the Klondykers wash out from $100 to $200 last fall on the bars and have it in nuggets from $2.00 to $10.00. The pure yaller stuff.

Tell Jim Pane that jack snipes up here is as big as buzzards and have a bill six inches long. Tell Al Bates I'll just be doggon if he hadn't ought to be on this trip too. Tell Pete King I have a better bird dog than he has got and he isn't a bird dog either. I guess it is in the air, dog can learn anything up here. Tell Finfrock, I don't mean John, that there is a squaw up here that looks like Jennie for all the world.

Tell Rabbit Goodman, Jimmie Welch, Jim Ballentine, Andy Leafgreen and Mr. Wiles that I would like to have them up here in the spring to hitch them up to this boat. I would like to see how they would look in harness and take a sketch of them. But tell them that if they do take a notion to come, for them to make up their mind to stay away from ma more than six months.

Mamma, I would like to have you up here now and go up on top of this peak with a toboggon and give you a start down it. I would like to see you go bumpety bumpety bump and take a sketch of you as you were bumping. Well, tell all the balance of the people that enquires about me that I will pay them a visit some time next winter or the summer after.

March 1st
Well it is coming in like a lion, I suppose it will go out like a son of a gun. It is snowing this morning and blowing and doesn't look much like traveling, but it won't last more than a week. We think now that we won't get away before the 20th of March. We will be just as well off to stay in St. John until then, only I want to get to the other side of the Portage and do some trapping before we start to prospecting. And to be there at the canyon when the bears come out, it is hard to tell when we will be on the move.

The weather is very uncertain up here at this time of year. Well, I don't know what else to talk about. I have said so much now I can't get it in one envelope I am afraid.

Twenty-eight pages and have three days more to write so I will stop for today. There was no mail come in, in February. We are looking for them every day.

Goodbye.

Thursday March 2nd
Some Indians have just come in with dog trains from the Nelson River, two hundred miles, with fur and they are on the war path good and strong. Some mony-as (white man) has killed their horses for meat to eat. There are lots of horses killed up here and eaten the same as beef. How would you like to have a horse steak for breakfast?

Friday 3rd
The mail man doesn't leave until the 8th, next Wednesday. Now mamma and kids, don't expect too much or imagine or make your calculations too high on my hopes. I might be over estimating or might not be fortunate enough to find a good thing up here. But what I have said about it is from the bottom of my heart even if

Hinkle's Poem

I don't find a speck of gold and I base my hopes and ambitions on the government reports on the formation of the country, on Dawson's report, the man that predicted the gold in the Klondyke and has surveyed all of this NWT for the government and on the gold that I see with my own eyes taken out all along Peace River on the sand bars.

Dawson says that when that eruption was, that the slide started from Circle City, Alaska and slid down from there into this part of the country and from Circle City down into the Copper River district in Alaska and that there are better indications in this part of the country than there was at Dawson City. He is a scientific man and now I am going to do my best to find it this summer and if I don't find it I will come home and make arrangements to come right back up here again with John Cantlon.

I wish you would have John Cantlon come up to your house and read this to him. It is a positive fact the gold is in here. It is impossible to be mistaken and it is in here in big chunks too. The reason it has not been found before now is, it is a hard country to get through. Thousands and million and millions of acres has never had a human foot on it and all of this unexplored country is right in the gold belt. It will be explored by someone and is being explored every year.

We are going up on that part that is not explored in the Omenica country between the mouth of the Omenica River and Fort Graham to the southwest, all of that country is unexplored. Nobody knows what is in there but God Almighty. Just below, south of there, is the Omenica country and the government report for the last thirty years in the Omenica is $60,000,000 in gold taken out.

So now if I don't find gold it won't be the gold's fault and if I don't find it this summer I want to come back with a man the next time. And I know that John Cantlon and myself could and would find it right up here in this God forsaken country if we had one summer to hunt it in. To do that we would have to come in, in the winter or leave Edmonton the first of February and to come in with just enough grub to last us on the trip with the money in our pockets to buy the grub after we got in here for it takes a whole year to get from Edmonton to St. John with an outfit.

That is the only way to come in, in this country, with the money in your pocket and buy after you get in even if you do have to pay a big price for the grub. Two men with $800 in their pocket after they get to Fort Graham can buy an outfit to last them one year and have enough left to get out of the country or two men could go to work on a bar and wash out enough gold in thirty days to buy them another outfit and stay the second year or summer.

Now you have my opinions, my hopes and all, so wait patiently until you hear from me again. I may have better news for you and I may not have so good a news, but you will get it just as it is, good or bad. I am as jolly as a young colt. Bring Mr. Clark over to the house and the balance of the men I have mentioned and read them what I have said. I will do my best for them all whether I come home with a million or busted flat as a pancake. That's all for today.

Saturday 4th
Well this is a nice day but it was 22° below zero this morning. Tomorrow I am going a visiting, two of the Suckerville boys are down and I am going home with them to spend the Sunday, will come back Monday. Just going for a walk and to see how they live in Suckerville. They have a fiddle up there and they say there is a champion chess player up there so I guess they can entertain me all right.

Well mamma and kids, so you won't be under too much suspense about me, I will say that you can look for me home about Christmas or sometime in December maybe, it is owed to the luck I have and the amount of grub I have by next September. I may stay over or I may be up in the mountains with a bright prospect in view and stay over the next winter and part of the next summer. So now be contented and I will do my best to get a gold mine and be home in December if I can or I might come home late this fall and stay the winter at home and come back in February. One thing is certain, I am stuck on this job and the prospect there is up here and if I don't find anything this summer I must try it again for a couple of years. That's all until Monday.

Sunday evening 5th
Just before supper. I didn't go to Suckerville this morning. It was snowing hard and snowed up until dinner so I didn't go. I expect you will get tired of hearing me changing my plans about getting out of here or getting on the move. But you must take into consideration that this is a long letter and was commenced in December and gives me a chance to alter my plans. Now I don't think that we will get away from St. John before the 20th of March as the weather is not suitable and very changeable and we have to wait until the snow melts and then freezes up again. We will be here now I guess until the mail man gets back. On leaving here I will write you again and leave it here to be sent out the first one that goes out in the spring. The mail man leaves Wednesday the 8th rain or shine. Has to be in Dunvagen the 15th.
Goodnight.

Tuesday 7th
And is the last day I will have to write to you so now I will have to bring this short epistle to a close. I have been a long time writing this letter and I expect you will get tired reading it but if you will take this letter and the one before this one and read them both over, you will know what I have been doing all winter.

Now mamma, on leaving here for the mountains and gold fields I hardly know how to tell you to notify all correspondence to me, the Hudson Bay Co. brings mail in this way as far as Hudson Hope, that is as far as they bring it this way. You will have to write me two letters at a time and address them like this, one of them address James Hinkle, Hudson Hope via Edmonton, Alberta, Canada in care of Hudson Bay Co. and the other one James Hinkle, Fort Graham via Ashcraft, B.C. care of Hudson Bay Co. or put it this way, James Hinkle, Fort Graham via Ashcraft, British Columbia, NWT care of Hudson Bay Co.

If you send me letters this way I will be sure to get one of them or both of them because there are Klondykers coming by Hudson Hope that will bring mail from Hudson Hope to Fort Graham and by the Ashcraft route. The Hudson Bay Co. brings them direct to

Fort Graham and as we will be about fifty miles from Fort Graham and maybe at Fort Graham we will get our mail. Now notify Mr. Clark and all concerned. Be sure and notify Mr. Tivnen.

Well as I guess I am completely wound up I will bring this to a close at the present. This leaves me in tip top shape, in good spirits, full of hopes and ambition and I do hope it will reach you all safe and find you all in good circumstances and getting along all right. I will write you a letter on leaving Ft. St. John which will be about the 20th of March and as often as I can find anyone going out after I leave here.

Give my best wishes to all inquiring friends. Write me often and big letters and always write two letters and send them both ways as I told you. We are having snow every day this month. I will expect big letters from Myrty, Harry and Presh and lots of them and more cheer up, be in good spirits and I will try and be with you Christmas or in December with my shirt tail full of gold nuggets or rocks. Many kisses to you all mingled with several squeezes. Goodbye for this time.

I am your Klondyker papa Jim

• • •

From Hinkle's Journal

March 8, 1899 Hamilton, Pierre and Manley left for Dunvagen with the mail, Hamilton will be back the 22nd. Manley went out of the country in disgrace, forged an order on Burbank or gave an order and then traded it out and did the same with Butch and then skipped out.

Thursday, March 9 Nice day all day, went over to the island to visit Jack and the old man. Dash and Patty had a fight, they fought for ten minutes, Dash coming out victorious and making Pat holler.

Friday, March 10 Warmer but snowing in afternoon. Harry came down.

Saturday, March 11   Snowing all day, went up the river hunting about a mile.

Sunday, March 12   Nice warm day, 32° above zero. Seven Indians with the old chief arrived from the Nelson River. Had beef steak smothered with onions for dinner.

Monday, March 13   Nice warm day but not thawing any. Had a whist party up at Hudson Bay, got beat.

Wednesday, March 15   5° below zero. Two Klondykers arrived from Ft. Graham, they meet their boss at St. John. They report one death at Graham, good traveling on the river with five feet of snow at Graham, the coldest it was this winter up there was 57° below zero.

Thursday, March 16   Nice warm day. Peters is sick, he has ruptured himself and has sent to Suckerville for Dock.

Friday, March 17   Day of Ireland, we had some fun all day. Two new arrivals in St. John from twenty miles above the Portage. All of us old citizens decorated ourselves in green, also all the dogs had green, there were several imitations of drunks all day. Everybody was drunk on tea and had a good time in general.

Saturday, March 18   It has been cold and has been blowing and snowing all day. Cashman took supper with us. Peters is no better.

Sunday, March 19   Going to Suckerville, it has stopped snowing.

Monday, March 20   Arrived in Suckerville in time for dinner. After taking dinner with Werth, went around to visit the boys, found Pat, Sam and Henry at home and awful glad to see me. Went up to Docks, found Bob there waiting on Jeff, Jeff is awful low and can't live more than a week. Stayed all night at Sams, had a good time, left for home at 10.00 A.M. Arrived at home for dinner. Peters is no better.

Tuesday, March 21   Nice clear day but not thawing. Travers Bros. have come down from the Hope. Says there is nothing to eat there but grease and bannock.

Wednesday, March 22   8° below zero, nice day but not thawing. Fritz spent the afternoon with us.

Thursday, March 23   6° below zero. Sam and Wert came down from Suckerville, took supper with me, after supper went down to Cashman's, stayed until 12. Sam got sick on some turnips I had for supper.

14

Fort St. John

Fort St. John, B.C. NWT

Sunday, March 26, 1899

My dear wife and children.

The mail arrived Friday bringing me two letters, one dated October the 11th, one January 3rd, bringing me the sad news of the death of my father. It is an experience one doesn't realize until he has it come on him, way off in a wild country, it seems to be so much sadder. I don't know what it is unless it is being away from the busy world so far. Everything so still, not even the chirp of a bird for three months and with but a few human beings, a dog and the cold still forest moaning once in a while.

With the news of the death of a parent, it changes one's feelings and takes a strong will to say, "Well, it was God's will to take him away." I have the consolation to know that my father was an honest man, a Christian man and know that he is an angel now with my dear mother. He had run his race and now is beyond all trouble.

It has been two weeks since I sent you two letters, stating in them that I would write again on leaving St. John. So now I will write as I have a chance to send this out in a few days by the Hudson Bay Co., freighters who are on their way up from Dunvagen now with supplies for their store here. They are coming on the ice with sleighs. Will be here sometime this coming week.

In my last letter I told you that we would be gone from St. John by the 20th but you will see by this that we are still in St. John. We have been delayed on account of weather. The same all winter, the snow is laying here yet with the thermometer from 10° below to 20° above zero (through the day) and not thawing one bit. It will be late spring.

Last year the snow was all melted off the first of March. This year the same snow that fell in November will be here the first of April but it can't last much longer. All I hated about it, I did not get to the other side of Hudson Hope the first of March to do some trapping but we will be there yet in time to trap the biggest part of April and in time for the bear when they come out of their dens. They will come out now the first big thaw.

There is a party of Klondykers on their way in here now, will be here this week with thirteen bob sleds loaded with tools and provisions with ten men going up the river sixty miles above the Portage who have found a quartz mine and we will follow them up and have a good trail after them.

Now I have some good news for you. I wrote you in my last letter some encouraging news about this country and now I have more of which is facts. It is this party I speak of coming in this week who are known as Dr. Potts' party from Chicago. They were in here last summer prospecting and found a quartz rock sixty miles above Hudson Hope. They took specimens out and had them assayed and it ran $64.00 per ton and now are on their way up here with tools, men and supplies and powder to work their claim.

$64.00 per ton is rich ore. The biggest stamp mill in the world which is at Juneau only runs $4.00 per ton and if I get up there and find a quartz that pays that well I will have what I started from Mattoon after. All I have to do will be to stake my claim, have it recorded, come home and notify my company that I have found what they sent me after.

We all look for a bigger excitement up here this summer than there was at Dawson City. It is up here sure, if I can find it and I don't think it will be hard to find. Not as hard as cutting stove wood for John Webber at 75¢ per cord or making brooms either. Of course it is hard work but mamma, I was raised up to hard work and when I have so much hopes ahead it makes the work easy.

This will be good news to Mr. White, Clark, Montague, Katz and all of them. I will write them and send it out with this letter. I have not been sick a minute since I left home, not even a bad cold. Peters is sick now and has been in bed for two weeks. He has been sick off and on ever since we left Edmonton. I don't know what to think about him. I don't think he will be able to leave St. John and I am certain he won't be able to work or do half the work I can do this summer.

But I have made up my mind that if he won't go out home that he will not stop my progress for he knows that he is not able to stand the work and trip and should go out as soon as the water comes. He looks bad, he coughs lots and two weeks ago he was lifting on a log and ruptured himself and has been in bed and the house ever since. He can just get up and down and that is all.

As soon as the weather permits I will take the outfit and go on to the other side of the Portage. If he is not able, when I am ready to go, he will have to wait and come later on, but I will insist on him going home for he will be of no earthly use to me in the condition he is in.

I can't tell yet what I will do, but I think I will buy horses and pack instead of going by boat. All my Klondyke friends here are friends sure enough, not like friends one would have in the States but everybody here, which is about twenty-five men are to one another better than brothers. If anyone does the least little thing wrong to his fellow man, he is dropped and looked down on. No one seems to want to do anything that would look little or injure his fellow Klondyker. Such a thing as sucking around and trying to find out or taking advantage or mislead one another is out of the question. It seems that we are all in here for the same purpose and it is the feeling of all that there is enough room and gold up here for all without taking advantage of anything.

One party from Montana who are camped at Suckerville five miles up on top of the mountain have thirty two horses, some of their men are on the Nelson River two hundred miles away, sick.

They are going after them as soon as the snow melts enough and bring them to St. John to send them home, that is if they are no better. And they have told me that they would see that I got up in the mountains, they told me that they would loan me horses to pack my outfit.

They are going the same way we are. One of them hauls us to the other side of the Portage for 3¢ per pound so there is nothing to fear among the white men up here. But some of the Indians are mean and treacherous. Some are all right but there are only a few of them — about five hundred scattered all around that are of the Beaver tribe and they understand that pale faces won't stand any foolishness and they are cowed down and about half of the whites up here are Indian fighters and know all their tricks.

I was awful glad to get the two letters from you, also two papers and the Journal. Also two letters from Mr. Clark and one from Kahn written in Chicago, but was awfully disappointed in not getting any letters from the children. Just one little piece of paper from Myrt written wide apart and nearly one whole side of it filled up with kisses of different kinds and that horrible excuse of hers that she did not have time to write much which she has said now in every scrap she has sent me for eleven months and sixteen days, but was going to write me a big letter next week. I don't think I will get it for the next year.

She meant that it will be the week that I will be one hundred miles from here in the Rocky Mountains shut out completely from outside recourses and I will never get her next week's letter unless she ties it to a carrier pigeon and sends it in to me that way.

I will answer your two letters now. The first one was dated October 11, '98. My log book says on that day I was doing this (Tuesday 11th of October. Cut two cords of wood, nice day, Grimstons are working on their chimney. Peters baked bread and piddled around all day, made a complete failure baking bread. We have company, the Grimstons.)

Your letters start off with the same old story that Harry was going to write to me but didn't. You said he went to the shop and Doyle had him answering questions all day but you didn't say what kind of questions. You left it blank on the paper. I guess for me to guess at and I can't guess. So that much information is lost and no good to me. He had better stay on the local now for it won't be as hard as through freight, until he gets stout anyhow.

You say Hardesty came home sick. Well I don't see what would make him sick up here where a better climate never was. I don't understand why he would mail that letter I sent to you when he was going right straight home. But he didn't go right straight home it seems. He was a week behind the letter. Well I suppose he thinks he had a good time at the company's expense. He was not fit for the trip no more than some old woman.

Well so far as me making a showing, you may be sure that it is the heighth of my ambition and if I keep my health I will make a showing if it is up here to get at. I think you are pretty well acquainted with my determinations to know that I will conquer or bust trying. The people are right to think that all that ailed Hardesty was homesickness for that was all it was or the biggest part of it. And he didn't like Peters.

I don't see why you didn't have a stand during the street fair. Why is it that Myrty didn't play? So Harry is going to have a stand next year is he? He will be in an awful fix next year if they don't have a street fair. He will be like the butcher when the customer asked him if he had any fish. Yes, he had some but it was all gone.

Did you go home with Hat? You said you were packed like sardines on the train so you must have been on the train with her.

So now comes the most difficult subject of all to talk about and I don't know how to begin or what to say or how to say it. The subject is, Myrty is not through with her shorthand yet. I have been living in the highest of hopes from the time I was camped at Edmonton last April until January 1st camped at the mouth of North Pine River that she would be all through and have a good position, but all my hopes are thwarted.

One year gone and not through yet and she begged me so hard at first to let her learn it and that it would only take three months. Well I don't know what to say about it unless she quit it and saves shoe leather and takes up something else that she can learn.

Don't say anything more in any of your letters to me about it. I don't want to have the subject to think about anymore.

Presh I see has the same old chronic disease, a hollow leg. Well I would rather he would have a hollow leg, a place to put it than to have a platform in his stomach that wouldn't hold much and have to waste his bacon and eggs, mangoes, mush, pie, etc.

It was pretty near six months from the time you wrote your letter until I got it — five months and thirteen days. Well better late than never. No, I have no letter from Tivnen since I left Edmonton, was sure I would get a dozen from him in this last mail, but not a word from him. I got two from Clark and one from Kahn. I was looking for a letter from White sure but didn't get any. That finishes the one of Oct. 11, '98.

I will answer the one written Jan. 3, 1899. There was not one of the children at pap's death bed but Lou and Neva according to your letter. It looks strange to me that Hat, Nora and George could not be there and it don't look right — so close and them not there or William or John either. Was John Hinkle at the funeral?

You want to look out Presh that all the girls don't fall in love with you. Someone might kidnap you. I will skip that part of your letter where you are coaxing, begging and digging Myrty to go to school. I don't want to talk about it.

That's funny about Hardesty had to go braking. I suppose he is giving me fizz for coaxing him away from his good job. What's the matter with his brotherhood that they don't get him reinstated? So they are going to have a time when I come home are they? Well tell them so am I. It seems that they all want me to be successful of which you thank all for their kind thoughts of me.

I thought it about time for Reed to kick up a fuss, I expected to hear it long ago. You said if I was there for Christmas you would give me a bottle of perfume but as it was I would have to get my musk of my own manufacture or of the rat. There is no rat up here but we have some squaws that would make good musk or some husky dogs or the Beaver. But Beaver come high $1465 per ounce. I could use Peters old socks.

I will try and get you a fur cap if I can, I will get the fur myself of a different kind, say a piece of bear, one I kill myself, a piece of martin, a piece of beaver, a piece of coyote, a piece of wolverine, a piece of lynx, a piece of silver fox (they are worth $125.00 per skin) and get the Indians to make it if I can get up to the Portage soon and do some trapping and hunting. I can get all of this I mention and I will.

Don't you worry about Dash not fighting good because he lost his toenails. I'll bet a million dollars that he can lick his weight in wild cats. He is the most all around dog I ever saw and everybody is in love with him and wants to buy him. The Hudson Bay man offered me $50.00 for him. I just laughed at him.

Here is what he is, all facts. He is a good hunting dog, good trailer, he is a good retriever. I have killed ducks across the river and he would swim all day to get that duck and bring it to me. We killed one hundred fifteen pheasants at Pine River Camp and he got everyone of them. He is a trick dog, a genuine clown, here are some of the tricks I have taught him.

He sleeps under the stove and wakens me up of mornings and the first thing he does is to shake hands. I have taught him to talk. I ask him, "Dash, do you love me?" He will give one bark. I say, "Dash, do you want to go hunting?" He will bark a dozen times. I will say, "Dash, do you love Peters?" He will just give a grunt. It makes Peters so mad. I say, "Dash, go get the gun, it is hanging over my bed." He would go and get it if I would let him but I always take it from him.

He will get my hat and bring it to me and here are two of the last tricks I have taught him. I will set down to the table with my hat on, he will come and take it off and put it on the bed. The other trick is that when I come in the shack and leave the door open, I say, "Dash, shut the door." He rares up against it and pushes it shut. So he is all dog and a good one at that. He weighs 65 pounds. Makes up with everybody except the Indians, he don't like a redskin.

You say that Presh's girl gave him a muffler. When are they to be married? You mention getting three letters from me dated the 9th

October, 27th October and the 12th of November. My next letter after that one of November 12th, I think was a sketch of our camp at Pine River. I wonder if you got it, you didn't say anything about it. It is real good, If you only get it have it photographed.

You say you write every two weeks. Well then I don't get them for this last mail, one of your letters is dated October 13th and the other one January 3rd, '99. So there is from October 13th to January 3rd when I didn't get letters. It looks strange that I would get those particular letters and not get any between them.

I got the two Commercials and the pieces of Star papers and the BSE Journal but I didn't get any clippings of my correspondence which you said the Mattoon papers copies. Also you said they copied the sketch of the river I sent to you and that you would send me the paper. I believe you are a little absent minded.

Well you had a pretty good Christmas dinner and I thought of you when I was eating my Christmas dinner, me and Dash. I will tell you what me and Dash had. I had roast rabbit, roast pheasant and bread pudding with whiskey dip and apricot pie.

I can't make out who you mean by old Amerous — that you had heard enough about her. I don't know who you mean and I have studied it ever since I got the letter. Why don't you write names in full. No one sees my letters but Dash and myself. They must be getting pretty low for women to go in a bar room. Now look here old girl, you aren't going to get any divorce either if I stay more than two years for I won't let you even if I have to take you with me. I expect to stay more than two years in this country if I don't strike it this summer, but I expect to come home in the winter and then come back again unless I hear of a big strike close this fall. I will stay until I can get to where the strike is and get me a claim.

You see I am just as well off if I don't strike it myself for if anybody else strikes it, all that are up here will have it too. I would guess all the prospectors in this part of NW not to be over a hundred fifty so if one strikes it there will be enough for all and every Klondyker up here is just as anxious for anyone to find it as he is himself. So you can make up your mind to take a trip north in 1900 instead of going to the Paris fair.

You needn't worry about my money. I could leave $500 lay anyplace for a week and it would never be touched unless some animal would take it to make a nest with. They don't steal up here. Whole outfits are cached in places and left for months and nothing bothers it. The Indians are noted for the most honest beings on earth. To show you, one of the traders of St. John, by name Mr. Burbank, has a store a hundred miles out in the hills and hollows from St. John in the Beaver Indian's settlement. The chief of that tribe catches fur and takes it to that store. There is no one at the store at all. Burbank is in St. John, has a store here and leaves it and takes bacon, flour, beans, for so much fur, and if any of this tribe gets in debt to the store and wants a plug of tobacco or anything else, he makes them go and catch the fur first before they can have a cents worth. So you see there are no crooks or SB's up here at all.

About the Shaw boys — you have formed the wrong opinion of them. In the first place neither one of them had sense enough to have found a gold mine if it had been sticking out on the banks of the river and they run their head against it. The next place they were too lazy to hunt for a gold mine and thirdly they or none of us have come through a country yet that we would be likely to find a gold mine.

Nothing but fine gold on the sand bars in the rivers. That's all there is to be found until we reach the main mountains which are fifty miles farther west from St. John at Hudson Hope. No, they went home because they only had grub enough to last them to the first of April and only had 40¢ in money. We bought them out of their flour and fruit.

I am surprised at Harry letting my dues go unpaid. I want you to keep them up without fail. Tell Reed to come up here and he can fight one of these mountains and he won't have to eat any vinegar. No, Peters don't trap anything. He hasn't got sense enough to keep from getting caught in his own trap. He is always talking about what he is going to do and what he is going to catch but has done nothing only killed a few pheasants and Dash helped him to get them.

Coming up on Slave Lake we were camped for three days in the mouth of Swan River. He took his gun up the river about a mile and all at once we heard him commence to shoot. He shot eleven times as fast as he could shoot and came running into camp out of breath. I says, "What is the matter Jack?" He says, "The river is lined with geese. I killed four and run out of bullets and had to come back for more bullets." Well we counted the shots on him and he shot eleven times (ask Hardesty). He said he killed four geese, we all ran up there with our guns. He had killed one goose and not another goose in sight so he wasted eleven balls for one goose and told two lies besides.

Then he has told the Hudson Bay man here at St. John that he killed four swans in the mouth of Swan River. The Hudson Bay man happens to know all about that part of the country and told me there never was known to be a swan on that river so that is three lies he told about it. That is just the way he is about everything and everybody is down on him. Everybody talks about him and he has become the laughing stock of St. John. He has been sick for two weeks and none of them comes to see him. He has not got a friend in St. John or at Suckerville.

They all say to me, are you going up the river with that cracked head? Everybody likes me, everybody tries to get where I am. Everybody talks good about me behind my back. Everybody wants me to join their party. I have lots of friends, half breeds and all, he has none. I play the fiddle right good and play most of the time and it entertains the men all these long winter evenings. Peters is never there, is always at home by himself. No mamma, you need not be afraid to show to all of them all I say about Peters — Montague or anybody. I don't say it to ridicule the man, I say it because it is fact and he won't try to amend nothing but on the contrary does worse all the time.

It does me lots of good to know that Mr. Clark takes interest in all my letters. There is one man that I liked the first time that I ever saw him and like him more every day. The first time I saw Mr. Clark to know him was on the Pete Hoben and Wible murder case and I was foreman of the jury that tried Hefferman and Engles and Myrty was born while I was on the jury.

None of you guessed the conundrum so I won't have to dig up to make a present. You goose, you might have know that it was a set of chess. I wanted you to guess it so I could get you a present out of B.C.

Well what got the matter with Mages, it seems as though you people can make changes out there and think nothing of it. To me it wouldn't have surprised me any more if you told me that Freads had moved to Honolulu.

You tell Peg Johnson that she is a damned liar. Len Gilcrist never told her that I was coming home, that she is like a great many more women who are in the habit of stretching it. Len Gilcrist has got no letters from me and I don't believe that she told Peg anything of the kind. She might have told her that she heard that I was coming home. Be it which ever way it is, it don't concern me a little bit. I am after gold and am attending to my business.

The whole petticoat government don't have any effect on me whatever. If I stay up here a couple more years I expect I would rather be with my gun, dog, pick and shovel than to be with a woman and will think they were only made and put on earth to bother men.

So you can tell Peggy old sock that here, Gilcrist can't bother me any. All that is bothering me is that if I find 500 lbs. of gold how I will get the blasted stuff out of here without killing my fool self for I will be sure to try and carry it all at one time.

Well that answers yours of January 3rd, '99 so I will rest. I have to answer Mr. Clark and Kahn's letter.

Monday, March 27
This is Monday 27th and will give you some more writing. Snowing this morning and is not thawing. Yesterday nice day. Will light my pipe and go up to Hudson Bay and play the fiddle.

I suppose you are anxious and have been waiting for me to say something about the women up here, how many and if there is any pretty squaws and so on. So I guess I will tell you. John Shaw is a half breed Indian and his wife is a squaw as ugly as sin. She goes by here every day with a papoose strapped on her back. Burbank is a trader and is a white man and his wife is a squaw, not very bad looking, about as dark as a creole. Old-man-looks-like-the-devil's wife is a squaw and is, I would judge by the wrinkles on her, about 89 and looks like the bark on one of these poplar trees. Old Mrs. Eat-the-butchers-beef lives with Mrs. Big-leg-like-a-horse. They are two old maids I think. Miss Eat-the-butchers-beef is six and a half feet tall and has only one eye and is about a hundred years old I guess. Mrs. Big-leg-like-a-horse is about three feet tall and has one leg big like you have seen on horses hind leg. That is all the women there are short of fifty miles. There is none to fall in love with. That is all for today.

Tuesday the 28th
It is snowing this morning just as hard as it can come down. It will soon be the first of April and it will soon be one year since I left home. Does it seem that long to you? I won't say myself. It is a late spring up here. I reckon it will quit some time. We will get away from here the last of next week.

There is a chance that I will get some more mail from you before I have to leave St. John if we don't get away for a couple of weeks. By that time there is liable to be some outfits from Edmonton and the preacher is to come yet who was to have been back in January. I am just as anxious now to get some more letters from you as I was before I got the last ones.

If I can get January and February's mail I can go away from here satisfied if they are good news from you. But I don't think now, from old reports, that I will be more than sixty or seventy miles from Hudson Hope. If I am not, it won't take long to go there and get the mail or to Fort Graham. Don't forget too, when you write me always write three letters — one to Hudson Hope via Edmonton, Alberta, Canada in care of Hudson Bay Co. and one to Fort Graham via Ashcraft B.C. in care of Hudson Bay Co. — no just write two letters. You understand that all letters addressed to Fort Graham goes by the way of Ashcraft. The letters addressed to Hudson Hope go by the way of Edmonton, sometimes are taken to Fort Graham by parties going up Peace River to Fort Graham. That is if I leave word at Hudson Hope for my mail to be forwarded up the river. That's all today. Mamma, add on your letters to me that are directed by way of Edmonton, ON PEACE RIVER.

This is Friday and the last day of March and we haven't gone yet. It is a late spring, snow is here yet — four feet of it and today, the last day of the month, is just like the first day was. The sun shines bright but not thawing a bit. We are looking for it all to come at once when it does come. It will be the middle of April before we get away from St. John and maybe longer. We are all somewhat disappointed over the late spring. That's all today.

Saturday, April 1st
April fool. Well nine days more will be one year since I left home. This is a beautiful day overhead but it isn't thawing one bit. Just now the Dr. Potts party pulled into St. John, twelve teams of them and ten men. They left Edmonton the 7th of February. They brought no mail as the mail man passed them at Dunvagen and brought it with him.

They will camp here over Sunday and pullout Monday for about seventy miles the other side of Hudson Hope where they claim they have a quartz mine that assayed $64.00 per ton. If it is true, which I guess it is, we will strike it ourselves up there this summer. We will pull out two days behind them if we can get word to our man at Suckerville to get the horses and sleighs ready. So I guess next week we will shake the frost off of our feet out of Ft. St. John and go up in the mountains where the bear and gold is. That's all today.

Sunday eve, April 2nd
Just at candle light and will have to finish this letter between now and tomorrow morning as this outfit that brought the Hudson Bay supplies in yesterday are going back tomorrow and I will have a chance to send this to you. It will take just about twenty-five days for it to reach Edmonton and five days from there to Mattoon So you see how much I miss it. About May 4th you will have it.

Well mamma up to this evening the snow has not melted a bit. The sun shines bright all day but the thermometer stands at 30° above all the time through the day. At night it gets cold. Yesterday morning it was 4° below zero. This morning it was 2° below zero so you see it is a late spring. There is four feet of snow on the ground now on the level.

But this Dr. Potts outfit are going to start on up the river this week as soon as their horses rest some and when they do go we will follow them up to the other side of the Portage so we will be that far before the ice goes out and we have a boat there. I am going to buy four horses there and sell the boat and go by pack horses when we get there. We are in the Rocky Mountains then and a boat is no good to prospect with in the mountains, must have horses, so as to prospect the small streams, the gulches, the hills and hollows.

I can't say when you will get the next letter from me but it will be when these men or freighters that are taking Dr. Potts party to the Omenica River return, they will meet us at the Portage and will send you a letter then and tell you how we got to the other side of the Portage.

Now I guess I have told you all I know and more too so I will close as I am writing Mr. Clark and Kahn a letter too. Let Mr. Clark know of you getting this letter and see if he gets one from me at the same time.

Some advice to the boys. Boys, don't forget the last words I told you when I bid you goodbye one year ago the 9th of this month. Take good care of your mother and sister. Stop before you go to spend a cent and think, "Does mamma need anything, does sister need anything?" Spend your money on them and you will live just as long and be a great deal happier at the end than if you spent it foolishly and you know too it is your duty you owe to them, to take care of them.

Direct your letters like this, James Hinkle, Hudson Hope (on Peace River) B.C. via Edmonton, Alberta, Canada, in care of Hudson Bay Co. and like this, James Hinkle, Fort Graham via Ashcraft, B.C. in care of Hudson Bay Co. You need not write them both alike but write them about a week apart. So now I will quit, give my best wishes to all friends. This leaves me as stout as Kid McCoy anyhow. Hoping I will hear good news from you in your next letter. Many many kisses to you all. Jas. Hinkle

• • •

FROM HINKLE'S JOURNAL

Monday, April 3, 1899 Warmer and thawing. Dock and Bob and Henry came down. Henry went after horses to take us to the Portage, was all up to the Hudson Bay tonight and playing the fiddle, Indians dancing a jig, everybody had lots of fun. Played a game of chess before supper with one of the Potts party, by name Bob, I beat him bad.

Tuesday 4 The Dr. Potts party left for up the river at noon, Shaw's man pulled out with the mail for Slave Lake Post, the Hudson Bay men went back fifty miles after their loads. Henry has not come from Suckerville yet with the horses. Two Indians arrived with dog train. Bob took dinner with us.

Wednesday 5 Warmer, 58° above zero. Henry has not come yet. Hamilton arrived at 3:30 P.M. from Hudson Hope. Pat, the Indian, arrived with fur. All the dogs, fifteen of them, had a fight. Dash cut his foot on the ax, he was not in the fight. Billy and Mrs. Burbank had a fuss about something written on a shingle.

Thursday 6 Still warmer, 60° above zero. It rained last night and today a little. The first of the season, the snow is melting fast. Don came back from Deep Creek. Henry has not come yet, I am getting tired of him and will cancel the bargain if he don't get a hustle on himself.

Friday 7 Henry and Sam came and are getting ready to take us up the river.

Saturday 8 Still thawing. Henry has gone up to Deep Creek after his horses, the Hudson Bay teams arrived, brought me one letter from Clark. Digby arrived from Pine River, Spencier has got the scurvy.

Sunday 9 One year ago I left home. Warmer today than any day, 60° above, snow going fast. Henry got back from Deep Creek with the horses. Dave leaves in the A.M. for Hudson Hope. Got a letter today from mamma and Myrty, lots of news from home, am answering them today.

Monday 10 Colder, snow melting some. Don left at 9:00 A.M., Wert and Johnson came down from Suckerville, Dock and Pete are getting ready to go the river on the ice. Sent two letters out today, one to Clark and one to folks at home. Been working all day getting things ready to start up the river in the A.M.

Tuesday 11 Started for up the river at 8:00 A.M. Got along all right for eight miles, then the snow got soft, snow and water ten inches deep every place, got stuck on some big rocks, had to portage mud Deep Creek. Finally about 7:00 P.M. found Don and Butch, Butch and Lamb went to St. John with dog team after Biff, Schultz and Foster are here in camp with a sick man with scurvy.

Wednesday 12 Got up at 4:00 o'clock to get breakfast to get an early start, just after I got a fire started it commenced to snow all over my bed, went into camp for the day. It snowed until 2:00 P.M. We expect to start in A.M. Henry is out after horses, Peters is cooking a pot of beans.

Thursday 13 Got up at 3:30, made biscuits. It froze good last night, we started at 6:00 A.M. Good going, made half way by 3:30 P.M. I was about played out, laid down and went to sleep on my bed out on the ice in the middle of the river. Don and Jack caught up to us, it snowed in the evening.

Friday 14   Had a good night's sleep, started at 6:00 A.M., made to Red River. We are in sight of Hudson Hope, eight miles from it.

Saturday 15   Left camp at 5:30 A.M., good ice, made within half mile of Hudson Hope, snow and ice played out, had to pack from there to on top of first bench at Hudson Hope. Don upset in the river trying to get farther, got all of his stuff wet but the flour. We are in camp for over Sunday.

Sunday 16   In forenoon packed the balance of stuff up to camp, in afternoon killed one pheasant, it rained some and snowed some.

Tuesday 18   Snowed all night, four inches of snow by noon, awful wet snow. Have been in camp all day and night by myself.

Wednesday 19   Quit snowing, sun shining, hot all day, snow all melted. We start in the A.M. for across the Portage.

Thursday 20   Left camp for the Cust House at 7:00 A.M. Snow thawing fast, got along all right. Arrived at Cust House at 3:00 P.M. Caught up with the Potts party, everybody is stuck here. It rained just after we got here, Don is here and Tom Shark.

Friday 21   Nice day but a cold wind. Don went up to Fritz's, twenty miles, I went down a mile in the canyon. Henry and Sam left for St. John. We bought six pack saddles off them.

Saturday 22   Went prospecting, found a good prospect, made a grizzly and am going to try it Monday.

Sunday 23   Nice warm day, Don is getting ready to pack up the river, Tom is out after his horse and can't find it, they are both mad, I guess because it is Sunday.

Monday 24   Nice warm day, the ice is breaking up in the river, snow is melting fast. Finished the grizzly and wheel barrow and set it up ready for work in the A.M. Don has gone with his horses light, is going to try and get them through and then take his stuff through on a boat. Pete has gone back to the Hope, Anderson leaves in the A.M. for Edmonton, am sending a letter out by him to the folks.

Tuesday 25   Nice day, bought six horses from Harkes for $165.00. Been washing gold today, have not got it amalgamated yet. Ice going out fast, had to move grizzly four times today. River is raising and ice jamming at the mouth of the canyon. Anderson has gone back.

Wednesday 26   Gold panned out about 60¢ for about two hours work. Harkes brought the horses up to camp, made a bill of sale and we accepted them. Tom and two of Fritz's men arrived in the evening. Don has gone on up the river trying to get his horses through.

Thursday 27   Cold wind all night with spitting snow all day, freezing all day. Peters has taken the horses up the river five miles to where there is good feed, took the shoes off them. Tom is hunting his horse.

Friday 28   Nice day until 6:00 P.M., then cold showers with lots of wind. River raised two feet, ice is jammed in canyon. Been washing gold until 3:00 P.M. Have quit it, the gold is too fine, can't make but about a dollar a day.

Saturday 29   Cold with snow showers all day. Went up in the A.M. to look after the horses, found four of them, couldn't find Sally and Buddy.

Sunday 30   Still cold with snow showers, a great big ice jam in the mouth of Canyon River, raised five feet, pulled the boat up the bank, Pete came, also Frank Anderson and Joe and two of Fritz's men.

Monday May 1   Snowed and blowed all night, ground covered with inch of snow, went up to look after horses after hunting all of British Columbia and part of Canada over. Found them chuck full up to the neck. Snowed all forenoon, got back at 2:00 P.M. Went and got some spruce boughs and fixed my bed. I am tired.

Tuesday 2 Still cold, windy and cloudy. Tom found his horse, Don came back, didn't get through the canyon, we are all going to pack up tomorrow.

Wednesday 3 Went up and got the horses, packed up after dinner, two hundred pounds to the horse. Left camp at 2:00 P.M., made five miles to where the horses are on feed, camped for the night. Got along all right considering green horses.

Thursday 4 Started at about 7:00 A.M. Made half way to Fritz's, went into camp at the mouth of a creek for the night. Got along very well considering.

Friday 5 Started early, made Fritz's by 5:00 P.M., had lots of trouble. Bad trail. Peters was ahead and got on the wrong trail. Got down a very steep hill and could not get back only with three of the horses. The other three could not get back up with their packs. All three of them fell down and rolled over and over down the hill with their packs on. Unloaded and carried the packs up the hill, loaded up and went a mile and ate dinner.

Saturday 6 Left our stuff at Fritz's, came back to Cust's House after the balance of the outfit, got in to Cust's House at sundown.

Sunday 7 Nice day but cloudy, Peters has gone to take the horses up to the pasture. Getting things ready to start in the A.M.

Monday 8 Got up before the sun was up, ate breakfast, went after the horses, found four of them together, hunted for an hour for Baldy, Give him up and started with the four, by chance I run into Baldy, tailed them all up and got into camp and are all ready to start after tea, made eight miles.

Tuesday 9 Started early, got along all right, made Fritz's, pretty tired. Don and Tom are gone, Lamb and Schultz caught up with us. Nice day and windy. First mosquitoes last night.

Wednesday 10 In camp all day repacking the outfit. It is a cold and windy day with spurts of snow. Lamb and Schultz arrived at dinner time, gone into camp for a week.

Thursday 11 Started after I baked bread, got about a mile, Nellie fell down the high bank with pack on, got pack off her and got her up and she rolled over and over down the steep bank to the river. Thought sure her neck was broken but came out all right except a bunged eye. Got her up on top once more and got along all right for six miles only. Peters don't know no more about picking out a trail or following one than some blind saw.

Friday 12 A.M. Up and had breakfast, Peters has gone to look up a trail. It has been snowing little showers all morning. Peters has got back, killed one pheasant and is cooking it for dinner. After dinner we will go back to Fritz's and bring the balance of the stuff up tomorrow. The mountains are high and rough, trail is very brushy but not hard to get along. Snowed hard in afternoon, big frost last night.

Saturday 13 Left Fritz's at 8:00 A.M., got to camp at noon. Lamb and Schultz packed up in afternoon.

Sunday 14 Nice day but windy, in camp over Sunday. Peters has gone up the river, am writing letter to folks.

15

Thirty Miles From Cust's House

Thirty miles up the river from Cust's House

Sunday May 14, '99

Dear Mollie and Harry, Myrty and Presh,

As my last letter was not a very long one or not as long as I expected it would be, there being a party going out (the government survey party) and I had such a good chance to send you a letter. I finished the last letter up in a hurry and will now commence another one continued from day to day.

We ate in camp over Sunday having packed all of our outfit from Fritz's yesterday evening. We are camped up on the side of a mountain, on the side the sun shines on and the wind blows through your whiskers. It is not cold and it is not any too warm. A cold wind blowing off the mountains and snow. We had duck and pheasant last night for supper and duck this morning for breakfast. I killed them yesterday evening. Had rice cooked with apricots and pearl barley and bacon for dinner.

We can only go twenty-five miles farther until the snow melts off. The farther up we get the more snow there is and we'll have to wait until the sun melts it sometime in June I suppose. We take half of our stuff up about six or eight miles at a time and then come back after the balance. By degrees we are getting there, aren't losing any time. By the time we get it all up twenty-five miles, maybe the snow will be all gone.

Cantlon nor anyone else has come to join us yet. I wish he would come if he is coming at all. It is hard work for two men or one man and a boy. Lamb and Schultz party are camped a quarter of a mile below us.

I would like to hear from you now but the Lord only knows when I will get a letter from you and I would like to know what is the matter with Tivnen. I haven't got a line from him for a year, not since I left Edmonton and I have written him a dozen times. I get letters from Mr. Clark regular and some from White, Kahn and Montague but none from Tivnen. I wish you would ask him if he has written any and how many and of what date. Something may be wrong, if there is I will find out.

Well Myrty old socks, this is our month of birthdays, yours the 27th and mine the 29th. Mamma did you know I was 47 years old the 29th of this month? Well I am just the same. I had a dream about you all last night. I thought I came home on a visit and I thought I was in the kitchen just a kissing and a hugging Myrty and I thought Mr. White came in and fell down over a bench to get to me and shake hands and I thought Mr. Katz and Mr. Montague and Mr. Tivnen and Mr. Kahn and Mr. Jantia and a whole lots of them were all leaning toward me with their hands reached out to shake with me and I thought Mr. Clark was setting down by the stove and saying, 'boys take your time to it, you will all have a chance to shake his fist' and when I wakened up, Dash was laying beside me with his paw across my breast. I says, "Dash, you done all of that". Well I will quit for today and take a stroll up higher on the mountain. Tra la la

Wednesday the 17th
Well we are camped on Eight Mile Creek, so marked on the map, about five miles farther up than we were Sunday, got here at noon with the balance of the outfit and have just got back from fishing, had fish for supper. I caught eight pounds. Gee whiz but if I'm not having fun.

Well sir, I laughed yesterday 'til I liked to have lost my breath. Back at the other camp in the evening Dash and I went bear hunting. So I climbed up one mountain next to camp and went up a canyon about a half a mile and I saw Mr. Bear away up on the side of the mountain. I couldn't get to him without climbing on another mountain about eight miles straight up so, gosh but I laughed, climbed up and got up within three hundred yards of his bearship, he never saw me and Dash at all. By gingo I split my sides laughing. He was a big fellow and as black as coal. Well I couldn't get any closer to him. Now Enoch, I wasn't afraid at all, but I couldn't get any closer on account of, well laugh, I guess I did. There was a small canyon between me and the bear so I knew I was too far most to kill him only by chance, so I says, "I will let you have it anyhow", so I raised the sights on my gun to three hundred yards and took a dead rest at him and waited 'til he got broad side of me and let him have it.

Well I wish you could have seen that bear anyhow and I wish you could have seen Dash and I wish you could have seen me. Joke on the mountain. Well I hit him all right. He whirled around and rared up in the air and down the side of the mountain he went end over end. Gee whiliker but I laughed and Dash after him.

Well I only crippled him so he climbed the other side of the mountain. Well if that wasn't the prettiest chase I ever looked at and I was up where I could see it all. Well Dash run him around on the side of the mountain three times and me a shooting at him but he was too far for me to hit him only by chance shot but I just kept cracking away and laughing as hard as I could.

Well I was afraid Dash would catch him and if he did, that would be the last of Dash for one swipe with that paw would split Dash wide open and you can't stop Dash from nothing after the first crack of a gun. Well finally the bear took straight up the canyon and Dash after him and he run him for about a half hour. I couldn't see Dash, bear or anything. Says I to myself, "Goodbye Dash, you have been a mighty good dog, but I suppose your mangled remains are too horrible to look at". So I called him and called him and finally I shot the gun off. In about ten minutes here he came plumb give out. I was so glad I took him up in my lap and let him rest and got him some snow to eat. Well sir, I laughed the way that bear was taken by surprise and the way he went down that hill, then I went to the camp. That's all for this evening. Ta Ta

Thursday 18th
We are still in camp at Eight Mile Creek. Thought I would let the horses rest up for another day. Peters has gone up the trail six or seven miles to see how it is. I am all alone in my tent — nothing but the trees, mountains, creek, wind and just me. We are twelve miles from the Ne-parle-pas rapids — will pull out for there in the A.M.

The weather is warm but not enough to melt the snow off these high peaks very fast. We can't prospect any yet for a month and by that time we will be up to where we commence to prospect at the Wicked River and the mouth of the Parsnip River and Omenica River for a few miles. Cantlon has not come yet. The Dr. Potts party went by here yesterday in boats. They go to the Aspeca River which is up the Omenica River a few miles. That's all for today. Haven't much to talk about. I will wait until I find a bear. Ta ta.

Saturday 20th
In camp for over Sunday. We are not making much progress, can't get Peters to make a move without just forcing him, he wants to rest the horses all of the time. They rest three days in the week besides Sunday and then he still wants to rest the horses more. He is the damndest bore I was ever with. I can't see what he is up here for but I will fool him this summer, he will not monkey with me this summer as he did last summer and get no place for I am going to travel this summer and get where I want to get if I have to divide up the outfit and hire a man to go with me. We have only got about six miles farther to go until I am where there is good prospects to find gold and he has got to go or else quit one or the other.

We are having some May showers occasionally but the snow is still on the tops of the mountains yet, we have plenty of time. But I don't want to let a day go by when it is nice weather, to keep on traveling for after while it will be hot and the flies and mosquitoes will be bad. I will quit for this eve and eat supper. Have cold beans for supper and I am going to fry some onions so ta ta.

Sunday 21st
I will write a little and tell you what I have been doing today. Now I went fishing so I did Myrty, it isn't wrong to go fishing on Sunday when a fellow is so close to a river is it? Now don't tell your Sunday school teacher about it. I did go so I did and I caught just one fish and I have just eaten it for my supper. It didn't taste any different from any other days in the week. Peters went up the trail a ways today. He killed one grouse, now that isn't goose, but grouse, and we had that for supper, had rice and stewed apples too.

If you folks will note and take my letters and put them all together you can see what I have been doing for a year every day pretty near, where we are now the mountains are very high and rough. The valley of the river is about a half mile wide, the mountains are all covered with trees. Small ones, spruce, poplar, some cedar and some birch. All of the tops of the mountains and half way down on both sides of the river are covered from a foot to three feet of snow yet.

The river has raised five feet since we left Cust's House. Lamb and Schultz party are in camp for a week back of us five miles. They are letting their horses feed up and rest. I don't think or expect to get any word from you until we reach the Parsnip River which is about fifty miles from here unless Cantlon overtakes us or by chance someone overtakes us from St. John or Hudson Hope. When we get to the Parsnip River we will have a chance to get mail. As that is the river that the Hudson Bay boats comes down to take their supplies to Fort Graham.

Well Myrty, I suppose that you are getting ready to celebrate your 20th birthday. Last May 27th I was at Athabasca Landing. This 27th of May I will be five hundred and eighty miles from there on Peace River in B.C. in the Rocky Mountains but ever thinking of you and on the 29th I will be just two days farther ahead I suppose. Well you have a good time and I will have a good time thinking about it.

Mamma did you know I was 47 years old the 29th of this month? But I can't catch you unless you stop a little while. See — it will be way past both of these dates before you get this letter, but you just refer back a little. I will quit for today. We took a load up the river in the A.M. about six miles, maybe ten. Have to go to where ever there is feed for the horses. Goodbye and don't tell anyone I went fishing today.

Tuesday May 23rd
Have just arrived with all of our outfit up to this place about sixteen miles above Fritz's and about thirty-five miles from Cust's House and are somewhat disappointed. But not discouraged a bit. I am after gold. Today we met Dan Killum and Lamb and Schultz coming back. Lamb and Schultz had gone up horse back to where Dan was and to where the main range commences about nine miles farther up than where we are now, to see what the prospect was for getting through. They were up there nine days and today we met them on their way back. Say they are going back thirty miles to Hudson Hope and go back on the old Graham trail and go straight to Fort Graham. It will take them two months to go that way and make Graham.

Well we don't want to go to Graham, only want to go to the mouth of the Omenica River which is sixty miles this side of Graham and only about fifty miles from where we are now. They were mad because we and Fritz's didn't come on up to where they were and help to cut the trail. Said they weren't going to cut a trail for Fritz's and him setting at his cabin waiting for them to do so. They weren't so mad at us for we were doing our best to get to them to help cut the trail but on account of having to double with our stuff we got along slow.

Now we are going on up there and if we can't get through with pack horses we will go back to the Cust's House and get our boat and get through that way and take our horses through light. There is only twenty-five miles of this bad place and we will wiggle through it some way.

It is awful warm up here right now but the snow is still on the mountains. The river is rising about a foot per day. Cantlon has not come yet and I don't believe now that he or anyone else is coming. That's all. I am setting yeast, going to bake in the A.M. Ta ta.

About sundown. I thought I had said everything but I didn't. Had supper and just got the horses all picketed out, doggon them, I couldn't keep them no place and the idea struck me that I would take the cinch ropes which are thirty feet long and tie them up, now I guess I won't have to run three miles in the morning to find them. This is the first time I have tied them up.

Mr. J.R. Peters of Seattle, Washington in the United States over on the coast has got the toothache, has had it for a week. I wish you could see me by gingo, I believe I am a red skin, anyhow I am as red as one.

Well this is a funny country up here. I don't know what it is good for unless it is to make Illinoisians and Washingtonians work and for it to hold the gold in. You couldn't make a half a mile a day if you would go any other direction than up or down this river. All back on both sides of the river it looks just like you had cut down a hundred acres of hay and stacked it all up in stacks all over it and some of them big and some little. Way back you can just see the tops of the biggest ones. I have been up as high as a mile and got tired and came back and thought what a funny world this is. The birds will light right on you, they don't know what we are. I guess that's all now. I am going to bed pretty soon. Ta ta.

Wednesday 24
I have just got done baking. There is no red skins around here. Have not seen any since left Cust's House. Peters has gone up the trail to see how and what it looks like. Nobody around but me and Dash and the birds.

Jack has come back. He says it is a proper SB of a trail the next four miles. So I guess we will have a time tomorrow. That's all today.

Thursday 25
Are in camp. It commenced to rain after breakfast and has kept it up all day. A real wet rainy day. I guess it has to do something to put the time in. I don't know but I think we are going to have a time getting through the next twenty-five miles and probably will take a month to do it and probably will have to go back and get

the boat and there will be a lot of hard work about it for two men. I wish we had another man and three more horses. We need them by all means.

I thought sure the way Mr. Clark talked in his last letter that they had sent a man to meet us, but it don't look much like it now for he should have caught up with us before this if he was coming. However we will do the best we can.

Tomorrow if it don't rain we will make Otter Tail Creek which is four miles. I don't know if it is marked on your map or not. It is about forty miles from the Cust's House and empties into the Peace River from the north side. Dan Kilman was up six miles farther than that with his outfit and cut some trail still farther than that but got mad and swore he wasn't going to cut all of the trail by himself for the balance of the Klondykers and I don't blame him much either. That's all for today.

About sundown.
I'm not done yet either. It just quit raining about 3:00 P.M. and I went up the trail a ways and it is as Mr. J.R. Peters says, a proper son of a gun. A mile from our camp we have to climb right straight up over a mountain and our horses can't pack over fifty pounds at a time so you see it is a proper something. It will take us all to get our stuff to the top. But I guess we can do it if we have to take pound up at a time. Just imagine us tomorrow, all of us, horses and all standing on end for about a day.

While I was up the river there was a boat come down with five men, one of them was Butch or the butcher that we was with all winter at St. John. He had been to Fort Graham and was on his way back to St. John and from there he goes home some place close to Montreal, Canada. He said he met Tom, that's the fellow that was with Don at the Findlay Rapids and that he would be back down the river in ten days. And if there was any mail at Graham for me he would likely have it. Butch said he saw the Hudson Bays boats on their first trip going to Graham and if you have sent any mail by Ashcraft I expect they had it. I wish I could have been there. Don't know when anyone will be up this way. Haven't heard of anyone yet coming. Well that's all, I will tell you all about it tomorrow. Bye bye.

Friday about 4:00 P.M.
I just got back about an hour ago. We took the horses up light to Otter Tail Creek where there is better feed for them and Jack has taken one horse and a week's grub and gone on up the river to see if we can get through first before we do anything else. Fun, I guess I am having fun.

Harry, you ought to be up here and help me to have fun, we all stood on end for a while going up. Just the same as if you would cut steps in a tree and drive six horses up it and then after while come down on the other side the same way. Old Sally the big kneed heifer slipped once but she caught again and got all right.

Well we went down the other side and right at the foot of the mountain is Otter Tail Creek, only thirty feet wide and thirty feet deep. We cut a tree and fell it across it so we could walk over. Tied a cinch rope thirty feet long to the — gee whiz but I laughed — tied to the one end of the horse and I had hold of the other end, my but I just hollered, and Jack would push them in and I would haul them across. Everyone of them but Dick went clear under. Cracky how I did laugh and haul in on the rope and say, "I baptize thee in the name of Otter Tail Creek".

Well after baptizing we turned them loose on the grass and Jack loaded up his horse and went on and I came back to camp, oh it was fun. But don't say anything about it, I don't want anyone else there to come up here unless you might tell Jim Gillespi. We will be in camp here a week. That's all today. Tomorrow is Myrty's birthday. My I would like to give you twenty stripes. Ta ta.

No I'm not done yet either. It is raining a cold rain and I have got a big campfire going and I am all by myself. I'm not afraid, no I'm not a bit afraid but it puts me in mind as though I was on the moon and couldn't get down again. It is awful nice to be a bum. A person don't get a bit afraid. If I could just have a bear or two come and visit me. But somehow they won't come. They say they are fond of music so I guess I will play the fiddle, maybe that will fetch them, I have been all alone since yesterday.

Another day
And I will put in my time today writing to Myrty. First thing I did this morning was to go up this canyon about a mile, I thought I might get a shot at a bear and I could have that to talk about. But nary bear did I see, so the thought struck me I would get some birch bark and write you a bit of poetry on it, so you will find on the bark what I said. It may not suit you but that is the best I could do.

Now you can have it printed into a song and get George Gibler to make the music to it and play it on the piano and probably can get a half a cent a copy for them. If I had some paper big enough I would make you a sketch of this place and all around here. But I will have to tell you about it when I come.

It is kind of lonesome here today, but I don't care, I guess it is because I am thinking of you. Peters will be gone four or five days. All I have to do is to eat and sleep and get lonesome and hunt and wait and look at the mountains and watch for bear and look at the river. The mosquitoes have come in great shape and sizes good and plenty, there are some the size of a Kansas grass hopper and they aren't afraid of me, have to make a smudge in my tent every night to scare them away.

Well I'll bet you are right now eating chicken for it is about one o'clock by this mountain. I will have to eat pig and pancakes for my dinner, have run out of fresh meat. Say if anybody asks you where was your papa on your last birthday, you tell them that he was in British Columbia cutting wood. After dinner I took the gun and ax and I thought I would go up and see how the horses were getting along and change the trail some on this bad place. Well I changed it and I cut and cut all afternoon 'til sundown. Just got back and have had supper. Oh but it is fun up here in this big large British Columbia cutting wood and looking after horses and climbing mountains and packing horses and unpacking horses etc. Oh it is a lulu. But I am after gold.

Well for a change it snowed a little today. It can do anything up here, all in one day too. Well old socks, the 9th of October will be eighteen months since I left home and that is the day our time expires unless they agree to keep us the two years. So our grub will run out the first of November and then I guess I will start toward Illinois if I can get down these mountains. Anyhow it will be cheaper for me to come home even if they do agree to extend the time.

But if I haven't found gold by the 9th of October and should there be a strike made around up here I shall fly to it first and then fly home. It will take me a month and a half to get home after I start. We have great hopes of finding a gold mine up here if we can only get to it. There is good reports from Wicked River and we are only twenty-five miles from that river now. It is on the river that the Dr. Potts party has a quartz claim instead of the Apeca River. So if we can get through these twenty-five miles am pretty sure of getting a claim or two anyhow. Well I guess I have said enough for today. I suppose your back is good and sore by the pounding you got today. Ta ta.

Another day

Have just got supper, me and Dash just got back from looking after the horses. It didn't rain today but it came pretty near. I haven't much to talk about. I am getting tired of being in camp so long. I am anxious to be on the move. Everything goes better. Time flies away and one can keep his mind occupied about other things besides home affairs and is not so lonesome.

I suppose you are wondering, why don't he prospect where he is? There is no use, we are not in the right kind of formation yet, not out of the sand stone formation. But I do prospect every creek and canyon as we go along and up in the mountains too but no indications have I found, only on the sand bars in the river and that you can find every place you try. From a dollar to five dollars a day can be made on the bars.

If we can make Wicked River we will be in a different formation and we'll do a great deal of prospecting on that river. I look for Jack

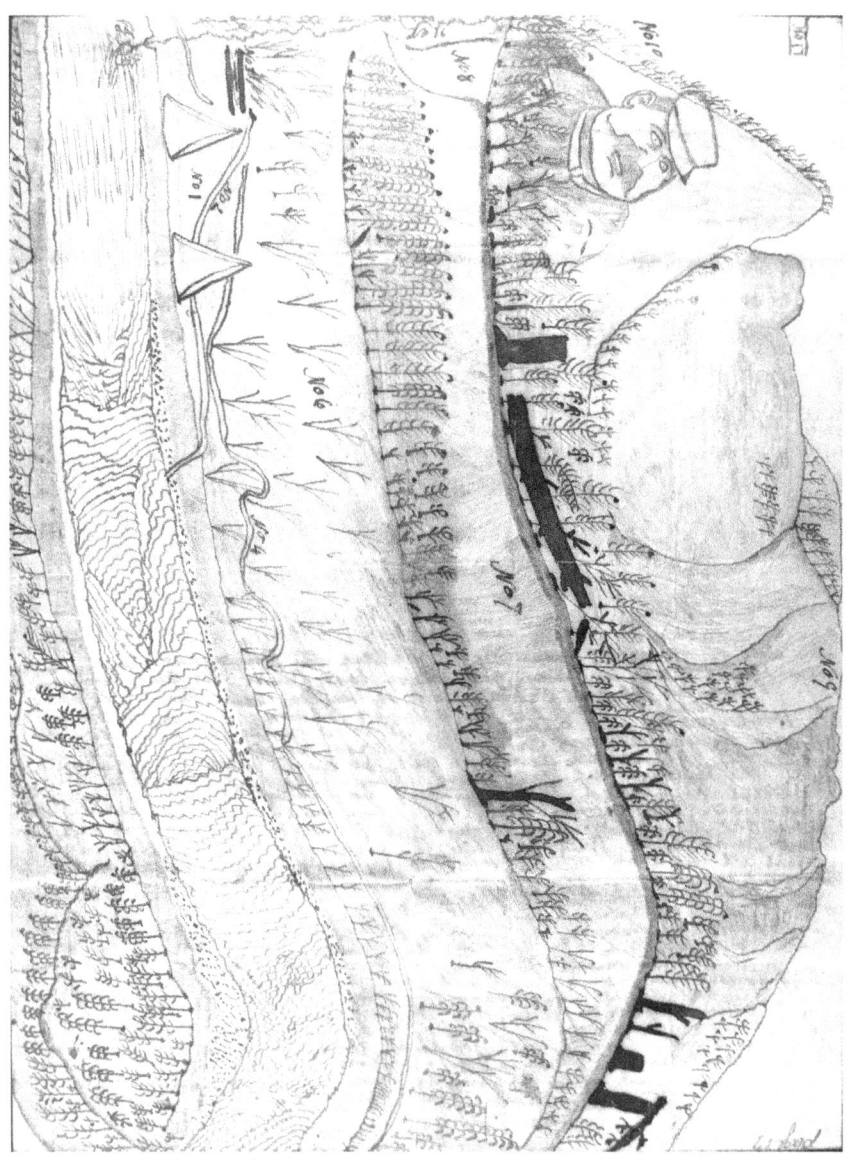

Cutting trails through the mountains

back tomorrow and will know then if we can get through. Well that's all today. Tomorrow I am 47 years old. Did you know it?

Monday afternoon — sun about three hours high, May 29th, 1899
Well who would have thunk it that 47 years ago I would be up here, right in this most beautiful, most ornery, most desolate, most uninhabitable, most hardest to get up and down country that I could have got into if I had of traveled the whole 47 years. But I am here and for a week or ten days I expect all by myself, me and Dash.

First I will tell you what I did all day. This morning I got up, got me and Dash our breakfast, which consisted of bread, pig and coffee. I wakened up at sunup and said to myself, "Hello Jim, how are you?" Says he to me, "1 am all right, how are you?" Says I to him, "I am 47 years old today." Says he to me, "Is that so?" Says I to him, "Yes, that's so, didn't I say so and how many times do you want me to tell you?" Says he to me, "Oh you needn't get rathey about it." Says I to him, "Well if I am rathey it is because I am old I guess." He he, goody goody, none of you get to pound me either, too far away. I had a notion to go and butt my head against a tree but not 47 times though.

Well after breakfast I and Dash and the gun and the ax went up the trail. First I finished changing the trail up at the bad place, then I went up to where the horses were to Otter Tail Creek. Just before you get to Otter Tail Creek you come to a bench or what you might call a step on the side of the mountain. It goes nearly straight down for an eighth of a mile and right at the bottom is the creek thirty ft. wide and thirty ft. deep. This bench runs around on the side of the mountain for three miles to a canyon and is where the creek comes down out of the mountains.

I went to the canyon and down the bench to the creek and ate my lunch which consisted of bread, pig and ice cold water. Right where I went down at the bottom, beaver had been working, trees were cut down by them quite recently. I watched a long time for to get to see one to get a shot at him but none appeared so after perambulating a while I turned myself around and started on the homeward bound. By the time I got up on the bench, I felt like I was a hundred and forty seven years old. But I wasn't so I got back a little while ago and had dinner.

I surprised myself, thinks I to myself, "This is my birthday, I must have something good to eat." I didn't kill a thing, pheasant or bear, moose or elephant so I could have a birthday dinner. Dash killed a young rabbit, it was about as big as a mouse so I says to myself, "That's too small, isn't enough to stink the skillet," so I will tell you what I fixed for my birthday dinner.

I put on a pot of rice, put some apricots in it with some sugar that I had for my dessert, I fried me some pig and I had bread and coffee. Well that was kinder slim I thought but it was the best I could do so I ate a little pig and bread and then a whole lot of dessert, then some more pig and bread and more dessert, finally I abandoned the pig and bread and just ate dessert altogether. I managed to get filled up pretty well anyhow and am setting in the tent writing this.

Tuesday 30

I would rather be hunting gold but I can't do a thing until Peters comes back and it is lonesome setting here without doing anything. Now I must go and bake bread. Say did any of you ever bake light bread in a bucket? Well I did, I just got done baking two loaves or two buckets full of bread. Now whoever heard of baking two buckets full of bread? Beats any stove or bake oven I ever saw.

We haven't got any stove and Peters took the Dutch oven with him, so I tried a scheme, I set yeast last night, this morning it was raised up nice so I didn't know what to bake it in, no stove, no nothing but a two gallon aluminum bucket, so I dug a hole in the ground the size of the bucket, filled the hole full of sand, built a fire on the sand, got it red hot, took sand out of the hole, put a gold pan on top of bucket, built a fire in gold pan and let her bake forty-five minutes and I had bread for your whiskers. Tell Mank that I want a job as cook for him when I come home, that I can get up more kinds, more funny kinds, more most palatable dishes than he and all the cooks ever have seen.

Well Peters has not come back yet. This makes five days he has been gone. He must have got lost or else gone on clear through to the jumping off place.

Well mamma and kids it is just sundown and Peters has not come yet. I don't know what to think. All kinds of imaginatives are whirling through my head. Suppose I be left all alone up here which if I was I couldn't turn a wheel. He took two horses with him and I have been up to where we took the other four every day and I have not seen them or heard them since he has been gone. He should be here this evening sure.

This is the first week since I left home that things look discouraging. I suppose that it is because we are going to have a hard time to get through these next twenty-five miles and because I am all alone for the last five days. Oh how I wish Cantlon was with me or someone. Well I will have to wait and see how it is all going to turn out. No one has come up the river since we arrived here last Wednesday and no one has gone down the river since Butch went down. I would give five cents to see the color of a man's hair. That's all for today.

Wednesday 31
I went up to where the horses are this morning, found Peters there in camp, got there last evening. He said he went up as far as Benard Creek on account of high water and awful swift. It is ten miles by the map from Benard Creek to Wicked River so we have decided to remodel our outfit so as to take it all at one load, the balance we leave here. Have just got done building a scaffold ten feet high to put it on. So then if we should come back this way we can stop and get it providing the bears have not eat it up.

We are just taking grub enough to last us until the 1st of October. Have to leave all of our winter clothes, sleeping bags, tools and some grub, some flour, some vegetables, nails, dutch oven, and lots of little trinkets that we may need but we'll have to do without them. If we didn't do this it would take us all summer to get any place by having to double.

Peters is camped up at Otter Tail Creek and will get the horses together and in the A.M. I will go up and help bring them down and probably leave camp some time tomorrow. We think we can get through this way and will undertake it anyhow. Anyhow I am getting tired of going up Otter Tail Creek every day having to climb a young mountain about a mile high every time I go.

Good place here for prize fighters to get in shape for a fight. You can exercise your muscles all right. Well I don't know of any more to say today so I will quit and get me and Jim some supper. Going to have pig and bread and bread and pig for supper. Slip me a kiss.

Thursday June the 1st

Tired, I guess I am. Yes I am tired. Oh it is so much fun up here to hunt gold, a fellow don't do anything else but work and get tired. But I mustn't forget I am after gold. This morning I went up to Otter Tail Creek to help Peters bring the horses down. Well I found him about three miles above the creek, had to cut a new trail up there so wouldn't have to swim the horses. After winding around in the wilderness, not forty years but four hours, we finally got a trail cut through and crossed the creek where it was knee deep.

Well we arrived at camp about 4:00 P.M. good and tired and have been working ever since, remodeling the outfit. Have got it all fixed up now with five months grub and can take it all at one load so now we will get along faster and if we have luck getting through the next twenty-five miles we will be on Wicked River in ten days and there go to prospecting.

At Wicked River is the Selwyn Mountains 6222 feet high and a different formation from Wicked River. To the Parsnip River is about twelve miles and from the Parsnip River to the Omenica is fifteen all good trail. We hope to find good pay dirt in that locality and if we find a quartz claim we'll stake a few claims and have them recorded and our eighteen months service will be over.

May the Lord see fit to give us luck enough to find it for we have earned it a dozen times. We start in the A.M. on our way rejoicing or falling down the mountains, I don't know which. We'll make three miles above Otter Tail Creek tomorrow and to Benard River the next day if everything goes O.K. Well that's all for today. You will hear from me later on. Ta ta.

Saturday morning June the 3rd
Well we are here I guess, I don't know though for certain, it might be a dream. But I guess it is so, I felt myself all over this morning and it felt like Jim so I guess we are here. We left camp yesterday morning about 9:00 with all our outfit, that is all we were going to take. Got along all right for the first two miles until we came to the bad place. After four of our horses doing the acrobat feat, such as walking trees, turning double somersaults, standing on end, first heads down then heads up doing the whole circus performance, we got to the top with a great deal of sweat, some profanity, but didn't know we said it.

All together we reloaded and started on for the other half of the journey. Just as bad only down hill instead of up but got along all right and got into camp on the river bank at 6:00 P.M. pretty well petered out but still in the ring. I laughed, well I just more than laughed. I wish Harris Clark and Joe Montague had of happened on us as we was doing the circus performance. Oh but it is fun.

The first performance was Mrs. Sally Bigleg and Master J.R. Peters of Seattle, Washington in the United States over on the coast. They started first, got up twenty feet. It being too straight up, Sally's load was too heavy and over she went backward, turned three somersaults and landed at the bottom in a pile of spruce logs, trees, brush and moss with pack on top.

First thing to do was to go to chopping wood, which I did, had to cut up three big trees — first have a log rolling before we got Mrs. Sally out, got her up with a few bruises, she was all together. Oh how I laughed, took her up to the top of first bench, light.

Next performance was Mrs. Nelly Harkes and Master Jim Memphis. Started, got along O.K. by resting every ten feet, got to top of first bench, unloaded so as to rest horses. Oh but it is fun to unload and to load up again.

Next was Mr. Dick Harkes, the strong man and Mr. Nig Hinkle, no trouble at all getting up. Next was Mr. Baldy Harkes and Jack Peters with a show in this part of program. Baldy had a notion he couldn't make it and stuck to it that he couldn't make it, after Jack Peters running several foot races through the brush, they give it up that Baldy couldn't make it. So unloaded half of his pack and went up the same as they do on a railroad.

Next was Mr. Buck Harkes and Mr. James W. Mc Hinkle. No trouble, got to the top O.K., loaded up and started for second bench. All got up O.K. Not quite so steep, started for third bench. Mrs. Sally Bigleg and Dick Harkes, Mrs. Nelly Harkes and Mr. Baldy Harkes got up all right.

Now comes the funny part of the performance. Billy Harkes met with an accident that usually don't happen to him for he is one of our best performers. About half way up the third bench he stepped over a log, got over balanced and down he came to the bottom over and over, knocking down small tress and finally landing against one, got him up and started again, got up all right second trial.

Now the funniest part of the show commences. Mr. Buckskin Harkes did the same thing, got over balanced and over and over he went to the bottom, lodging with his rear end straight up against a tree, his head and neck bent right around under his body with pack on top. I says to myself, "We will only have five horses now and will have to leave some more grub." Well the only way to get him up was to cut the tree down he was lodged against, so I cut it down. He turned one more somersault and stood up on his feet.

Then I did laugh. I laughed because his neck wasn't broke and I laughed at the position he was in. Well I let him blow a little, loaded him up and he got up O.K. The balance of the trip for the day was all right so far as turning somersaults was concerned.

We got down the other side all right, got to the creek (Otter Tail) and figured some more baptizing but got over all right and landed in camp at 6:00 P.M. all pretty well tuckered out. And as there is good feed here we will probably stay here a week as we can't get through here yet on account of the snow, it is four feet deep in places yet.

6:00 P.M.
Well this has been a cold and awful windy day. It rained a little while and then snowed a little while, been in tent all day. I don't know what else to say so I will quit and see what happens tomorrow. You had better slip me a kiss or else I will forget how it goes. Ta ta.

Sunday 4th
Still windy with occasionally a little snow and a little rain. The trees are just commencing to bud, some of them got frost bitten and will have to bud over again. There is no fruit through here except wild strawberries and gooseberries, they are in bloom now. Haven't seen a soul since Butch went down the river ten days ago.

No Indians through this part of the country and no game except bear and pheasant. Lots of bear and pheasant but have not killed a bear yet, they are hard to get — always away up on some high cliff or steep mountain and can't get close enough to get a shot at them. At this time of year, later on they come down along the river to get berries. Maybe I will get a whack at one of them. Very few birds through here, some snow birds, a few whiskey jacks and a few eagles.

The river has been up so high for the last three weeks that have not caught any fish, not since left Eight Mile Creek, are living on pheasants, pig and bread with fruit on Sundays. Please send me up by delivery boy 10¢ worth of green apples and 10¢ worth of celery and have him charge it to Frank Kernes. I haven't much to talk about today and as my letter will be so big before I have a chance to send it out I will lay off a day or two.

That's all today, don't forget about the kisses.

Monday 5th
It has been raining all day so I have been laying around in the tent. We will stay here a few days yet and let our horses get fat and we want to prospect some up Otter Tail Creek and another creek about as big, half a mile from Otter Tail, hasn't got any name so I am going up tomorrow and call it Jim Memphous Creek. It comes right down over the mountains and I may find quartz up in it. Be

a joke on the gold if we did not have to go any farther wouldn't it. Well I hope so, that's all today.

Tuesday 6th
Well I'm not lagging much but I guess I'm not saying much either. I have just got back from up Jim Memphous Creek, I went up about three miles. Of all the God forsaken countries this takes the shoe bread. That creek runs right up between two mountains and every bit there is a perpendicular fall of twenty feet and logs, brush, moss as soft as a feather bed and rock. Well it is too ornery for birds to stay up that creek.

Didn't find any gold, I went clear to the top of it but I couldn't see out for the trees and brush, lots of snow up there. So I set down and ate my lunch and then come back so in the A.M. we hike out of here and will go to Benard River which is ten miles, all good trail except a quarter mile and that is fallen timber. Will have to cut some wood there I expect. We will not stop until we get to Benard River. We can make there by 4:00 P.M. That's all today. I will say something at Benard River.

Wednesday 7th
About 4:00 P.M. Have just arrived at Benard River, got along all right, and the next thing on the program is to make a raft and get our goods across Benard River and then take the horses across light, it is not so deep but awful swift and a horse couldn't stand up in it with his pack on. It is about forty feet wide according to the map.

If this is Benard River, we are about eight miles from Wicked River and are right opposite the Woolsey Mountains. At least there is one on the south side nearly out of sight and has got a hump on it like Woolsey has on his back and about five miles above the Neparle-pas rapids we think. No one has been up or down the river so we can find out any information. Tomorrow we will make a raft and get our goods over the B.R. and then look ahead a few miles and cut a trail and look for feed for the horses.

That's all today.

Thursday 8th
Been nearly all day making a raft, got it done and I tried it first but on account of water so swift could not pole it across. So then went to work and fixed a rigging on it and made a set of oars. Got everything all ready and I jumped on board and tried to row it across and that was the best I could do. So now in the morning Mr. J.R. Peters of Seattle, Washington will try it and see what he can do.

Somewhat discouraged about everything. Two men aren't enough to make this trip and as we have got a hard piece of ground to get over ahead of us for twenty-five miles and as it is getting along in the summer and haven't found any gold yet I am somewhat discouraged, it is awful hard work, harder than going by boat, that is with only two men. Every time we pack our horses we put two hundred twenty five pounds on a horse, one hundred on each side and twenty-five on top.

It is in one hundred pound packages and you lift a hundred pounds up on a horse or high as your head and hold it there while you tie it. It is hard work. Then nearly every day we get from two to four horses down, that is they stumble going up the steep places, get over balanced and tumble over and over down to the foot of the hill, then we have to unload them for they can't get up with their packs on them so we have to unload them and load them up again.

Then we have to go some, to get five miles of a morning before we find them, as feed is pretty scarce and they go until they find it. We always do a day's work before we start and then we come to a river like Benard River, there is three or four day's work making rafts, getting the goods across and then hunt the horses up and get them across, so take it all, it is hard work. But I wouldn't care for the work if we were making any progress.

We are where we can't get any word from anybody unless someone comes down the river going to St. John. We don't know a thing of the whole world, only what little of B.C. we are in. I would give $500 to get a letter from you and to know that you are all right. It takes a man with nerve to stand this, no babies need come up here for they would die with a broken heart. But you know me, I have a determination about me, that I can't get shod of until every effort is exhausted, so I have a few efforts left and will use them all up first, before I climb a tree.

No one has come yet to join us and I have give it up that they will. I was sure that the way Mr. Clark talked, someone was coming and he has had time to have got my statement about the matter, that I sent him I think in February, to have sent a man and he be with us. I do want to make a success out of this trip so bad I would be willing to work twice as hard as I do if I could make it successful for all concerned.

There is gold up here in this God forsaken place if I can only get to it. We would have been all right if we would only have gone the Ashcraft route. Would have avoided all of this hard country to get through. But it is too late now to talk about it. If we only make a mile a day we will get there some time this summer. Well I have said enough for today. We'll see what turns up in the A.M.

Friday 9th

Fourteen months today that I have been away from home. It seems like fourteen years and this is a blue Friday to me. Everything looks blue, I went up this Benard River twelve miles this morning to see if I could get across it some way and the farther up you go the worse it gets. I cut two big trees down and fell them across thinking I could get across that way but they didn't reach across so I had the fun of seeing them splash in the water anyway.

Peters said last night, oh yes, he would go across this morning on the raft, so this morning as usual he took sick. I knew he would or he would have some excuse. He always takes sick when we come to a bad place. He has been telling everybody at St. John this last winter that he had put in bridges, some of them two hundred twenty six feet high. I told him this morning that I didn't think he could make a bridge across dry land or he could contrive some way to get across this little stream that you can stand on one side and spit across.

I can get across it if the water wasn't so cold, it is ice water, for I would swim across it easy. Once I was across we could get a line a hold of the raft and we could pull the raft back and forth that way and haul our stuff over that way but I don't see no other chance only to wait until the water gets low and then wade it with gum boots.

It will be a long time between this letter and the last one you got for it is no telling when we will get out of here and it is no telling when anyone will be along to send it out and should they come now it would take two months for the letter to reach you. I suppose you will think I am dead but I'm not and Lord only knows when I will get a letter from you. I hope that you all will be careful with your health and not get sick. Well that is all for today.

6:00 P.M.
Well I'll just be doggon mamma and kids, if here isn't Tom and the two other men from Fort Graham. Well I never was so glad in all my life to see a man, I had a notion to kiss them. They are on their way out to Edmonton, are out of grub and there isn't a bit in Graham to be had for love or money.

They just got ten pounds of flour per man to come down the river on so now I will have a chance to send this out by them. They say that the people up at Graham will starve if the Hudson Bay don't bring in a supply. They have been in once this spring but with only two small boats and what they brought in didn't last a day for all the Indians are in there with their winter fur and gobbled up the grub.

Well Tom says we are twenty-five miles from Wicked River and that the Dr. Potts party are located one mile above Wicked River on the south side of Peace River, that that is where they have their claims. Now we are going to try and make there and if we do we will be apt to find some claims too. He says though that the trail is bad from where we are to Wicked River but that we can get through.

We are not on Benard River as we thought now but Otter Tail River instead, that's what Tom says anyhow. We will use his boat to get our stuff across while he is here. Now mamma I am all right in every respect, good health, haven't been sick a minute, only have the blues some in the last few days but am somewhat over them now after seeing Tom. I will start for home as soon as our time is up. Have not heard a word from anyone since in February and then it was from you and Mr. Clark. I will send Mr. Clark and Mr. White a letter with this. See if they get them and let me know what I say in this letter. Have not got a word from Mr. Tivnen since I left Edmonton. I don't understand why it is that I don't get letters from him. I have written him twelve letters.

Now mamma I still think that if we can get through these next twenty-five miles that we will get a gold mine but don't build up on it too much for it is a hard country to get through and only two men to do it but I am doing my best and will do my best to make a success out of this trip for all concerned. If I fail it won't be because I didn't try or because I didn't want to for the men that sent me up here. I do honestly hope I will succeed.

Now I can't tell you when you will hear from me again but whenever I have a chance to send a letter out I do it. I always have one partly ready. So do be careful with your health, all of you, don't get sick for I can't hear from you very soon, but write often, I may get them some day unexpected.

Harry, take good care of yourself and if you are railroading take your rest and be careful on the road and please don't go near the gambling places. Presh, you do the same and take good care of your mamma and save all of your money. Myrty my dear dear daughter, I don't know what to say to you, if I had a hold of you a minute I would kill you I expect with kisses. You must be careful too, and don't get sick and take good care of your mamma and I will be home before long and take care of you all.

Mamma, now you are not to work at all, the kids will do your part of the work, won't you kids, yes of course you will. So now I will stop with this letter, the mountains are still covered with snow, the weather is fine though only the mosquitoes are bad. Give my best wishes to all, everybody that asks about me. This leaves me and Dash all right. Many many kisses to you all.

From your Klondyke Jim and Dad

16

Otter Tail River

In camp at Otter Tail River, B.C.

June 6th, '99

Mr. William White
Dear Friend and brother,

I have just time to say a few words. I have had no letter from you I believe since January. I have written you several but some of them I sent in my wife's letter on account of stamps being short.

I am well and hearty and am within twenty-five miles of Wicked River but Bill, it is H. L. them twenty-five miles we have gone through and the next twenty-five is just like the last ten. Up one mountain and down another one, have to cut our own trail, but we are getting there slowly. If we can get through to Wicked River we will put in some time prospecting in that locality. It is there that the Dr. Potts party are at work and claim they have quartz that assays $64.00 per ton.

I am hopeful of finding something yet but we ought to have another man. But it's too late to send one now I guess. I wrote you a letter some time ago asking you to see if you could send me the Traveling Password, that is if I am still a member. I would like to have it so it would be good in October and the winter.

I will let you know of any luck I have just as soon as I can send it out to you. You must hear my letters read I send to my wife, or part of them anyhow. I told her to read you my letters, would have written to you oftener if I had of had stamps and paper.

Give my best wishes to all of the boys and tell them that Jim Memphous is as red as any darned red skin they ever saw and about as tough looking. My best wishes to your family and you. Write me often. I have to stop now and send this out by this man. Goodbye from

Jim Hinkle

• • •

OTTER TAIL RIVER, B.C.

June 13th, 1899

My dear Mollie and Kids,

I just sent you a big letter out day before yesterday by three Klondykers that were going out, hoping that you will get it all right. I will now begin another one and first will tell you that I am more than discouraged on account of we can't get through the next twenty-five miles with pack horses and we can't take our stuff through by boat. That is, two men can't, all at one load and we can't get our horses through by swimming them back and forth on account of there is not a speck of feed for them short of thirty miles. It would take eight or ten days to get through and they would starve in that time.

If we had another man and boat we could leave our horses where they are and take the outfit through all right and prospect around the Selwyn Mountains which is just opposite Wicked River and in that locality, for a couple of months and am almost certain we would find something good. If we could hire an Indian we would but there is none in this part of the country to hire so I am discouraged for once on this trip.

We have decided to man a canoe and one man take two months grub and go through there and prospect and the other man stay with the outfit and horses. We are making a canoe now. One man can paddle a canoe along the beach with that much load all right and can get through in about ten days. Peters will go and I will stay with the outfit. It will be a lonesome job but that is the best we can do.

I will make a trip to Hudson Hope in the meantime to get the mail and maybe go to St. John. We are on the wrong trail anyhow. If we had of went the Ashcraft trail we would have been all right and could have got some place. But as it is we are almost completely stuck. We can't do a thing short of ten days except make the canoe and be ready on account of Peace River is on its high horse and the water is high.

This is Wednesday morning June 14th
Peace River is still on the rise and if it raises one more foot we will have to carry our outfit back on a beach about as far as it is from your house to the depot. That will be nice won't it, carrying a hundred pounds at a load for our flour and some other stuff is done up in hundred pound packages. But it is a ground hog case. We are on the west side of Otter Tail River and our horses are on the east side and a mile and a half up Otter Tail on pasture. Besides, we would have to swim now to get them across.

Well everything is blue this morning but we are at work making a boat for Jack to go up the river in to the Selwyn Mountains or to Wicked River. He will prospect there for a couple of months and see what the Dr. Potts party has. I will stay with the horses and outfit and in the meantime take two horses and go to Hudson Hope and maybe St. John to get the mail. I can't do anything else.

I just got back from up Otter Tail River on this side. I went up a mile and a half where the horses are but didn't see them and I wish you could see the trail I had to take to get up there. Just one solid mass of underbrush and moss a foot thick. It was all Dash could do to get through. But by crawling and walking logs, climbing trees and falling down I managed to get there and back.

To make things more pleasant we can't do a thing until the water goes down for we have to take two horses and go back twelve miles where we cached part of our outfit and get the rip saw, the nails and tools and pitch and oakum to build the boat with and we can't get down on account of the river has raised in places and covered the trail up so here we are. All of this gives me the blues and would the devil too I guess.

As soon as the boat is made and Peters gets started, I will move down to where all of our outfit is and then take two horses and go to Hudson Hope. See if there is any mail and if there is none there I will go on to St. John. It will take me eight days to go but that's all I can do and I want to hear from you so bad.

Thursday 15th
Well we are here and I guess stay here for a while anyway until the river quits rising and goes down. It is just about full from bank to bank and is raising about three inches per day. Nine inches more and we will have to hike back an eighth of a mile to higher ground. I like to pack hundred pound packages through the brush (in a pig's eye).

We will be safe enough where we are tonight I guess unless it comes down in a pile, then I suppose we will have to get up in the night and climb a tree. Didn't look for this raise until the last of the month. But the snow is melting and it has to hike out of here sometime. There is lots of snow on the mountains yet, just the tops of them.

Say did you know that when we are setting around the camp fire of evening at sundown that you folks are in bed or ought to be and it is midnight there at Mattoon? Well that is fact, sun sets here at about 9:00 P.M. and raises right after it sets a little bit. It is trying to catch itself I guess. I wonder how far north it is to the jumping off place. That's all today.

I am like a fish out of water, can't set still, stand still, lay still or be contented any way I fix it. I write a little bit, sketch a little bit, walk around a little bit and don't know what I am doing. I said that was all for today but it ain't. Now I have something else to say.

As soon as we make the boat for Peters to go up the river in, we have decided that I will take the horses and the outfit down to Hudson Hope and stay there until Peters comes or I hear from him. I think the way this thing is staring me in the face that it is the first step toward going home. However, I will stay a couple of months at

Hudson Hope. By that time it will be September and we will know if we have found a gold mine or not and if we haven't found a gold mine by that time and don't hear of a strike being made in this country, it will be time to start for Illinois before the ice comes.

I am just giving you a few hints of the way it might be. At Hudson Hope I will be where I can get mail from you once in a while and can send mail to you oftener by the Hudson Bay. The river is still on the rise about an inch an hour. Have not moved yet and aren't going to this evening even if we have to climb a tree. But I think tomorrow we will move north about one eighth of a mile.

This is Friday the 16th
Well we haven't moved yet. The river is still on the rise though, but only about two inches a day, got about six inches to go on yet before we have to move. Do you folks know what a dugout is? Dugout is a noun because it is a name of a canoe because it is cut out of a poplar log. There you have it in grammar. Well a dugout is a log (poplar is the best because it shapes easier) about eighteen feet long and twenty-four inches wide and made into a canoe by chopping it all out but a shell just like a sugar trough.

Now you got it and that's what we have been doing all day, digging out a log. We are making a dugout instead of a boat, can do it quicker. So we cut down a poplar tree that is twenty-eight inches across and it is eighteen feet long and have got it most done, will finish digging tomorrow. Then it will take a couple of days to smooth it up, then as soon as the river goes down Peters will go up the river to Wicked River and the Selwyn Mountains and I will take horses and the balance of the outfit down the river to Hudson Hope. I am tired and I have got two great big blisters on my hands so that's all for today.

Saturday 17th
Have been digging all day on the dugout and have got done all but putting the finishing touch on it and at last the river begins to fall. It fell four inches since last night. Don't have to hike out of this camp for a while yet. For a change it snowed a little today. By the middle

of next week I will be on my way to the Hope unless the river takes another spell of rising. But if I can get down thirty miles it can raise all it wants to. I guess it won't get over the tops of these mountains and you had better have some letters at Hudson Hope for me when I get there or there will be the darndest fight when I get home you ever read about. That's all for today. Tomorrow I am going up to salt old Buck if I can get across Otter Tail River. Bye bye.

Sunday morning June 18th
Well this beats all the country I ever saw for different kinds of weather. Now yesterday it was cold and windy and raining and snowing a little all day. This morning the sun is shining bright and warm. Last night it rained hard half the night, just as hard as it could pour down and this morning all of the tops of the mountains are covered with a new coat of snow. The next thing I look for is Peace River for freeze up and I will go a skating. Well I guess it has to be, what is to be will be, if it never comes to pass.

The river fell six inches last night. If it will just keep falling I will be on my way to Hudson Hope by the last of the week, anything to get out of this most lonesome, most solemn, most disagreeable, most miserable, low degrading, ungodly, Godforsaken place around Otter Tail River in B.C. We have been here eleven days and it seems like eleven years. I haven't got much to say today so I will wait until evening. I didn't find anything more to say so that's all for today.

Monday 19th
Of course this letter will be two or three months old when you get it and I will be down to Hudson Hope before I send it out I expect. But it tells you what I am doing each day. Well the river is going down slowly. I have been all day remodeling the outfit, taking out what Peters will take with him and getting the rest in shape so I can load it on the horses.

Say how would you like to be three million miles from no place with six horses and a dog with nothing to talk to but the horses and dog and yourself. I suppose you folks will think, "I'll bet he talks to himself, " but I don't. Peters does though.

Well altogether it is quite a romance of a trip, good place to play solitaire. There is a bird up here that I call the piano bird. The darned thing is always singing and it goes just like anyone running the scales on the piano. I will see if I can make the notes as he sings them and Myrty, you can practice on it. I think it is in G sharp.

Well by tomorrow I will be on my way down the river if the water keeps going down. We have got the dugout done and I will get out of here before another high water comes which will be in about ten days after this one. That's all for today.

Friday 23rd
I arrived here yesterday evening about 5:43 P.M. but you don't know where I'm at no more than a rabbit. Well I'll tell you. I am at the camp where I got the birch bark to write Myrty that great piece of poetry where the big tree is with the duck's nest. I left Otter Tail River Wednesday 21st about 1:00 o'clock, all by myself and Dash and six horses with the outfit for Hudson Hope.

I went up to find the horses and Peters was to bring the balance of the stuff over Otter Tail River in the dugout. Well after running my legs off up to my knees and climbing three sets of mountains, ten miles from camp I found the horses in behind a young mountain, standing among a patch of fallen timber sound asleep. I got them to camp at noon and there Peters was on the other side of Otter Tail and no stuff over. He isn't worth the salt that's in his dough.

He says, "I split the dugout, a big crack in it and it will take me all day to fix it, can't you pull the raft up and come over and get it?" Well anything to get started so the raft was down the river about a fourth of a mile and the water as swift as a mill race.

I says, "Yes, I can do anything, I can do it all." So after an hour's hard pulling in ice water up to my waist, I got it up and crossed over and brought the stuff and him over. Now he had split the dugout a little crack that wouldn't leak a pint of water through in six months.

All the trouble was he was afraid the dugout would fill with water and sink and drown him. Well he helped me to load up and I got started about 2:00 P.M. to go eight miles over the worst piece of trail we have gone over. I got along all right until about three miles. Then the trail runs close to the river bank and the bank is about twenty feet high and Nelly of course, she had to step off and down she went to the bottom, pack and all, clear into the water. Well I got her up and after digging a road up the bank to get her up I got her up on top again. Now I had done a big day's work before I started. Oh it is lots of fun to go to the Klondyke.

Just then two men came down the river from Graham. They stopped and helped me to get started. I told them I would camp five miles below. They said they would go on down and camp there too. Well I got there about 7:00 o'clock and found them there, but one of them came back to meet me and help me. They are two of the nicest men I have met in this country. One of them gets down on his knees of a morning just when he gets up and prays.

Well the next five miles is still worse trail than the first eight. It is where we had so much trouble going up and the horses tumbling down so much so I asked the men could I get one of them to go with me down to Hudson Hope and help me and I would pack their stuff across the Portage from Cust's House for nothing.

Well they said that one man couldn't manage the boat but they would both help me over the next bad trail and they would stop at my next camp and take part of my stuff down in the boat. You know the next camp is where we left part of our outfit and I intend to stop there and take it all down to the Hope.

Well we started in the morning and it took me two hours to cut and find the trail through to the high bench where we have to go up and where the creek runs at the bottom of the bench where we baptized the horses going up. Finally we got through to the bench and across the creek all right except Sally, in crossing, got down and went clear under, pack and all. The water was so swift it took her off her feet. Well I hauled her out, second baptizing for her and got them all over and we started to go up the mountain, each man leading two horses.

I went first and got up about two hundred feet with Buck and Nelly and Buck got to plunging and down he went and over end to the bottom, pack and all. Well I told the other two men to go on up with their horses and they got up all right, and to unload Dick and bring him down to pack up Buck's load. Finally we got them all up on top but I was completely give out, I couldn't do a thing for a half hour. My legs and arms cramped so that I couldn't move and we all had to rest.

After we got rested we started for the camp about three miles and the men went back to get their boat and would go on down and stop at camp and take part of the outfit down in the boat. Well I had to rest four times before I got to camp but did finally get there just ahead of the men, too tired and sick to unload the horses. It is the first time I have been sick since I left home. I wasn't sick but had the cramps and was give out.

Well they took part of the stuff and went on down the river and one of them is coming back to meet me and help me, so today I am resting up and will start in the A.M. and make down to the next camp. I don't know but I guess I will make down to the Hope some way. I am over the most part of the trail but it is awful hard work for one man to pack six horses by himself and get them along. I have to take them up and load the head one.

Now you folks I guess, knows what tailing up horses is. I tie the halters fast to each horses tail and that's the way I go single file as the Indians do. Anybody would take me for an Indian anyhow. I am so stiff and sore this morning I can only just drag myself around. I had to get up in the night and rub my legs with pain killer. That and the skeeters together, I put in a very pleasant night, in a pig's eye.

Saturday 24th
And I am here and I don't know how I got here either. Maybe it is a dream. I am at Fritz's old camp. Got here about noon. Well back at the camp where the duck's nest was and where I said I would rest — that day the two men went down eight miles to Eight Mile Creek and came back on foot to help me. I had just got done eating dinner. I was praying that they would come back and help me but not that day for I wanted to rest.

They said, "We have come back to help you over this next bad trail. "What?" I says, "today?" "Yes." Well I didn't know what to do,

I was too tired to move and I was afraid if I didn't go they wouldn't help me any more after walking back eight miles. So I says, "Well, I will try it but I am played out," so I got the horses up and we loaded up and there was a mile of new trail to cut on account of high water so one of the men went ahead and cut trail until we caught up to him, then we stopped and I cut a while.

We got through the cutting part, then we got to the digging part. Say, did you ever work on the section? There was five hundred yards along a steep-cut bank that we had to dig a new trail up on the side of the bank. Before the water was up we went down on the bar. Well we got it dug and got the horses over it all right and made Eight Mile Creek at dark. No, I guess I wasn't tired.

So this morning the men helped me to load up and I got to Fritz's about noon and they went on down the river to the Cust's House and one of them is coming back to meet me. But I couldn't move out of this camp before Monday morning for all of B.C. and Canada throwed in. I am taking a rest and don't forget it. I have got my mosquito bed up and I am getting under it writing this right now and the sun is about two hours high and I am too tired to say anymore today.

Sunday 25th

Just after dinner. Well I have been all day trying to catch two fish that I can see in the mouth of a little creek by my camp. I tried bacon and dough for bait and they just laughed at me, 'cause it was Sunday I guess. So I went up on the hill and caught some grasshoppers and I put the hopper and hook right down by the fish, too tempting, had to take a nibble at it anyhow and I hauled him out. It was fourteen inches long and as much as I can eat at one meal and I am going to have him for supper.

Well this is a nice day and hot and the skeeters and gnats and flies and ants are about to take me alive. I will hike out of here in the morning for the Cust's House but I don't think I can make it in one day. I look for one of the men back this evening or tomorrow. If he comes this evening I can make it to Cust's House tomorrow.

The tops of the mountains are still covered with snow. I guess it stays on all summer or else it is petrified. It might be salt.

Well Peace River is on her high horse again. It has raised two feet since I left Otter Tail. I don't care, I am by all the bad places. It can raise twenty feet if it wants to. Say my Myrt, you had better have some letters at the Hudson Hope when I get there if you know what's good for you, black rascal. That's all today. I am going a fishing, don't tell anybody.

Monday 26th
The man hasn't come and I got the horses up and loaded up and got started and got about half mile and it commenced to rain and the farther I went the harder it rained. I just kept on going. Well sir, I wish you could have seen me and the six horses and Dash hiking up the sides of those mountains, down through the brush, over creeks, some of them young rivers. Well I was wet and I wanted to stop and go into camp and there was no place to stop, no feed for horses, no nothing but mountain, valleys, brush and wet. So I kept on hiking until I made it to the cabin which is seven miles from Cust's House. There I unloaded you bet.

I was wet and cold and hungry and tired and mad and I had my matches in my hip pocket and they were all wet and I didn't know where the other ones were. Such a time I had. Well I found the matches and built a fire and dried myself. It rained all night and until 9:00 o'clock Tuesday. I packed up at noon and started for the Cust's House, met the two men five miles from Cust's House, got there about 4:00 P.M. and glad of it.

So this is Tuesday the 27th
And I am at the Cust's House and it is raining and I am in the tent and I don't care if it does rain. Tomorrow I load up and take a load over the Portage to Hudson Hope. I will have to make two trips and I will finish this letter and send out by them.

Well if Peters don't get me word from up the river 'til October there will be nothing for me to do only come home. I guess you think it is time but I want a gold mine before I come and I am going to have it if it is to be had. I feel almost confident that we will find a good thing where he is going. It is in there some place.

If he gets me word that he has found it, then I will take two horses and grub and go back to Otter Tail, then by boat up to where he is and we take all the claims the law will allow us. Don't send any more letters by way of Ashcraft. Send all your mail to Hudson Hope via Edmonton. I guess that's all for today, will finish the letter tomorrow and send out by men. Ta ta.

Wednesday June 28
Just after supper. I arrived here with the two men at Hudson Hope about an hour ago with their stuff and as much as I could bring of my own. I will go back tomorrow to Cust's House and the next day will bring all of my outfit to Hudson Hope. It is a good trail but awful big hills to go up and down. It is twelve miles across it. Well there is no one at Hudson Hope. Not a soul but me and Dash and the six horses. The Hudson Bay store is shut up for the summer and the river has been so high that Klondykers can't get up. As soon as it goes down there will be parties coming in often and I am going to go in the freighting business.

That is, pack outfits over the Portage to Cust's House and pack parties that come down the river, and their outfits over to the Hope. The regular price is 2¢ per pound or $2.00 per hundred. My six horses can pack a thousand pounds per trip. Will leave a notice at Cust's House to that effect and stay at Hudson Hope so if anyone at the Cust's House wants me they can come over and say so.

This is a nice place to stay, not lonesome, up two hundred feet from the river. I am going to make garden. I have radish, lettuce, cabbage, beets, turnip seeds, good place here to plant them. Come up in about a month and get some radishes. If they aren't big enough we will eat the seed.

Well I must finish this as the men are going to start early in the morning and take this letter out and mail it. I am sound and well but awful tired. No man in Mattoon could or would begin to do what I have done in the last seven days. But I am about through with it now and I can rest up.

I hope I will get lots of good word from you from the first one that comes up from St. John. Send all of your mail to Hudson Hope via Edmonton in care of Hudson Bay Co. I will quit now for the skeeters are about to take me. Give my best to all. Let all read this letter that you want to let read. Many kisses to you all. I will send you a letter out by everyone that goes out from here. Goodbye and God bless all four of you.

Your Klondyke Hubby and Dad

• • •

FROM HINKLE'S JOURNAL

Thursday, June 29 Left for Cust's House, arrived there at noon, stayed all night in the Cust's House, no I didn't either, the skeeters were too bad, slept out on the grass.

Friday, 30 Got up before sun up, got breakfast, saddled the horses and started with the balance of outfit for Hope, got along all right except Buck, Baldy and Sally didn't want to go, kept raring back and breaking halters. Got to the Hope about noon, put a big tent up and have gone into camp all by myself.

Saturday, July 1 Nice day, four more horses around here and the stallion is fighting my horses and run them down the river three miles, me after them with the gun. I shot the stallion in the fore shoulder and leg and he don't run my horses no more. Bull flies are just awful bad, have to keep a smudge all the time for horses, they feed at night and stand around smudge in daytime fighting flies. River is still on its high horse. Skeeters bad. Killed two robins for supper.

Sunday, 2 90° in the shade and mountains covered with snow. Baked bread this A.M. Had bean soup and fresh light bread for dinner, baked ginger cookies. It is threatening rain, it is thundering all around. The skeeters are just simply awful. Have a smudge in the tent all of the time. River not falling a bit.

Monday, 3   Rained hard last night, the air is just black with skeeters. About 10:00 o'clock the horses came in covered with them, built a smudge for them, they have been here the balance of the day. Hot in the afternoon, 100° in the shade, river is just the same.

Tuesday, July 4   Rained all night and up to the present time at noon and still raining a steady rain. This is a bad day for celebrations, me and Dash and the horses were going to have a flag raising but had to abandon it. No one drunk around here today. River is just the same. Cooked a pot of beans and dried moose meat, had bean soup, apple sauce, ginger cakes and tea for dinner.

About 6:00 P.M   This is a fourth of July long to be remembered by me, it has rained all day, awful lonesome, can't step outside of tent on account of skeeters, they would actually kill a human if they had no protection. It has stopped raining, have not seen the horses today.

Wednesday 5   Rained nearly all night and has rained all day up to sun down and still raining. Horses came in this morning on the run. I jumped up to build them a smudge but they couldn't wait, started off in the bush on a gallop. Have not seen them today, they are almost crazy and I expect will wander off for miles. River is still the same, no arrivals at Hudson Hope yet, awful lonesome. Can't step out to do anything without the skeeters will just cover you black. Have made a mosquito net over my hat and I wear gloves every time I go after water. It is thundering right now.

At dark, two men came in from the Cust's House soaking wet and nearly ate up with skeeters. I was in bed, got up and built a fire, loaned them some dry clothes, got them some supper and finally got them dry and all went to bed.

Thursday 6   Rained all night and up 'til noon, it has now stopped raining and I start for the Cust's House in the A.M. to portage men over. Had a mess of greens for supper.

Friday 7   Nice morning. River raising fast. Horses came up to smudge, caught Billy, Dick and Nelly and left for Cust's House at 10:30, arrived there at 1:00 P.M. Got boat ready, loaded up and left Cust's House at 5:00 P.M., arrived at the Hope at 12:00 midnight but it was getting daylight. Got along nicely but had to stop often and rest Billy, he was pulling the boat. Skeeters awful bad.

Saturday, July 8, 1899   The men left for St. John at 9:00 A.M. Sent a letter out to folks by them. Nice hot day.

4:00 P.M.   Two men just arrived with eight pack horses from St. John, have come up to portage Dr. Pott's party over the Portage. River still on the raise.

About 6:00 P.M.   Dr. Potts arrived. I have lots of company.

• • •

OTTER TAIL

July

J.M. Hinkle
Dear Sir,

Dr. Potts arrived here yesterday about 2:00 P.M. and gave me some mail. He remained about two hours and gave me all the news. He also told me about Sommers* turning back from Peace River crossing. The best thing he could do. I do not think they will send him any more money.

---

* The Mattoon Mining and Investment Co. sent Sommers to replace Hardesty who had returned to Mattoon the previous September. Sommers was unable to locate Hinkle and Peters and finally turned back.

Now about the best I think you can do is remain there until I return. I am all O.K. and have made two trips up Otter Tail about thirty miles. It took me four days to walk it. I did not take any blankets, just grub, gun and mosquito bed and it rained every day. Each time when I came back, Peace River was too high to go up it.

So I have about decided to make the third trip up Otter Tail as I have some very good samples and all free milling ore and one fine vein of copper. Thirty miles from here is a good place to prospect as one can find anywhere so I am in no hurry to leave. But I want to get up to where Dr. Potts is so I can get some assaying done. I had a long talk with him.

Now today, I tried to go up Peace River but I cannot make it until it falls two feet more. If it doesn't fall two feet more soon, I will take a pack and go on foot. Dr. Potts told me he would come over and take me over in a canoe if I came. I am in just as good a place if not better than where they are. I will be down September 1st and if I have anything good I want to get out and back to it this fall. So if I find anything good I may be there some time in August.

Are you going to try and haul the boat over? Or can you get a boat there? We will want a pretty good size boat or large raft if we will go down by water. Can you sell the horses or will we have to take them out? I will get up to where Robb is inside of two days if I have to walk. So just do the best that you can and I will rustle every day. I thought I could get up Peace River today but after working all one half day I did not get five hundred yards, there is no place to walk.

Today I went up Otter Tail to where the horses were to try and get a moose. There is an old one and two calves over there and I have been trying for three days to get a shot at them but can not get near enough. I got a bucket full of strawberries and just got back just as this man came along. You had better write out some of the company you know and have them take Sommers back as he will only be an expense to them. I will write a few lines to Mrs. Peters and a few lines to Clark.

Yours
J.R. Peters

17

Hudson Hope

Hudson Hope, B.C.

July 8, 1899

My dear Mollie and Kids,

I just sent you a letter out a few days ago and I have another chance to send you this one so I will write it in a hurry and it will be short. I will say nothing about business. I have just got done portaging two men over from the Cust's House who are just down from the Selwyn Mountains. You know that is where we were trying to get to with pack horses and could only get as far as Otter Tail River which is thirty miles from Selwyn Mountains or Wicked River.

They are on their way out of the country with their prospects (in quartz) to have it assayed. You know there is where the Dr. Potts party are located. These two men have staked claims there and they think they have a good thing and so do I.

I left Peters at Otter Tail River with a boat and as soon as the river goes down he is going up to the Selwyn Mountains to prospect and to stake claims. He will send me word down to Hudson Hope by everyone that comes down of what he is doing and whether to come up to him. He sent word down by these two men from Otter Tail River that he had been up Otter Tail River two weeks prospecting and for them to tell me that he had found some good quartz up Otter Tail River.

Now if he sends word down for me to come up, I will take three horses and go up as far as I can with them in low water which I think I can get within fifteen miles of Selwyn Mountains with horses. If I can't get clear through, then I will make me a dugout and go the rest of the way by boat.

Mamma, you can tell all of them that I am in better hopes than ever of finding something good, so there is all probabilities that I will go back up there and if I do we will stake all the claims we can get a hold of and get samples of the quartz and bring it out to the States and have it assayed and be home late in the fall, some time in November, maybe sooner. So now you can figure accordingly.

I am well and in the best of health only I'm almost ate up with the skeeters. I have no word from you since February, There is no one at Hudson Hope but me and the river has been on its big horse for over a month. Consequently no one can go up the river until it falls. As soon as it falls the Hudson Bay boats will be up and Klondykers too, and they will bring the mail up. This is a lonesome job but I don't care if I can only get a gold mine for me and the men that sent me up here and I have great hopes of doing so.

It keeps me busy building smudges for the horses. They are almost wild on account of the skeeters and bull flies. I do hope I will get good word from you four soon. I pray every night for all four of you. Haven't missed a night since I left home and the good Lord has answered my prayers that I asked of him of myself, and I believe he will also of you four.

Take good care of yourselves, don't get sick and I will be home before long now. Give my best to Mr. Clark and family, Mr. White and family and Montague, Karnes, Cantlon, everyone of the men that are connected in sending me up here and tell them all that I am doing my best for the good of all although it is awful hard work, harder than any work I ever did. But I don't care as long as I have health and grub to eat.

This is all, the men are ready to go, they go straight to Edmonton and out to Ottawa, Canada as soon as they can and then come back to their claims this fall. They have to hustle so many many kisses to you all. I am your

Jim and Dad Hinkle

• • •

FROM HINKLE'S JOURNAL

Sunday, July 9, 1899   The two men have been all day hunting horses, didn't find them, sent Joe, the Indian out, give him $5.00 if he would get them, he found them in an hour. Rained a little all day and rain storm at night.

Monday, 10   Raining nearly all day, hired one of my horses out to pack Dr. Potts over the Portage, they left for the Cust's House at 2:00 P.M. Sold my shot gun.

Tuesday, 11   Rainy in forenoon, in afternoon nice and sunshiny. Men have not come back yet from over the Portage, horses all came up to smudge this afternoon.

Wednesday, 12   Men got back at dark last night. Nice warm day, skeeters not so bad but bull flies awful bad.

Thursday, 13   Nice hot day all day, flies awful bad. The two men left for St. John about 4:00 P.M. River on the fall a little bit. A large black bear swam over the river from south side yesterday, we got after it but didn't get a shot on account of brush so thick. Dash trailed it for a while but then give up.

Friday, 14   Clear and hot all day, baking bread in the evening. No arrivals at Hudson Hope today. River going down slowly.

Saturday, 15   One more long and lonesome day gone. Been busy all day fighting bull flies. Am building smudges for horses. Been very warm all day, 110° in my tent. River has gone down about one foot, it is threatening rain. Had strawberries and ginger cakes for supper. Rained in evening.

Sunday, 16   all day, thundering and threatening rain all day, sprinkled in afternoon. Flies awful bad, all the horses up to smudge but the crippled one has not been up for two days, think he is dead, killed by flies and skeeters. River gone down one and a half feet.

Monday, 17   At 4:00 A.M. two men of Dr. Pott's party arrived at my camp, by name S.R. Stevens and E.F. Svenson from Cust's House with three more of the party at Cust's House. They stayed with me until 1:00 P.M. Got horses up and went over to portage them over.

Tuesday 18   Didn't sleep any last night on account of skeeters, commenced to get ready to start for the Hope at 6:00 A.M. Got horses all packed and Billy and Dick to the boat and we started, pulled the boat about two hundred yards and broke down, saw that two horses couldn't pull the boat so I left it there and went on to the Hope with men and the balance of their outfit. They are making a boat at the Hope. They was to pay me $30.00 for bringing boat and outfit over, but only got $15.00 for what I brought over. The nights are cold and days very hot.

Wednesday, 19   Nice day, rained in afternoon. The five men are building a boat, got it done. Skeeters awful bad.

Thursday, 20   Got up at 4:00 A.M. Cloudy, got breakfast and built a smudge for horses, set around until 8:00, then the men got up. Got breakfast, took me and Dash's picture with the fiddle, gave me goodbye and was off for Ft. St. John. Dash took a big cry, he actually cried and for a long time. I felt so sorry for him, had to watch him to keep him from following them down the river.

About 11:00 A.M.   Another man came over from Cust's House from Graham, belonged to Dr. Nichol's party, a Norwegian, he packed over a hundred pounds by doubling every few miles. I am having lots of company, let 'em come, the more the merrier. This man has nothing, just enough to get out of the country with one dollar in money. He is staying all night with me and goes down the river in the A.M. on a raft. Rained after dinner.

Friday, 21 Nice day, 110° in the shade. The Norwegian left about 9:00 A.M. on a raft, will bring my mail up from St. John if any there, for $10.00. Pretty lonesome around camp today. Had biscuits and greens for dinner, strawberries for supper. It threatened rain all afternoon, sprinkled a little. Brought me a letter from Peters.

Saturday, 22 Rained and thundered a little all day, picked some gooseberries.

Sunday, 23 One long and lonesome day, thunder showers all day. Picked a quart of strawberries. Hot days and cold nights, mosquitoes are not so bad but have to keep a smudge all of the time. The river is falling gradually.

Monday, July 24, 1899 Nice day, 110° in tent, threatened rain. It has been a long and lonesome day. Did my washing, had greens for dinner, skeeters awful bad today.

Tuesday, July 25 Nice hot day. About noon, Peters came and about 2:00 P.M. one of the Potts men came. Rob, with five of the Pott's party are at the Cust's House, going out of the country. They want me to come after them which I will do in the A.M. Then we will start for St. John and on our way out of the country. Peters said today in his talk that if the company did not send him back that he would come himself and that he wished they wouldn't send him back. He is not working for the company but for Peters. Baldy is sick this evening, the flies have just sucked the blood out of him until he is too weak to walk.

Wednesday, July 26 Couldn't sleep last night thinking about Peters, never went to sleep until daylight. Got up, got breakfast, left with horses, all but Baldy, for Cust's House to bring some of Pott's party over. Arrived at Cust's House at 3:00 P.M. in the rain, rained until sun down.

Thursday, 27 At Cust's House, went to bed at sun down, laid there until 11:00 o'clock, couldn't sleep for skeeters. I and Jimmy got up, built a big smudge and sat around it like two bums until got sleepy, got our blankets, laid down by fire and went to sleep, got up at 3:00 A.M. Jimmy got breakfast and I got the horses all up, ate breakfast, loaded up and started for the Hope, got to the first hill and Dick stopped to eat grass on the top of hill and kicked his foot into the side of his pack, turned the pack on him and down he and pack went to the bottom.

Got him up and started, got ten feet and Sally's pack turned on her and over she went pack and all to the bottom. I didn't do a thing but swear at everything I looked at. Got her up and loaded up and all hands started once more, had no trouble, arrived at the Hope at 12:00. Peters was to have bread baked and have dinner for us, as usual he did not have anything ready. No, I guess I wasn't mad! It was a nice cool day.

Friday, July 28 Mr. Rob, Spalding, Milow, George and Jimmy the cook, made a boat and left for down the river at 5:00 P.M. After that I had a set-to ....

Note: At this point a page had been torn out of Hinkle's Journal, eliminating the balance of July 28, all of July 29 and the following page had the last part of July 30 on it but had been erased. However, the following words were discernible through the erasure: "Peters for the first time, give me a statement."

The next entry was for Monday, July 31

Monday, July 31 Well, we are on our way home, got horses up about 9:00 A.M., loaded up and made Red River about 4:00 P.M., twelve miles. Had no bad luck, very rough trail but got along nicely, just had supper. I picked a quart of raspberries, had pheasant and berries for supper. Nice clear day and skeeters awful bad.

Tuesday, August 1 Very foggy, loaded up and started about 7:00 A.M. Heavy dew, nice trail and arrived at Half Way about 5:00 P.M. and found it impossible to ford with horses, will have to make a raft and raft the outfit over and then swim the horses. I never was so discouraged in my whole life. It will take us all day tomorrow to get across, I am almost in the notion of leaving the horses, make a raft and tear out for Peace River Landing.

Wednesday, August 2 Commenced raining, rained 'til 2:00 P.M. I went up Half Way River to see if there was another trail, didn't find any. Jack cut logs for raft. At 10:00 A.M. took Nelly and went to find Dick, Baldy and Sally, found Baldy back on trail about a mile. Dick and Sally went on back, tracked them for five miles and give them up, they have gone back to the Hope. Afternoon, Peters took Nelly and some grub and went after them. I am building the raft.

• • •

These were the last words my Grandfather Hinkle ever wrote.

18

Questionable Assertions

St. John

                August 13

B.H. Tivnen
Mattoon
Dear Sir:

  We left Hudson Hope and reached Halfway River August 1, river being too high to ford, we started to make a raft. Aug. 3rd two of our horses started back on the trail. At noon I took a horse and Hinkle told me that I would have to go to Hope for the horses and it would take me three days and to take plenty of grub. I told him I thought I would catch them at P.M. which I did and camped for the night about twenty miles from camp. Aug. 3rd I reached camp about 1:00 P.M. and found Hinkle's dog there and a horse loose with a pack saddle on. The horse came to me and I noticed the saddle being very wet. I thought something was wrong.

  Before I cooked anything to eat, I went up to where I cut the logs for a raft to see if I could find Hinkle, not finding him there I went along the river and found fresh horse tracks going into the river. Also about 1/4 below found where the horse had come out of the river and rolled in the sand. I spent all afternoon looking for him.

Aug. 4th a Mr. McFee, a government rig and guide arrived and he helped me search for him that day and not finding any new information, they went up to Hope and arrived back at Halfway River Monday last and advised me to raft the outfit and swim the horses which I did. I also found where the horses had come out of the river and then crossed back. I have been hunting for Hinkle since Aug. 3rd and failed so far to find any new information.

I have just arrived at St. John and will leave horses and outfit here and return with some Indians and search Peace River from Halfway River to St. John, thirty miles. I have come to the conclusion that he tried to swim the river on a horse and lost his balance and is drowned. I was in hopes for several days that he had reached this side of the river and not having anything to eat and not expecting me back for two days had started for St. John for grub. But he has not been here.

I also had six men look for him from where the horse went into the river to St. John and they reported no sign of him. I have offered a reward for him or his body and will remain here and search for him as long as I think there is chance of finding him.

I met Dr. Potts of Chicago, Ill. going out this A.M. and he is waiting for this letter. We had decided to return and were on our way to Edmonton and expected to reach there in September with our samples and make a report to the company. But now I am so broken up I do not know what to do. Am all alone and I will have to make the trip to Edmonton with six horses alone as I can not sell them here.

It is not probable that he went out in the woods and got lost as his dog would not have left him. I am sure that he was at camp an hour before I arrived as the camp fire was still burning and the coffee was warm. His gun was in the case and I find nothing missing but him and the clothes he had on. Will send a message also by Dr. Potts to be sent you from Edmonton, Will write every chance I have to send mail.

From what Hinkle told me before we left Hope he had about $130.00 and spoke of trying to sell something we would not need and then divide up the money. There also, he told me he had sold some things and had taken in some money packing parties over the Portage while I was away prospecting. His money, I am satisfied, is on him as he always carried it in his pocket.

I have $100.00 and expect to be broke before I leave here as one cannot get any help here unless one pays well for it. I think I can make Edmonton with the six horses. I will keep enough grub to do me out. Write me at Edmonton what to do as I think I will reach there in September. No use to address me here. I was never so badly broken up in my life. Notify his family please as I never met any of them.

J.R. Peters

St. John, B.C.

August 13, 1899

H.S. Clark

We were on our way out and Hinkle is either lost or drowned. He disappeared from camp thirty miles above St. John while I was away hunting horses August 3rd and so far has not been found. I think he tried to swim a horse across Halfway River and is drowned as I found a horse at camp with a pack saddle on and the horse had been in swimming water as the saddle and pads were very wet. I wrote Tivnen full particulars today. Also sent a message. I have now looked for him six days and had six men look the river for thirty miles and could not find him. I am going back with some Indians to look for him.

I am so broken up that I don't know what to do. Please notify his family and have my sister to write my wife that I expect to reach Edmonton some time in September. I will have to make the trip alone and take six horses as I can not sell them here. Write me at Edmonton what to do. I have some good samples and will bring them out. Dr. Potts is returning to Chicago, Illinois and I send this out by him. He is hurrying me. I think I can make Edmonton (600 miles) alone but I am very lonesome since Hinkle disappeared.

Yours
J.R. Peters

> Rates $2.00 per day
> Alberta Hotel Free Sample Room
> Jackson & Grierson Free Bus
> Proprietors Livery in Connection

Edmonton, Alberta

August 28, 1899

B.H. Tivnen, Esq.
Mattoon
Dear Sir:

I have just sent you a telegram from Peters and am now enclosing this letter. He asked me to send you my Chicago address in case you or the Life Insurance people wished any further information about poor Hinkle. You had better, on receipt of this, put in claims against insurance company as time limit is about up and I do not think there is any possible chance of his being alive. Although his body had not been recovered when I was at St. John August 13th, it is a practical certainty that he was drowned in the Halfway. I will reach Chicago either September 3rd or 5th and will be there for a very few days only. If you wish to see me, wire me making appointment there for the 6th or 7th. Address me care of S.D. Stryker, 194 Fifth Ave.

Yours truly
James M.C. Potts, M.D.

From the Mattoon *Daily Star*

September 1, 1899

CONFIRMED
HINKLE EITHER LOST OR DROWNED

The first report that Prospector Hinkle was dead is partially confirmed. Later reports say he is either lost or drowned. Still later news practically says Hinkle is dead.

From the Mattoon *Daily Star*

September 30, 1899

VERIFIED
IS THE SAD NEWS OF HINKLE'S DEATH
EDMONTON PAPER GIVES ACCOUNT OF SEARCH
Brave Prospector Lost His Life in Water

The sad news of James Hinkle's death is verified by an Edmonton newspaper that contains an account of the diligent search made to recover the body. Mr. Peters, Hinkle's partner, did all possible to recover possession of the body, but to no avail. The Edmonton Bulletin of September 21st, has this to say of A. McFee, a miner who assisted in the search. The article relating to Hinkle reads as follows.

Mr. McFee gives further particulars as to the drowning of Hinkle, of Mattoon, Ill. in Halfway River, on the trail from St. John to Hudson Hope. Hinkle and his partner J.R. Peters, were corning down the river from Mt. Selwyn at the junction of the Findlay and Parsnip Rivers, where they had staked out quartz claims. They had reached the crossing of Halfway River and camped on Aug. 2. Peters went back to a stream called Red River to look for some of their horses which had strayed. While he was away, Hinkle was to try the ford across the Halfway on horseback. When Peters returned he found the fire burning at camp and a meal partly prepared. Not suspecting any mishap, he ate his dinner. Some time after, he noticed one of the horses with a pack saddle on and apparently having come out of the river. He then began to search for his partner, but without avail. When Mr. McFee reached the east side of Halfway on Aug. 2, Peters was still camped on the west side. Mr. McFee and Mr. Cook, of Buffalo Lake crossed the river on horseback. It was swimming deep. Peters then told them what had happened. They searched and found where the horse had gone into the river, and also where he had come out on the same side further down. He had gone in where the river was narrow and therefore deep and where there was a cut bank on the opposite side which the horse could not climb. Mr. McFee went on to Hudson Hope to complete his examination of the trail and returned to the Halfway on the 6th. A Montreal party that was coming down the river on a raft, also landed at the Halfway on the same day. All hands searched again and found where the horse had come out of the water on the east side and then returned to the west side, leaving no doubt as to Hinkle's death. Peters then gave up the search and returned to St. John. But there he hired another man and went back again to search, but without avail. Peters then came down to Peace River Crossing and Mr. McFee passed him on his way home.

Edmonton is the metropolis of Alberta, and headquarters for all prospectors in the Northwest Territory.

Hinkle was a very powerful man and could withstand the ravages of disease and hunger, but the account shows he was drowned and there is little hope that he succeeded in escaping.

From Mattoon *Daily Star*

September 30, 1899

FOUND!
THE BODY OF JAMES HINKLE DISCOVERED
IN THE WATERS OF FAMOUS PEACE RIVER
Remains Were Interred at St. John N.W.T.

At last news has arrived setting at rest all doubts as to the fate of James Hinkle, the popular railroad man who left this city 19 months ago to find fortune in the barren and cold northwest regions. A telegram from Edmonton, Alberta reads as follows:

Edmonton, Alberta, September 29, '99.

B.H. Tivnen, Mattoon, Ill.: — Body of Hinkle found and buried at St. John. I will leave for Mattoon Tuesday. J.R. Peters.

Thus ends the sad story of the mining expedition that was started out of this city. Three men left for the gold fields in the early spring of 1898. There were Charles Hardesty and James Hinkle, both well known railroad men, were accustomed to making lots of money, and J.R. Peters, of Arcola who had spent some years in Alaska. Hardesty came back long months ago, broken in health and spirit and was compelled to go to Colorado for his health. Hinkle met his fate trying to ford a river and Peters is left to make the return trip of 5,000 miles by himself. Certainly the expedition has been a most disastrous one and two families will never forget it.

Last spring Lee Summer left to join the party. He got well into the frozen regions, but failed to find those who had preceded him. He is an old mountaineer, having seen rough service in both Old and New Mexico, and no one has ever been uneasy about him. How long he will be absent no one can tell as he is plucky and, if there be prospects of success, may be gone ten years.

However, it is proper to comment on the foolishness of people getting the gold fever. Outside of Peters and John Cantlon, there was no one in that stock company who knew so much about mining as does a turkey hen about baths in Paradise Valley. Hinkle and Hardesty had good positions and were not the proper men to send to the new country. True, both were strong, steady men, but inexperience told on them.

EDMONTON N.W.T.

Oct. 2, 1899

G.M. Beals Wm.
Mattoon Lodge No. 290
Mattoon, Illinois

Dear Sir and Brother,

Yours of Sept. 21st to hand and contents carefully noted. I enclose two copies Edmonton Bulletin which contains about all that is known about the death of Brother Hinkle to date. I have seen McPhee (have known him for twenty years). He says

Peters is a KP, was rusty in the Blue Lodge work but was fairly well up in the higher branches of Masonry. McPhee is a KM. Peters is here. I saw him today. He told me all McPhee did about Bro. Hinkle.

Peters claims to have been made in Oakland Lodge, Oregon, was not sure of the Lodge No., thought it was 24, is a charter member of Ellenborough chapter No. 5 and Ellenborough Commandry No. 11, Washington. Was for ten years on bridge work on the Northern Pacific on the western division. Met Hinkle Illinois. Did not go to Potts claim but Peters did and staked a claim, remaining with the camp and horses along the river bottom.

Peters had six good horses at St. John which were taken to Peace River Crossing 250 Miles below St. John. Peters told McPhee, Hinkle had about $140.00 in cash on his person when drowned. Hinkle told him so as they had some business talk a few days before at Hudson Hope. At the time of the accident, Hinkle was on his way to St. John and Peters was helping him with the outfit, it being Peters intention to return to work the claim while Hinkle came out (presumably on business). By today's Bulletin you will see the body of Bro. Hinkle has been recovered. Grimston, one of the finders, camped close to Hinkle and Peters last winter. So there can be no mistake about the identity of the body. The other man, Pearll, I know well.

From all I can gather from people and correspondance from St. John, Peters did everything possible to recover the body and made provisions for taking care of it in case it was found after he left. And is my opinion on the information before me, Peters is straight and not a shadow of suspicion of foul play should attach to him as to the death of Bro. Hinkle. Peters goes south to Chicago tomorrow. He has Hinkle's dog which he is taking back to Mrs. Hinkle. Tonight

I am writing to a Brother at Peace River Crossing, 350 miles NW from here. If there is any new developments he will be informed of it as he is a Sergeant in the NW Mounted Police.

Fraternally yours,
James U. O. Donald S W
Edmonton Lodge No. 53
G R M A F & A M

Ft. St. John B.C.
J.R. Peters, Esq.
Mattoon, Illinois

Dear Sir:

Having found the body of James Hinkle, I am dropping you a few lines to let you know what we have done with him. We buried him at St. John, could not take him down to the Crossing being too damaged. Animals did not do anything to him. We found his body, his pipe, handkerchief, and money bag. His money amounted to $145.86. We dried it out and paid to Mr. Grimston and Pearce $100.00 reward for finding him. The rest went to expenses and funeral as you will find enclosed. I am forwarding you his pipe, handkerchief and money bag by mail.

I remain yours truly,
John P. Gaudet

Money of the late Mr. Hinkle
By cash	$145.86
To reward to Mr. Grimston and Pearce	$100.00
Paid to three boatmen to go up $5.00	$15.00
To one w. blanket for body	$5.00
To lumber for coffin, canvas and nails	$10.00
Paid three men to dig grave and make coffin	$15.86
	$145.86

FROM THE MATTOON *DAILY STAR*

November 1, 1899

IN MEMORIAM

A tribute to the memory of James Hinkle, who lost his life by accidental drowning in Halfway River, British Columbia, August 3, 1899 by the stockholders of the Security Mining and Investment Company of Mattoon, Illinois.

Whereas, it has come to our knowledge that James Hinkle lost his life by accidental drowning on his way home from a prospecting trip in British Columbia, and

Whereas, from a long personal acquaintance with James Hinkle before, and during his association with us, we learned to honor, love and respect him, as an honorable and upright citizen, worthy of the highest confidence, and in whose daily life and conduct we recognized that true friendship to all, and that devotion to his wife and children which endears his memory to all who knew him.

Therefore be it resolved, by the stockholders of the Security Mining and Investment Company, of Mattoon, Illinois, that we extend to the widow and children of our deceased friend our deepest and most heartfelt sympathy in their bereavement, and

Be it further resolved, that we do hereby pledge ourselves that we will always be mindful of the faithful services, privations and hardships endured by our deceased associate, James Hinkle, in his devotion to the interest of the company, and whose untimely death has cast a gloom over the prospects of our enterprise.

Be it further resolved, that the foregoing resolutions be spread upon the records of the company, and that a copy of the same be given to the family of the deceased. Passed by a unanimous vote of the stockholders at a meeting held in Mattoon, Illinois on the 30th day of October, A.D. 1899.

Louis Katz, President
Bryan H. Tivnen, Secretary

515 Clarke Ave.
Westmount, Montreal

Dec. 7, '99

Mrs. Mary E. Hinkle
Mattoon, Illinois
My dear Madam,

 I have today received four letters addressed to my brother Digby, and opened it in case it should require an immediate answer.

 I got a letter from my brother Digby, written on Oct. 23 telling me the sad news of your poor husband's death by drowning. He wrote very briefly and gave me no particulars but said that he expected to come out of the country from Lesser Slave Lake and arrive here in time for Christmas. He has not yet arrived nor have I any further news of him. But you may rest assured that as soon as he reaches Edmonton I will forward your letter to him and I know he will write you and tell you everything that he knows about the sad occurrence.

 I myself was one of the party last year. I left them to come out last winter. I knew your late husband and liked him as we all did very much and I am more than sorry to hear of his death. I respectfully extend to you my most hearty sympathy in your bereavement.

 He was a fine manly fellow, always so full of life and hope of making a good strike. And always so good tempered, we were together so long and so intimately that I am exceedingly sorry to hear of his death.

 I may say that I met a man named Hamilton (of Montreal) last week who has just returned from that country and he had heard of your husband's death as having happened at the Halfway River where he and Peters were camped. According to his account, Jack Peters went out to hunt and poor Jim went with a horse during his absence to try and find a place where they could cross and did not return. He was afterwards found by my brother. The horse returned to camp 3 days afterwards. I do not think there was any foul play of any sort.

However, I shall let my brother have your letter as soon as ever he comes out and meanwhile I remain

Yours very sincerely
S.G. Grimston

19

Later in Mattoon, Illinois

by Martha J. Bates

Approximately two months later in Mattoon, Illinois.
Peters returned to Mattoon, Illinois and was questioned extensively by the members of the Security Mining and Investment Company. One of the meetings was open to the public and quite a number of the Mattoon townspeople attended. After hearing his story, many of them were of the opinion that Peters had killed Hinkle and thrown his body into the river. They said he made up the story and then couldn't keep the facts straight. Each time he told it, he had a different version.

Peters had brought back Hinkle's diary and his personal belongings. Among them was a chamois skin bag about four inches wide and twelve inches deep. In it were three small gold nuggets about the size of the end of a thumb. Mollie and Myrty were of the opinion that it had been full at one time. They had intended having a pin or ring made out of them but an elderly woman who rented a room from them stole the nuggets so they, too, were gone.

Peters called on the Hinkle family to return the personal belongings and to pay his respects. He also brought Dash with him to turn over to the family. Dash had never been in Mattoon before and had never met any of the Hinkles except for his loving master, Jim Hinkle. As they walked into the house, Dash immediately went

Hinkle's mining license

over to where Mollie and Myrty were sitting and sat down on the floor between them. He instinctively knew that these people were close to his dead master.

During the course of the conversation, Mollie Hinkle, Jim's wife, asked Peters,

"Did you stake a claim?"

"Wellll, no-o-o," he answered.

"Why didn't you?" Mollie asked.

"Welll," he stammered, "my license had run out."

"Why didn't you stake a claim on Jim's license?" Mollie asked.

"Well", he hesitated, "his license had run out too."

"No it didn't for I have it right here, I found it among his papers and it was renewed in July, 1899."

"Well I didn't know that," Peters said quickly.

Those were not the days of intensive investigations. Long distance communications were impossible and it took months for mail to reach its destination, which made it impractical to delve into this incident from such a long distance. Someone said he drowned so that was the easiest way to leave it — there were too many other deaths under strange circumstances during the gold rush.

A day or two later, on a return visit to the Hinkle home, Peters knocked on the door and Dash growled and barked and would not let him enter. This, above all else as far as most people were concerned, put the guilt on Peters.

Peters was in Mattoon for perhaps a week or ten days while he was being questioned. He then left town and as far as is known, no one ever heard from him again.

Dash lived comfortably with Mollie, Myrty, Presh and Harry until he died several years later of a natural death.

It was evident Peters was dishonest and Hinkle did not trust him. On February 21, 1898, Hinkle wrote in his journal, "Made an invoice of the outfit today and are 100 pounds flour short, think Peters has sold it."

Peters had threatened to kill Hinkle several times. There were several notations in the journal that had been erased, some in ink, in which case it looked as though the paper had been scraped with a knife in an effort to make the words illegible. I'm sure that Peters dared not throw the journal away after Hinkle's death for fear his family knew he was keeping one and it would look too suspicious if he disposed of it. So he went through it quickly to try to erase the items that he did not want others to read.

On December 30, 1898, there was one such notation which had been scraped with a knife but with a magnifying glass, these words could be discerned. "Had a fuss with Peters, he wanted to kill me on the spot. I told him to get his gun and knife and go to it. He growled like a dog." Another day he wrote in his journal, "Peters came at me with a knife."

The hard work in the cold, rain, snow and freezing temperatures, along with the loneliness, took its toll on both of them and the fact that Peters said very little and kept to himself made the situation even more intolerable. A notation in the journal on October 22, 1898, after they had all seen a bear, said, "Peters got the shotgun first, then a club, then he thought of his rifle — he pretty near had one of those spells again. One more year and he will be bug house right."

The last letter written by Hinkle was a short one with the date of July 8, 1899. Since he always started another letter as soon as he finished one, there would almost certainly have been a partially written letter among his possessions, which Peters probably threw away. That letter could have given many clues as to their last days together.

The July 8 letter stated that the Dr. Potts party were on their way out from the Selwyn Mountains where they had staked claims and Peters was on his way up there to prospect and to stake a claim. He had sent word to Hinkle with Dr. Potts that he had found some good quartz.

Peters returned on July 25th and Hinkle noted in his journal that day, "We will start for St. John and on our way out of the country. Peters said today in his talk that if the company did not send him back that he would come himself and that he wished they wouldn't send him back. He is not working for the company but for Peters."

That could have been the beginning of their final argument. Perhaps Peters tried to convince Hinkle to not tell the company about the good find because he wanted to come back on his own.

On July 26th, Hinkle wrote in his journal that he couldn't sleep for thinking about Peters and he didn't go to sleep until daylight. I'm sure that he would have told Peters that he had no intention of telling the company anything except the truth. But also on July 26th Hinkle had to go to the Cust's House to bring some of the Potts Party over as he had promised.

On July 27th, he went back to the Hope where Peters was and got mad at him because he did not have the bread baked as he should have.

On July 28th, all the other men left for down the river and Peters and Hinkle were alone and Hinkle said in his journal, "After they left I had a set-to .... " and the rest of the words had been erased and the next page had been torn out, eliminating the rest of July 28th, July 29th and part of July 30th which had been erased but one could make out through the erasure, "Peters for the first time give me a statement."

This should have been a time of great happiness since they were at last going home and they did have something to report to the company if a claim had been staked but now it is quite puzzling whether that had been done or not.

Those last few days must have been filled with deep resentments and hostility, Hinkle's seething anger at Peters wanting to tell the company they had found nothing and Peters knowing that Hinkle would indeed tell the truth.

So perhaps Peters was wondering, planning and conniving about what he could do to get out of this and how to shut up Hinkle when they returned. On July 31st and August 1st they started their trip out of the country. On August 2nd they decided they would have to build a raft to cross the river since the water was too high. Peters cut the logs for it in the morning, then left to find the horses. Hinkle's last words in his journal were, "I am building the raft."

Epilogue

by Martha J. Bates

In 1903, Myrty was married to Harry W. McNaught in Indianapolis, Indiana. They had a boy and three girls of which I was the youngest. I subsequently married and my only child, Marcia, was born in 1942. In 1943, after the war started, my husband was no longer able to get gasoline to drive his insurance route throughout the county so he accepted a position with a construction company that was helping build the Alaska Highway. He was to work in the offices in Edmonton, Alberta, Canada.

My small daughter and I moved there as soon as we were able to obtain housing. I had always heard the stories of my grandfather and now we were actually living in the city from which his journey originated. I became very interested in this fact and asked my mother to send some of grandfather's letters to me. The letters then were forty five years old, the writing was very small since he tried to conserve the paper and I felt they should be copied word for word, for the preservation of the contents. I spent the next two years in my spare time painstakingly trying to make out each word and copying all the letters along with his journal.

During the two years we were there, my husband contacted the Catholic Church in Peace River in an attempt to find a burial record of grandfather. We received this reply.

THE IMMACULATE CONCEPTION CHURCH
Peace River, Alta.

November 18, 1943

Dear Mr. Bates,

In reply to your inquiry re the burial place of James Hinkle, I fear it will take some time before interesting particulars can be gathered. At the time you mention, "about 1898", there was no residing priest at Fort St. John, the nearest residence being at Spirit River (Alta.), a few hundred miles away. I presume the burial record, if existing, could be found at the Catholic Rectory in Spirit River. I have written to the pastor about your request and shall send word to the actual pastor at Fort St. John in hopes that some old timer may still remember the sad event you refer to.

Any bit of enlightening news which I may receive will be forwarded to you without delay. Personally, I can be of little service since our local records date no farther back than 1916.

Trusting that your search will meet with success eventually, I remain,

Sincerely yours,
E. Beaucage, O.M.I.

CATHOLIC RECTORY
Peace River, Alta.

Nov. 30, 1943

Mr. R.J. Bates
Edmonton, Alta.

Dear Sir:

To complete my previous note concerning the death of James Hinkle, I bring you a few more particulars which are not brightly enlightening.

As I told you, the church records regarding Fort St. John district in 1898 are officially at Spirit River, but temporarily at the Bishop's House in McLennan, Alta. Unfortunately, these, I am told, do not contain any burial records covering those early days. Only Baptisms and Marriages are therein registered.

My letter of inquiry sent to the actual pastor at Fort St. John (Fr F. Otterbach, O.M.I.) met with partial success. Father tells me that an old poineer of the north, "Old Man" Beaton by name and a legendary figure at the Fort, claims that he arrived at Fort St. John on the day of James Hinkle's burial ...! Naturally, I cannot guarantee the statement.

I should advise that you contact this "Old Man" Beaton directly or through Father Otterbach in order to verify the exact location of your grandfather's grave.

Hoping that this bit of information may be of some service to you, and conveying my hearty best wishes,

I remain,
Yours sincerely,
E. Beaucage, O.M.I.
pastor

In the meantime my husband and Father Beaucage became good friends through their correspondence with each other.

CATHOLIC CHURCH RECTORY
Peace River, Alberta

June 17, 1946

Dear Bob,

I wonder if the "please forward" will be of any use this time ... or, are you still at home ... planning another trip?

Your April letter remained unanswered because I was awaiting Joe Apisasin's return from the "bush". Father Jungbluth finally interviewed the swarthy gentleman and sent me the findings. Presuming charitably that you have behaved properly in the meantime, I am hereby rewarding you with my translation of Joe's message. As you can see, Jim's death had apparently little in common with the "Shooting of Dan McGrew".

(Joe Apasasin was the young Indian to whom Hinkle gave $5.00 to find the horses. Also, Father Beaucage did not know the particulars of Hinkle's death.)

I took the liberty of informing Father Jungbluth that you would like to have the grave located and marked before Joe himself 'kicks the bucket'.

Nothing new or thrilling around here, save long days of precious sunshine. I am still minus a car, because eastern strikes applied brakes to all deliveries and even forced factories to close. My 'round robin' appeal for funds turned out to be a 50% success. Consequently, I've been pinching nickles and pennies in an attempt to meet the sky-high price of the "cheapest" car on the market, a Ford coach. It costs $1400 - $1500 around here. Trifling matter, of course!

All my dough being sunk in this enterprise, there is none left to complete the church according to plans or dreams of mine. And I do need a car!

I am still all by myself and am getting used to my unpleasant company. I must be improving in character or simply going nuts gradually. Who knows?

Here's hoping that you have landed an A-I job with light, pleasant work and a fat salary. Should you be in Hawaii, may the ideal weather and the glorious sunsets appeal to your artistic soul. On the other hand, may the "hula-hula girls" behave with reserve whenever you meet! Henceforth, Martha may have to keep not only one but both good eyes on you for your own good. Good luck!

As ever sincerely
E. Beaucage, O.M.I.

Epilogue / 303

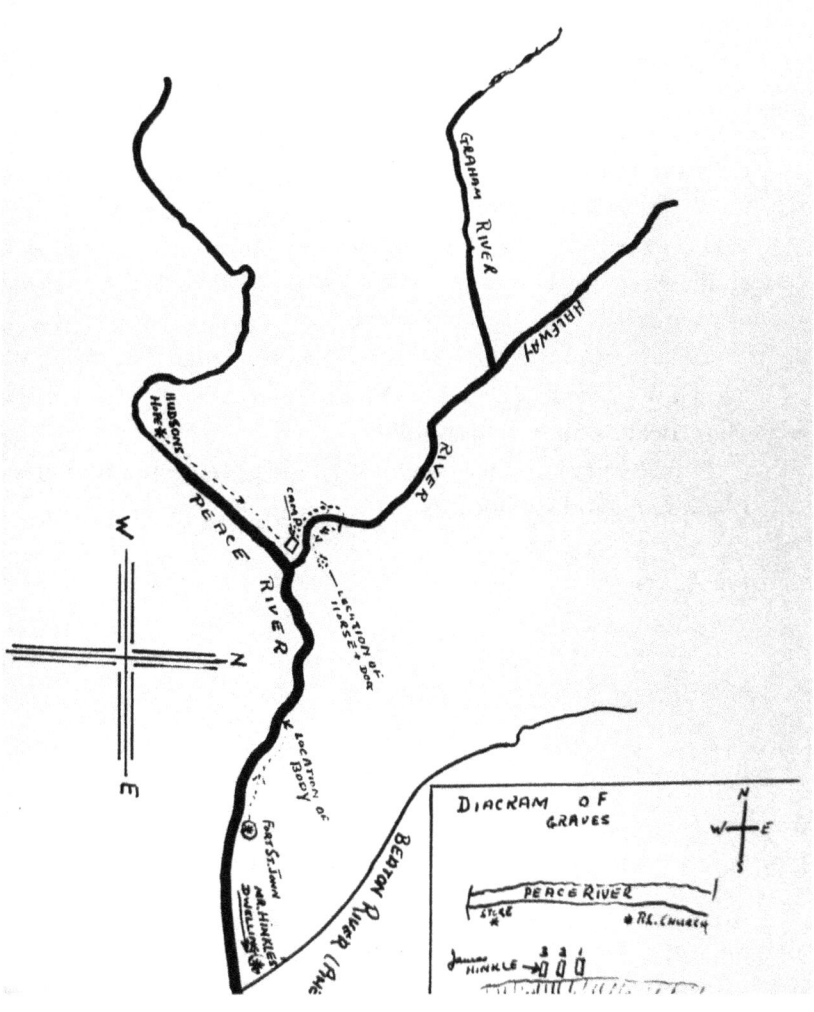

Diagram of graves

This is the statement Father Beaucage enclosed in his last letter.

Re: James Hinkle

One summer day, a long time ago (1899) a saddled horse without rider arrived at old Fort St. John. I, Joe Apasasin, recognized the horse as Jim's. (Hinkle)

Three weeks later, Jim's corpse was found in the Peace River about three miles from the Fort. I saw the body of which no bones were broken.

To my mind, Jim was drowned while fording the "Half Way River", swollen at that time (i.e. high water), The Police and "Old Man" Beaton shared this opinion.

I buried Jim Hinkle, and although the grave is now unmarked, I believe I could still locate the spot.

Joe Apasasin

Message obtained through the kindly efforts of Fr. E. Jungbluth, O.M.I., Fort St. John

E. Beaucage, O.M.I.
Peace River, Alberta

After two years, we moved back to the States and my project was set aside. However, in 1952 we returned to Edmonton for another two years since my husband was to work in conjunction with the construction of a chemical plant there.

I was able to get in touch with Father Thomas P. Sheil, O.M.I. of Fort St. John who also talked to the old Indian, Joe Apasasin. They made a sketch for me, showing the location of Hinkle's grave and the fact that two other men were also buried there, John Shaw and Isadore Ferguson, both men whom Grandfather had known.

Martha, Marcia, and Myrtle, Edmonton, Alberta., 1952

My mother was able to visit us while we were living in Edmonton at this time. I had a nice surprise for her, I intended to drive her to Fort St. John to see the area where her father was buried.

The three of us started out, my ten year old daughter, Mother and I, along the dusty gravel roads and arrived in Fort St. John in less than two days, covering the same distance it had taken Grandfather almost a year to travel.

As we drove along, my mother was very silent and I tried not to intrude upon her thoughts. I'm sure she was trying to imagine her father trudging through the woods and pulling the heavily loaded boat down the rivers, camping in the cold and snow at night and realizing the hardships he endured. I believe she felt very close to him in that serenely tranquil and beautiful setting.

Peace River Valley

Myrty near burial site in 1952

As we stopped at various places along the way, we always engaged in conversation with the old timers we would see, on the chance that they would remember events of the past.

When we reached Fort St. John, we learned that Joe Apasasin was out on his trap lines far away. However, we had the sketch he had drawn and were able to locate the approximate area where Grandfather was buried which was a great satisfaction to my mother. She said that this was the highlight of her life and had never in her wildest dreams, thought that she would ever be in this same area where her father had been.

After returning home, she wrote to her brother Vernon Hinkle who was called Presh in the letters. This is what she said: "As I stood there viewing the beauty of the surrounding hills and the river flowing quietly through the green valley below, I thought, with tears in my eyes and a throbbing heart, where in all this world is there a more beautiful, more peaceful resting place for our dear Papa. It is a picture I shall never forget. When I closed my eyes that night all I could see was the valley where lies our Papa whom we loved so dearly and who risked his life and lost it for our sake. That lovely scene that nature prepared for his resting place was far beyond anything I expected to see."

www.ingramcontent.com/pod-product-compliance
Lightning Source LLC
Chambersburg PA
CBHW051748040426
42446CB00007B/268